*St Antony's Series*
General Editor: **Jan Zielonka**, Fellow of St ⌐
Research Fellow of St Anthony's College, O⌐
at Oxford.

Recent titles include:

Cathy Gormley-Heenan
political leadership and the northern ireland peace process
Role, Capacity and Effect

Lori Plotkin Boghardt
kuwait amid war, peace and revolution

Paul Chaisty
Legislative Politics and Economic Power in Russia

Valpy FitzGerald, Frances Stewart and Rajesh Venugopal (editors)
globalization, violent conflict and self-determination

Miwao Matsumoto
technology gatekeepers for war and peace
The British Ship Revolution and Japanese Industrialization

Håkan Thörn
Anti-Apartheid and the Emergence of a Global Civil Society

Lotte Hughes
Moving the Maasai
A Colonial Misadventure

Fiona Macaulay
Gender Politics in Brazil and Chile
The Role of Parties in National and Local Policymaking

Stephen Whitefield (editor)
POLITICAL CULTURE AND POST-COMMUNISM

José Esteban Castro
water, power and citizenship
Social Struggle in the Basin of Mexico

Valpy FitzGerald and Rosemary Thorp (editors)
economic doctrines in latin america
Origins, Embedding and Evolution

Victoria D. Alexander and Marilyn Rueschemeyer
art and the state
The Visual Arts in Comparative Perspective

Ailish Johnson
european welfare states and supranational governance of social polic

Archie Brown (editor)
the demise of marxism-leninism in russia

Thomas Boghardt
spies of the kaiser
German Covert Operations in Great Britain during the First World War Era

Ulf Schmidt
justice at nuremberg
Leo Alexander and the Nazi Doctors' Trial

Steve Tsang (editor)
PEACE AND SECURITY ACROSS THE TAIWAN STRAIT

James Milner
REFUGEES, THE STATE AND THE POLITICS OF ASYLUM IN AFRICA

Stephen Fortescue (editor)
RUSSIAN POLITICS FROM LENIN TO PUTIN

**St Antony's Series**
**Series Standing Order ISBN 978–0–333–71109–5 (hardback) 978–0–333–80341–7**
**(paperback)**
(outside North America only)

You can receive future titles in this series as they are published by placing a standing order. Please contact your bookseller or, in case of difficulty, write to us at the address below with your name and address, the title of the series and the ISBNs quoted above.

Customer Services Department, Macmillan Distribution Ltd, Houndmills, Basingstoke, Hampshire RG21 6XS, England

# How Gangs Work

## An Ethnography of Youth Violence

James A. Densley
*Assistant Professor, Metropolitan State University, Brooklyn Park, Minnesota*

*In Association with St  Palgrave Macmillan*

First published 2013
First published in paperback 2016 by
PALGRAVE MACMILLAN

Palgrave Macmillan in the UK is an imprint of Macmillan Publishers Limited, registered in England, company number 785998, of Houndmills, Basingstoke, Hampshire RG21 6XS.

Palgrave Macmillan in the US is a division of St Martin's Press LLC, 175 Fifth Avenue, New York, NY 10010.

Palgrave Macmillan is the global academic imprint of the above companies and has companies and representatives throughout the world.

Palgrave® and Macmillan® are registered trademarks in the United States, the United Kingdom, Europe and other countries.

ISBN  978–1–137–27150–1    Hardback
ISBN  978–1–137–57293–6    Paperback

This book is printed on paper suitable for recycling and made from fully managed and sustained forest sources. Logging, pulping and manufacturing processes are expected to conform to the environmental regulations of the country of origin.

A catalogue record for this book is available from the British Library.

A catalog record for this book is available from the Library of Congress.

Typeset by MPS Limited, Chennai, India.

*For Alex*
*In search of a world free from gang violence*

# Contents

# About the Author

James A. Densley is Assistant Professor in the School of Law Enforcement and Criminal Justice at Metropolitan State University, Brooklyn Park, Minnesota. His teaching and research interests include street gangs, organized crime, violence, and theoretical criminology. Densley is trustee and director of Growing Against Gangs and Violence, an educational partnership with London's Metropolitan Police Service. He earned the D.Phil. and M.Sc. in Sociology from the University of Oxford (St. Antony's College), the M.S. in Teaching from Pace University, and the B.A. (Hons) in Sociology with American Studies from the University of Northampton. He has published studies in the *European Journal of Criminology, Crime & Delinquency, Global Crime, Social Problems,* and other leading social science journals. Densley's articles have appeared in newspapers and magazines, including the *FBI Law Enforcement Bulletin, Police Review, Policing Today,* and *The Sun.* This is his first book.

# Preface

From 2005 to 2007 I taught special education in the New York City public schools. I was a 22 year old Englishman in New York who needed to stay on the right side of US Immigration and Customs Enforcement while paying down a sizable student loan. Teaching was never my planned destination. A little lost in the throngs of people riding the Brooklyn-bound A train one afternoon, I caught a glimpse of a simple black and white advertisement posted around where the transit map should be, that read: 'You remember your first-grade teacher's name. Who will remember yours?' And those eleven words forever changed my direction of travel. The subway ad promised a one-time tax-free stipend during training, a competitive starting salary plus health insurance and retirement plan, even tuition assistance toward earning a graduate degree. All I had to do was teach.

It was almost too good to be true. With barely a second thought, I signed up to the NYC Teaching Fellows, an alternative teacher certification program that took earnest graduates like me and, in an effort to plug the teacher shortage and bridge the achievement gap, provided a quick on-ramp to needy inner city schools. I reported for duty at a middle school in Hunts Point in the South Bronx, a neighborhood that 30 years ago seemed to exemplify the bleakness of poor urban places and today still lies in the poorest congressional district in the United States. The principal handed me the keys to the classroom and told me to teach. I did. Then reality set in. Youth half my age but twice my size looked right through me. I was not the center of attention.

My students were distracted. The source of their distraction was gangs. The symbolism of the graffiti on their desks and in their notebooks, the tattoos on their necks, and the clothing on their backs was visible even to the untrained eye. The airport-style metal detectors and small army of police officers that greeted me that morning suddenly made sense. In the weeks that followed, I separated fights, mediated conflicts, and learned about children dealing drugs out of backpacks and carrying weapons in playgrounds. I witnessed first hand how events outside the school disrupted the learning process inside the school. During a routine exercise of 'Where do you see yourself in ten years?', for example, one of my students, a self-proclaimed 'blood for life', answered he would either be dead or in prison for killing his estranged father. It was an education.

When I later taught in Manhattan's Lower East Side, the *idea* of gangs distracted my students more than gangs themselves. It was here, coincidentally a few blocks from the Five Points district vividly portrayed in the movie *Gangs of New York*, that youths divorced from gangs would spend their Halloweens warning me not to drive home at night, lest I be violently victimized by gang members. As my students had it, All Saints Day was annual gang initiation day and prospective gang members would be out in force, driving on busy roads at night with their headlights switched off or on high beam. Any motorist who responded by blinking their headlights to warn oncoming traffic would be purposefully followed home by the gang, attacked for perceived disrespect, and, in most versions, murdered in cold blood. Hence the subway was safer than the expressway.

The 'lights out' gang initiation is in fact an urban myth. The tale originated in California in the early 1980s and spread throughout the United States during the Clinton years with the help of fax machines and the Internet (for a discussion, see Best and Hutchinson, 1996). That I first heard the story from a cohort of streetwise and otherwise savvy teenagers a decade after police and municipal leaders very publicly denied it, demonstrates the pervasiveness of gang mythology. Indeed, I heard it again at least three more times during the fieldwork for this book, only then gang members were allegedly cruising the streets of London, England.

My old students inspired this research and remind me always of why it matters. After all, gangs cause damage beyond that which is measured by traditional law enforcement and criminal justice indices—damage measured in the lost productivity of otherwise capable young people, the deterioration of once stable social institutions, and the loss of precious public resources expended in efforts to repair the damage caused. My students taught me that gangs exist as both real and imaginary threats. But they also taught me how to spot the difference between the two. With so much misinformation out there about gangs, this book sets out to make sense of them in straightforward, rational terms. The implication is that lessons learned in New York carry over to London and vice versa. And to understand 'how gangs work' you must take the road less travelled and work with gangs.

# Acknowledgments

Many people contributed to this research and book. First and foremost, my sincere thanks to the nearly 200 individuals who agreed to be interviewed and observed during the fieldwork, but cannot be named because of my promise to preserve their anonymity. This would be a bound volume of blank pages were it not for their courage, dedication, honesty, and insight. For this, I am forever grateful.

This book grows out of the research I did as a doctoral candidate in the Department of Sociology at the University of Oxford. I owe a great debt of gratitude to many great minds at Oxford, especially Heather Hamill, Diego Gambetta, and Federico Varese, who modeled a profound sense of academic integrity and challenged me to look at my data in new and exciting ways. Thanks also to Gabriella Elgenius, Christina Furr, Thomas Grund, Declan Hill, Lindsey Richardson, Andrew Shipley, Alex Sutherland, and Valeria Pizzini-Gambetta for fun and feedback along the way.

Formal and informal discussion at numerous conferences—notably, the National Gang Crime Research Center's 15th International Gang Specialist Training; the 2011 Inter-Ivy and Sorensen Memorial Sociology Conference at Harvard University; the Second Annual Postgraduate Criminology Conference at the University of Cambridge; the 105th Annual Meeting of the American Sociological Association; and the Workshop on Recruitment into Extra-Legal Organizations at Nuffield College, Oxford—helped the ideas in this book to mature. I am grateful to all those who participated.

I am greatly indebted to Ian Buchanan, Wolfgang Deicke, and others at the University of Northampton who encouraged me to apply for Oxford in the first place. I am also grateful to Alex Stevens for examining the work upon which this book is based and later collaborating with me to improve upon it. Many of the ideas for Chapter 1 developed under his tutelage. Special thanks go to Scott Decker for sage advice, my colleagues at Metropolitan State University for their vast reserve of patience and knowledge, Rebecca Diederichs citation assistance, David Squier Jones for indexing assistance, Paul Iovino for great ideas, and my teammates at Growing Against Gangs and Violence, especially Allen Davis and Nick Mason, for translating theory into practice.

For understanding forgotten emails, missed birthdays, and long nights at the computer, I'd like to thank my family and friends. Without their contributions and support this book would not have been written. My parents Jan and Andrew and my sister Jo were a constant source of strength and deserve extra credit for their vigilant collecting of secondary sources. My in-laws Jo and Jim, moreover, made me a home away from home during the writing stage and celebrated every word I committed to print. But words cannot express my gratitude to my wife, Emily, for sharing in the agony and ecstasy of every aspect of this project. I wish I could say that this research was supported by fellowships and grants from wealthy donors. Alas, Emily sustained this research almost entirely, working 70-hour weeks or more while I hung around on street corners. God only knows what I'd be without her.

Finally, my sincere thanks go to the editors of the St Antony's Series, Jan Zielonka and Othon Anastasakis, the anonymous reviewers, Mritunjai Sahai and the MPS Production Team, MPS Limited, Chennai; and the team at Palgrave Macmillan, especially Julia Willan and Harriet Barker, for their professional advice and assistance in polishing and publishing this manuscript.

I published a shorter version of Chapter 2 as 'It's Gang Life But Not as we Know it: The Evolution of Gang Business' in *Crime & Delinquency* (Sage, 2012); parts of Chapter 3 as 'The Organisation of London's Street Gangs' in *Global Crime* (Taylor & Francis, 2012); an earlier version of Chapter 5 as 'Street Gang Recruitment: Signaling, Screening and Selection' in *Social Problems* (University of California Press, 2012); and odd phrases here and there in 'Ganging up on Gangs: Why the Gang Intervention Industry Needs an Intervention' in the *British Journal of Forensic Practice* (Emerald, 2011). As usual, responsibility for the contents of this book lies solely with the author. All mistakes are mine.

# Introduction

In August 2011, the eyes of the world were set on thousands of young people as they took to Britain's city streets and engaged in unprecedented scenes of civil disorder. A peaceful demonstration over the fatal police shooting of a young black man in Tottenham, north London, spiraled into four days of riots and looting, five deaths, untold economic damage, and nearly 4000 arrests. Via rolling news feed and grainy home video, Britons perused the charcoaled remains of local landmarks and public vehicles. They navigated a sea of broken glass and thrown projectiles. They relived exuberant raids upon steel-shuttered retail stores. They bore witness to indiscriminate acts of violence, mostly concentrated within eyeshot of a depressed post-war council estate. Less than one year away from hosting the Games of the XXX Olympiad, London was burning.

Those five days in August put gangs firmly back in the headlines and on the political agenda. Gangs were scrutinized six months prior when five-year-old Thusha Kamaleswaran was paralyzed after being shot in the chest by gang members pursuing who they thought was a member of a rival gang cowering in her uncle's convenience store (Laville and Taylor, 2012). Public outcry over this incident spurred the demand that police and public officials acknowledge and begin to seriously address London's growing gang problem. But it never came to fruition because the wider public was largely insulated from the internecine violence of gangs. That is until the riots.

If the Kamaleswaran shooting was the spark, the riots were the fire. In response to allegations that gangs had suspended territorial rivalries to coordinate the disorders over smart phones and social media, Prime Minister David Cameron (2011) made tackling gangs his 'new national priority' and launched a 'concerted, all out war on gangs and gang culture'. It was the kind of rhetoric the public has come to expect from 'tough on crime' law and order politicians who favor individualized explanations for aberrant behavior over critiques of social structure (Blair, 1993, p. 28). Had the government blamed the riots on social exclusion and social deprivation it would have implicated itself. By blaming gangs, the coalition instead implicated others. And it worked because the media thrives on simplicity and sweeping generalizations, and most Britons have little or no direct experience of gangs but remain frightened and fascinated by them in equal measure.

According to Metropolitan Police Service (MPS) intelligence (2012a, 2012b), there are an estimated 250 active criminal gangs in London, comprising of about 4800 people. Of these gangs, 62 are considered as 'high harm' and commit two thirds of all 'gang-related' crime; that is, 'any offence committed where the victim or suspect is identified through MPS indices as being a member of a gang'.[1] The gangs range from organized criminal networks involved in Class A drugs supply and firearms to street-based gangs involved in violence and personal robbery. Based upon 'daily scanning processes' and 'dip sampling' of only 100 cases from the small proportion of crimes that leads to detection of the offender, the MPS concludes that this relatively small number of people is responsible for approximately 22 percent of serious violence, 17 percent of robbery, 50 percent of shootings and 14 percent of rape in London (Metropolitan Police Service, 2012a, 2012b).

Aside from the obvious problems of definition, which I shall address later, when the flames eventually subsided and more sober inquiry ensued, we learned that less than 20 percent of those responsible for the riots came from gang backgrounds, and even where gang members were involved, they did not play a central role (Home Office, 2011). Journalists on the Right reported this as, 'one in five Londoners arrested during the riots was in a gang!' Journalists on the Left led with, '*only* one in five Londoners arrested during the riots was in a gang'. Either way, the government had conflated youths dressed in hooded sportswear with 'criminality, pure and simple'. Worse still, the government seemed intent upon developing populist policy around gangs without first developing proficiency with the issues.

The riots and their aftermath invite questions that have intrigued gang scholars for decades: what is a gang and how does it differ from organized crime or crime committed alongside groups of friends (a category into which a substantial amount of all juvenile delinquency falls)? Are 'gang' activity and 'gang member' activity conceptually distinct? What is the nature and extent of gang organization? What is the role of media and technology in gangs? Why and how do young people join gangs? Once they join, can they ever leave? What works in gang prevention and intervention? Such questions are at the heart of this book.

In answering them my aim is to challenge popular misconceptions about gangs as amorphous collectives of hoodies and hoodlums, 'unhappy, unloved, and out of control', perpetrating wanton acts of crime and violence (Mayer, 2008). This book demonstrates that gang members are to large extent rational agents who optimize under the constraints of their harsh life conditions. Gangs, in turn, are rational organizations that evolve to punish fraud and fault but reward industry and ingenuity. Like mafias, some gangs are 'a species of a broader genus, organized crime' (Varese, 2001, p. 4). I appreciate, in the words of the late astronomer and astrophysicist Carl Sagan (1980), such 'extraordinary claims require extraordinary evidence'. The rest of this chapter thus is structured first to ensure we are speaking the same language when it comes to gangs; and second to describe the data sources and methods upon which such claims are built.

## Gang, defined

Gangs—and the hysteria surrounding them—are not new to Britain (Pearson, 1983; Davies, 1998). If Robin Hood's band of Merry Men is 'an archetypical, early Nottingham gang', then British gang history dates back to the Middle Ages at least (Schneider and Tilley, 2004, p. xv). But as Stacy Peralta's (2009) documentary about the rise of the notorious Bloods and Crips implies, gang life as we know it is 'Made in America'. So too is our knowledge about it. Since David Downes (1966) famously declared British gangs nonexistent, attempts to understand gangs in the British context have been curtailed by the 'Eurogang paradox'—the denial that there are 'American-style' gangs in Europe, based on a 'typical' American gang with functional role division and chain of command; a model that is not actually typical of gangs in America (Klein, 2001, p. 10).

Only in recent years have gangs in Britain received any scholarly attention (see Batchelor, 2009; Centre for Social Justice, 2009; Deuchar, 2009; Hallsworth and Silverstone, 2009; McVie, 2010; Young, 2009), but studies have been marked by rhetorical debate as to whether gangs in British cities are shapeless gatherings of peers (Aldridge and Medina, 2008; Bannister et al., 2010; Bennett and Holloway, 2004; Bradshaw, 2005; Mares, 2001), or are more structured groups that coerce 'reluctant gangsters' into their ranks (Pitts, 2008), or are even exaggerated and—at least partly—imaginary productions of the predilection for 'gang talk' among the academics, police officers, and policy makers who 'need' gangs in order to justify their very existence (Hallsworth and Young, 2008). Barry Goldson's (2011) recent edited volume further enables the central protagonists to reprise and intensify the debate about 'gang-land' and 'gang talk', with John Pitts (2011) and Simon Hallsworth (2011) talking past each other again—Pitts insisting that gangs exist and Hallsworth responding that the problem of street violence is not reducible to the gang—when in fact both propositions can be true. Unsurprisingly, gang processes have until now been largely ignored.

Gangs still go against the grain of British criminology, which has traditionally focused on oppositional rather than subordinate youth formations that lack a criminal *raison d'être*, such as the neighborhood- and style-based subculture movements of the 1960s and 1970s (see Campbell and Muncer, 1989). British criminologists struggle with or challenge the term 'gang' because no precise or parsimonious definition exists and gangs have a tendency to bring out the worst in criminal justice policy and practice (Alexander, 2008; Hallsworth and Young, 2008; Sharp, Aldridge, and Medina, 2006; White, 2008). As an example, the Insane Clown Posse hip-hop group is currently suing the US Department of Justice for classifying their fan base, or 'Juggalos', as a gang (Michaels, 2012). Closer to home, the *Evening Standard* once published the names of 257 London gangs as obtained from documents 'leaked' by analysts at Scotland Yard's Specialist Crime Directorate, only to retract the list when it discovered that parts of it were incorrectly copied from an open source website and benign groups 'posturing' on the Internet were included (Davenport, 2007).

To paraphrase the author David Frum (2009), if the gang is a mirage then interventions based on that mirage can only lead us deeper into the desert. But 'action sets' (Sullivan, 2005), 'troublesome youth groups' (Decker and Weerman, 2005), and other euphemistic gang alternatives are no less ambiguous or ill defined. According to 'rap's poet laureate' (Hagedorn, 2008, p. 142), Tupac Shakur, for example, one is 'troublesome' if they're 'young', 'strapped'—that is, carrying a firearm—and 'don't give a fuck'. Which just so happens to be the same 'thug life' stereotype that those embroiled in debates over the utility of the word gang wish to avoid.

Since entering common parlance, the gang epithet has become convenient shorthand for social commentators to describe a range of collective behaviors, from 'crime that is organized' to 'organized crime'. But as the economist Thomas Schelling (1971) explains, the two are conceptually distinct. The former encompasses crime that involves cooperation, functional role division, planning, and specialization. The latter involves monopolistic control exerted by one criminal group over 'the production and distribution of a given commodity or service' (Varese, 2010, p. 14). The mafia as industry of private protection thus represents the quintessential 'organized crime' (Chin, 1996; Chu, 2000; Gambetta, 1993; Hill, 2003; Varese, 2001).

Very few gangs meet the essential criteria for classification as organized crime (Decker, Bynum, and Weisel, 1998; Howell, 2007; Weisel, 2002). The drug-selling gang famously described by 'rogue' scholars Steven Levitt and Sudhir Venkatesh (Levitt and Venkatesh, 2000) does so because it offers a variety of tangible illegal goods and services to its patrons and aspires to be the sole suppliers of them in a given domain (see Varese, 2010). As Mac Klein (2004, p. 57) observes, however, the gang concept 'implies a level of structure and organization for criminal conspiracy that is simply beyond the capacity of most street gangs'. He adds, 'most street gangs are only loosely structured, with transient leadership and membership, easily transcended codes of loyalty, and informal rather than formal roles for the members' (p. 59). Gangs are limited in their efforts to organize, Klein argues, because they are susceptible to random violence and their members are developmentally too young and too conspicuous to engage in organized criminal activity.

For comparison purposes, Klein's 'consensus Eurogang definition' (durable and street-oriented youth groups whose involvement in illegal activity is part of their group identity; see Klein and Maxson, 2006, p. 4) is sufficiently general to capture the essence of gangs described in this book. The notion that crime is integral to the group's reason for being, for instance, lends support to my argument that gangs have evolved from 'associations of criminals' to 'criminal associations' (see also Morselli, 2009). Nevertheless, Klein's treatment of outcomes such as 'durability' and strategies such as 'street orientation' as invariable features is problematic. Being 'street-oriented', for instance, may simply be a variable attribute that depends upon the business of the gang (street-level drug-dealing, for instance) or, indeed, the weather. The consensus Eurogang definition thus is a lot like water, 'it takes on the shape of whatever contains it' but 'slips through your fingers when you try to hold it' (Tsang, 1998, pp. 209–10).

That no two gangs are exactly alike in form and function—the dictum of seminal gang researcher, Frederick Thrasher—holds as true today as it did when it was first said in 1927. But the gangs in this study do share some prevalent descriptive features, which is where I get off the definition merry-go-round. First, they are all self-formed associations of peers that have adopted a common name and other discernible 'conventional' or 'symbolic' signals of membership (see Gambetta, 2009b, p. xix). Second, they are comprised of individuals who recognize themselves (and are recognized by others) as being 'members' of a 'gang' who individually or collectively engage in or have engaged in a pattern of criminal activity. Third, they are not fully open to the public and much of the information concerning their business remains confined within the group—gangs are, in Martín Sánchez-Jankowski's (1991, p. 28) words, 'quasi-private' and 'quasi-secretive' organizations. Fourth, disputes within the group cannot be settled by an external 'third party' as established by the rule of law.

The third and fourth descriptors here are precisely where the problems of trust lie that shape and influence gang processes. More on those later, suffice it to say that gang processes often overlooked in the annals of gang research (for a discussion, see McGloin and Decker, 2010) are front and center throughout this book.

## Data sources and methods

'You never really understand a person until you consider things from his point of view ... until you climb inside of his skin and walk around in it', says Atticus Finch, the protagonist of Harper Lee's (1960) Pulitzer Prize-winning novel, *To Kill a Mockingbird*. In the spirit of suspending what you think you know about others and seeing the world through their eyes, I spent two years from January 2008 to January 2010 embedded in communities and neighborhoods inhabited by gangs and in frequent contact with gang members on their own turf. This book represents my best effort to take into account their perspective and to understand the view of the world held by those in gangs using native terms and categories. During my fieldwork, one gang member commented:

> If you just wrote your book from what you've heard, like from all these conferences and so-called experts, people would not take that serious. People would read the first page and think, 'where did you get this from?', bam and not read it. But, 'cus you've heard what we have to say and you're going to quote us, you've got proof, like bam, people are going to think 'yeah, he did his research, he spoke to so and so, he spoke to gang members and he's got his research properly'. So people will take this serious.
>
> Member 43

I hope he is right.

There is a long tradition of ethnographic gang studies (Short and Strodtbeck, 1965; Thrasher, 1927; Whyte, 1943), but emphasis on my methods is necessary because there is no established, traditional way of organizing and reporting qualitative research. The data are derived primarily from face-to-face interviews with the self-nominated 'members' ($n=52$) and 'associates' ($n=17$) of 12 London gangs, drawn from six of Greater London's 32 boroughs—severely socio-economically deprived geographic areas recognized both in the media and in the literature as being inhabited by gangs and with relatively high rates of serious violence (see Table I.1). These data are supplemented by countless unstructured conversations and observational hours, but also triangulated against media reports and interviews with the parents and siblings of gang members ($n=15$); young people aged 16 to 24 not affiliated with gangs but living in the same areas ($n=27$); and representatives from law enforcement ($n=28$), prosecution, courts, prison, and probation ($n=17$), health, education, and social services ($n=22$); and the voluntary and community sector ($n=20$), who answered my questions from their specific position *vis-à-vis* gangs.

Qualitative methods provide a snapshot rather than a portrait of processes and peoples, but they are appropriate given the sensitive nature of the subject matter and the challenges inherent in gang studies. After all, research is 'the art of the feasible' and access is the primary obstacle to gang research (Blaxter, Hughes, and Tight, 1996, p. 145). As popularized in the best-selling book, *Freakonomics* (Levitt and Dubner, 2005), Sudhir Venkatesh was practically taken hostage by gang members when he tried cold calling them in the stairwell of a Chicago housing project (see also, Venkatesh, 2008). Martín Sánchez-Jankowski (1991) even fought with gang members to gain their approval, which is certainly 'not an ethically acceptable way of doing research, even if the results had proved interesting' (Sullivan, 1994, p. 1642).

Thankfully no one held me captive or challenged me to a duel during the fieldwork for this book. For ethical reasons, I neither hid my being a sociologist from people nor my intentions regarding the use of data collected. From the gang member's point of view, however, someone who looked like me and sounded like me was either a government administrator or police officer. Worse still, a local crime reporter.[2] I still needed people who could convince them otherwise.

Early in my fieldwork, a church pastor advised, 'If you want to know gangs, you've got to know every hairdresser, every barber, every Deejay ... the youth workers, the faith workers, the networkers, the movers and the shakers in the community. They can help you'. Heeding this advice, I befriended people (sometimes by chance, often by design) who sponsored my entry into gangs and guaranteed my safety within the broader community.[3] I interviewed these 'gatekeepers' and intermediaries en route; indeed, many of them saw my interviewing them as an

Table I.1  Demographic statistics for the research setting

| Location | Area (sq. mile) | Population[a] | Population density (sq. mile)[a] | % Black and minority ethnic[a] | Rank in terms of average deprivation[b] | Un-employment[c] | Number of gangs[d] | Homicides 2000–10 (London rank)[e] |
|---|---|---|---|---|---|---|---|---|
| *London* | *607* | *8,174,000* | *13,466* | *40* | – | *9%* | *250* | *1,693* |
| Croydon | 33.6 | 363,400 | 10,163 | 28 | 125 | 10% | 4 | 69 (8) |
| Hackney | 7.4 | 246,300 | 28,495 | 56 | 2 | 9% | 10 | 100 (4) |
| Haringey | 11.4 | 254,900 | 19,668 | 33 | 18 | 10% | 6 | 77 (6) |
| Lambeth | 10.4 | 303,100 | 26,382 | 38 | 19 | 10% | 11 | 131 (1) |
| Lewisham | 13.6 | 275,900 | 19,047 | 34 | 39 | 10% | 8 | 62 (10) |
| Southwark | 11.1 | 288,300 | 24,633 | 38 | 26 | 11% | 6 | 102 (3) |

*Sources:*

[a] 2011 Census.

[b] Department for Communities and Local Government (2007). NB: Out of the 354 local authorities in England, where '1' is the most deprived. Hackney is in the 1 percent most deprived boroughs, Haringey and Lambeth in the 5 percent most deprived, Lewisham and Southwark in the 10 percent most deprived, and Croydon in the 25 percent most deprived.

[c] London's Poverty Profile (2012).

[d] Author's compilation.

[e] MPS Borough Level Crime Figures 2000/01 to 2009/10 (Wikipedia, 2012a).

opportunity to first screen me before referring gang members for interview. These interviews also helped me to develop probes and prompts, which later supplemented my core questions as a means to seek further elaboration, clarification, specific examples and so on.

My reliance on gatekeepers of course introduced potential sources of bias and numerous research challenges. Some contacts were wary of 'gang' research and did not want their participation in it to be perceived by others as a tacit announcement of a local 'gang problem'.[4] Other contacts rescheduled meetings at short notice and conducted them in multiple sittings or in remote settings. Some changed roles or moved away during my fieldwork, thus relinquishing them of the authority to broker access to gangs and gang members as agreed. Still others got ill or injured and entered into prolonged periods of hospitalization and rehabilitation during my fieldwork. Practically everyone I met promised greater access to gangs and gang members than they actually delivered. To ensure my fieldwork continued uninterrupted I worked across multiple networks and maintained a variety of separate contact chains. With hindsight, this approach maximized the breadth of data collected and provided an important check on internal validity.

Gaining access to some interviewees was a case of going through all six degrees of separation. Gang youth were identified through a snowball or 'chain referral' sampling technique (Biernacki and Waldorf, 1981), which despite its limitations (see Petersen and Valdez, 2005) is common in field studies of gangs and other reticent or 'hidden populations' (Heckathorn, 1997, 2002). The 'vouching' intrinsic to snowball sampling enabled earlier respondents to verify the legitimacy of others as gang 'members' or 'associates' and thus their eligibility for interview (Decker and Van Winkle, 1996, p. 41). A gang member is defined here as someone who identified himself or herself as being a member of a gang (such as through verbal statements, tattoos or correspondence), but also successfully answered a series of screening questions concerning the overall orientation of the gang they were claiming. They also had their identity 'vouched for' by a minimum of one other gang member.

This study differs from some British gang studies (for example, Alexander, 2000; Pitts, 2008) in focusing on the experiences of people who claim the identity of a gang member for themselves, rather than having it placed upon them by others. They described themselves as committed to their gangs, rather than 'drifting' between conventional and criminalized activities like Anthony Gunter's (2008) research participants. Gang associates, by contrast, are prospective gang members who, through talk, conduct or behavior, displayed a specific desire or intent to join a gang. Gang associates neither recognized themselves nor were recognized by others as *bona fide* gang members, yet they offended with gang members and were associated with them by law enforcement and criminal justice agencies, or community information.

The ethics committee of the University of Oxford approved this study. Of course, research on gangs that leaves out crime 'leaves out a critical part of the phenomenon' (Sánchez-Jankowski, 1991, p. 16). To avoid any compromising situations, interviewees agreed not to disclose anything that only the two of us knew; not to provide identifying details of criminal activity (dates, addresses, and victim profiles, for example); and not to discuss the specifics of scheduled offences. As a result, I really only learned about things that others knew and could have reported if they were so inclined. All research participants gave informed consent but for reasons of confidentiality, interviewees are identifiable only by the code 'Member' (for gang members) or 'Associate' (for gang associates) and a randomly generated number (for example, 'Member 7' or 'Associate 10'). All 12 gangs have likewise been given pseudonyms derived from the NATO phonetic alphabet (see Appendix 1).

My fieldwork concluded at the point of informational saturation. For gatekeeper and other key informant interviews, little documentation was needed beyond a topic outline informed by the 'Eurogang Research Program Expert Survey' (Weerman et al., 2009) or *aide-mémoire* containing a few brief, very general questions. The gang member and associate interviews followed a semi-structured format, but in practice, this often became open-ended, with an average duration of two hours but a range of 30 minutes to five hours. All interviews were largely performed in pre-arranged public settings, such as classrooms, cafés, pubs, parks, playgrounds, even the alcoves and stairwells of tower blocks.

Gang members' willingness to talk did not surprise me—as a teacher, I understood that young people can be hesitant of highly structured and directed discussion, but they are enthusiastic conversationalists; particularly when their own lives are under discussion. Given the topics under investigation and the fact that gang members typically associate a tape-recorder with the words, 'what you say may be given in evidence', however, it was not always possible or appropriate to record the interviews; in which case I took extensive notes by hand. Such notes were later supplemented with any contextual information that was difficult to document at the time. Audio files ($n=31$) were transcribed. All files ($n=69$) were coded thematically. Please be aware that quotations recorded by hand and used in this book are not strictly verbatim, but rather faithfully reconstructed: in no way do they distort the language or intentions of interviewees.

Differences in the reliability of what was learned from the interviewees transcribed versus interviewees recorded through note-taking was minimal as confirmed by the interviewees who were interviewed more than once and using both methods (*n*=19). As Mark Fleisher (2005), among others, have argued, however, the interview material that one gets with gang members in one-off encounters is substantively different from the narratives that emerge in interviews that result after numerous encounters in the context of ethnographic research. Given that some interviewees revised prior statements once they came to know me better, texts derived from face-to-face interviews must be interpreted as co-productions of the interviewer and interviewee (Holstein and Gubrium, 1995).

Sample demographics can be found in the appendices of this book. Interviewees were predominantly (77 percent) males with an ethnic identity associated with the Census category 'Black or Black British' (93 percent), a mean age of 20 (range: 13–34), and a three- to four-year average period of serious gang association (range: one to 14 years). A total of 58 interviewees were 'active' at time of interview while 11 had 'retired' from active gang duties; 19 had served time either in an adult prison or young offender institution.

It is important to highlight some limitations of the data. First, I rely largely upon retrospective accounts. The problem with retrospective accounts is of course that they are contingent upon memory, which is selective and fades with time (Sudman and Bradburn, 1973). Generally speaking, salient events are recalled more easily than events that are frequent or mundane. With hindsight most people also tend to rationalize their motivations (Viterna, 2006) and may do so in accordance with their own interpretation of the interview situation.

Second, black young people are disproportionately represented in my sample. This reflects the fact that current resources—and therefore the starting points for chain referral—are almost exclusively focused on the black community. I do not claim that gangs are a specifically black phenomenon, but the data do allow me to explore the views of black gang members of the effects of ethnicity and racial discrimination.

Third, who I am is a potentially potent source of bias. But it could equally be argued gang members accepted me because of who I am. Because I was different from them, for example, gang members did not perceive me as a threat;[5] my interest in their lives was perhaps even peculiar enough to intrigue. Having lived in a number of multicultural cities, from Leicester to London in Britain and New York to Minneapolis-St Paul in the United States, moreover, I felt comfortable speaking and interacting with people from different ethnic backgrounds. My experience as a teacher also appropriately moderated my affect. Teaching indeed lent me some credibility in the field, particularly among youths fascinated by American gang culture and for whom my living and working in New York City was a source of prestige.

As Sveinung Sandberg (2008) found among the young drug dealers he met in Oslo, Norway, gang members are skilled in the language of the professionals with whom they come into contact; the language about them, not the language their experience lives in (see also, Hallsworth and Young, 2008). In the interview situation, it has been assumed that gang members' general 'mistrust or wariness' of others exacerbates the possibility of understatement, exaggeration, concealment, or outright deception that exists in any conversation (Sánchez-Jankowski, 1991, p. 24). Others note a tendency for 'mythologizing' and the exaggeration of interviewees' roles in violence and the group (Decker and Van Winkle, 1996, p. 49). In an effort to mitigate these risks and tendencies, I adopted a theoretical and methodological perspective that prioritized my interviewees as active architects and narrators of their own experiences, thus enabling them to express their own 'repertoire of narratives' (Sandberg, 2010).

Any data presented in descriptive form represent generalized patterns that came out of the fieldwork. Any idiosyncrasies noted in relation to these consistently observed generalized patterns are identified as such. Quotations are employed throughout the book as examples of these patterns or idiosyncrasies. The reader is advised that some gangs are discussed in more detail than others, which reflects both the level of access I was afforded and the amount of secondary data available with respect to such gangs. In addition to police data, for instance, I relied upon a range of cultural sources for verbal, visual, and written descriptions of gang argot, names, territories, rivalries, and alliances, including web pages and social networking sites used by gang members. Unsurprisingly, some gangs have a greater public profile than others.

## Theoretical framework and chapter outline

The gang novice and gang expert alike should find something of interest in this book. **Chapter 1** explores the implications of my interviewees self-reported motivations for gang membership, including the search for safety and security in contexts where families are stretched to their limit, government protection of rights is limited at best, and the search for meaningful occupation in contexts where opportunities for education, employment, and training are curtailed. This chapter places gangs in the context of social, economic, and cultural exclusion, and draws parallels between the profiles of gang members and the profiles of the people involved in the 2011 UK riots.

**Chapter 2** examines the extent to which gangs seek to regulate and control the production and distribution of one or more given commodities or services unlawfully. The chapter thus contributes to longstanding debates over the form and function of gangs outside of the United States (Klein et al., 2001; Decker and Weerman, 2005; Van Gemert, Peterson, and Lien, 2008), the nature and extent of gang evolution (Weisel, 2002; Ayling, 2011), the role of gangs in the drugs trade (Bjerregaard, 2010), and whether or not gangs constitute a form of organized crime (Decker, Bynum, and Weisel, 1998; Decker and Curry, 2002; Decker and Pyrooz, 2011b). The chapter describes an evolutionary process within gangs wherein gangs become increasingly formal groups with more structured organization, roles, and functions as they evolve toward a business model. This chapter focuses on the fluid and dynamic nature of gangs; the sequential actualization stages they go through; the role of internal and external factors in organizational change; the impact of drug distribution on gang organizational structure; and the acquisition of 'resources', including violence, necessary to govern markets.

**Chapter 3** pries open the 'black box' of gang organization (see Decker, Katz, and Webb, 2008). The chapter examines group size and (sub) group interaction, hierarchy and leadership, organizational mobility, incentives, rules, and sanctions for violating the rules—measures implicated in prior research for understanding the nature and extent of gang organization (Decker and Van Winkle, 1996; Decker, Bynum, and Weisel, 1998; Decker, Katz, and Webb, 2008). The chapter explores how gangs use incentives to curtail selfish behavior and how life 'on road' is essentially a 'ratings' game or tournament for those who wish to compete for the chance of promotion. How youths earn ratings, how ratings are regulated, and by whom, are also discussed. The chapter further sheds light on the role of prison in facilitating gang exchange and the role of women in gangs, drawing a distinction between female gang associates who perform a supportive or sexual role and *bona fide* female gang members who employ violence in the defense of the gang and its territory.

**Chapter 4** examines the role of media and technology in gang life, including the use of smart phones and social networking sites both in 'gang member' and 'gang-related' activity. This chapter further explores the expressive *and* instrumental role of music in gang members' lives, the connection between violence in the media and violence on the streets, and how gangs as organizations seek association with the symbolic elements of popular culture that best promote their image. This chapter specifically looks at the appeal of the American gang for British gang members and elaborates upon Marcus Felson's (2006) 'street gang strategy' by examining the media myths that gangs, for protective purposes, borrow and cultivate in order to appear more dangerous than they really are. The use of popular culture references within the symbolic organization of gangs, I argue, is one way in which gangs overcome their secrecy constraints, verify to outsiders their status as a gang, and advertise their qualities to prospective members.

Through application of signaling theory to the strategies gangs and their prospective members adopt during the recruitment process, **Chapter 5** answers one of the most crucial unanswered questions in the literature on street gangs: why, in any given pool of individuals with similar sociological profiles and motivations, do only some gain entry into gangs? The chapter outlines the primary trust dilemma that gangs face in their uncertainty over the quality of recruits. Given that none of the desirable trust-warranting properties for gang membership can be readily discovered from observation, gangs look for observable signs correlated with these properties. The chapter also outlines the secondary trust dilemma that gangs face in their uncertainty over the reliability of signs because certain agents (for example, police informants, rival gang members, and adventure-seekers) might mimic them. Much like a peahen trusts that a peacock is a good mate because his extravagantly large and colorful tail is hard-to-fake, the signs gangs look for must be equally hard-to-fake.

If you've ever wondered why someone would dare permanently tattoo his or her face with gang symbols; or wear conspicuous gang insignia when crossing notorious territorial boundaries; or post extravagant acts of violence on YouTube that, in this digital age of perfect remembering, can be used as evidence against them; or pick a fight with someone much bigger and stronger than they are; or tout a criminal record like a badge of honor; this chapter has the answer: the above are all hard-to-fake signals of proficiency and perseverance that gang recruiters interpret like lines on curriculum vitae. In displaying them, prospective gangsters burn bridges back to mainstream society; they show rather than tell gangs that they have exactly what it takes to become the next big thing on the street stage.

**Chapter 5** argues that gangs overcome their informational handicap ex-ante by screening and selecting among prospective members based on 'hard-to-fake' signals. The study of recruitment into gangs lends itself to signaling theory, but given its complexity, it is incumbent upon me to take a moment to explain what exactly signaling theory is.[6] In a nutshell, signaling theory is concerned with differentiating between the honesty and the costliness of a 'signal', or any observable feature that a sender purposefully displays to modify a receiver's beliefs about something or someone (Maynard Smith and Harper, 2003). When a gang member (the sender) takes off his shirt to reveal his gang tattoos (the signal), for example, he is 'signaling' his status as a gang member to someone (the receiver), who, assuming he understands the signal, will respond according to his own status in relation to the gang member.

'Strategic' costs or 'handicaps', such as resource expenditure, predation, and risk are one way to ensure that a signal is perceived as honest. 'Indices' (Maynard Smith and Harper, 2003) or 'automatic cues' (Gambetta and Hamill, 2005), such as one's accent or phenotype, are another way, not least because it is impossible for those without the quality being signaled to successfully mimic them (Cronk, 2005). To avoid confusion between strategic and efficacy costs, Chapter 5 describes 'hard-to-fake' signals and how if they cluster together to point in the same direction, they come close to discriminating between 'right' and 'wrong' types (for a discussion, see Gambetta, 2009a).

**Chapter 6** moves on to the subject of gang desistance, yet another widely discussed but little studied aspects of gangs (see Decker and Lauritsen, 2002; Decker and Van Winkle, 1996; Pyrooz and Decker, 2011; Pyrooz, Decker, and Webb, 2010). The argument is that gangs are obliged to let their members 'retire' under certain conditions because an unhappy or reluctant gang member is a potentially disruptive or unproductive gang member. These conditions stipulate that (a) gang members possess a reason for leaving that can easily be 'sold' to the gang at large, and (b) retirees subject themselves to some form of ongoing monitoring, remaining proximate and passively loyal to the gang post-desistance. Desistance is a complex process that like recruitment is shaped by the constraints of illegality and secrecy that gangs work within. Gang members retire for many reasons, but it is how they present themselves in retirement that matters most for their success and survival.

**Chapter 7** examines what works in gang intervention and prevention, with emphasis on the government's move toward finding American solutions to British problems (including zero-tolerance police gang units, civil gang injunctions, Operation Ceasefire, and other public health models) and my own experiences designing and developing the 'Growing Against Gangs and Violence' partnership with London's

Metropolitan Police Service. This chapter further advances some implications for policy and practice by addressing whether or not sufficient attention is being paid to the theory or rationale underpinning gang prevention and intervention, its components, and the intended target group population.

Finally, the **Conclusion** reflects upon both the overall processes and particulars of this study, draws parallels between street gangs in London and elsewhere and street gangs and other extra-legal groups, and offers recommendations for further academic inquiry.

## A walk on the wild side

The 2011 UK riots got everyone asking, 'how do gangs work?' I suspect not everyone will like my answer. But this is my truth. And as a sociologist tired of watching his beloved discipline turn more and more inward and become more self-referential and combative and postmodern and irrelevant and intentionally difficult to read, I hope it motivates others to leave the office in search of their own. At the very least, I hope it starts a conversation. *Carpe diem.*

# 1
## Gangs and Society

Not long after the 2011 UK riots, I co-wrote a paper for *Policing Today* questioning the role of gangs in urban disorder (Densley and Mason, 2011). I argued that by attributing the riots to gangs, the government had conflated the actions of gang members as individuals ('gang member' activity) with the actions of gangs as organizations ('gang-related' activity); a subject to which I shall return in Chapter 3. Gangs were present at the riots but not controlling them, I said, in part because gang identities ceased to be relevant in such a context. If anything, the riots actually disrupted conventional gang activity because gangs lost control of their markets. The perceived suspension of normal rules instead presented gang members with an unprecedented opportunity to acquire consumer products for 'free'. In the words of Philip Zimbardo (2008, p. 8), author of the infamous Stanford Prison Experiment, 'You are not the same person working alone as you are in a group.'

My thinking about the riots was informed not only by my training as a sociologist, but also via an experience I had as a secondary school student when I was a face in a crowd out to avenge one Year 11 classmate who had been assaulted by a group of boys from a rival school because he was judged to be wearing the wrong colors on a bus that crossed catchment areas. Dressed in school uniform and apoplectic with rage, we descended upon the bus stop brandishing skipping ropes, field hockey sticks, rounders bats, Bunsen burners, utility clamps, workplace utility knives, and whatever else we could salvage as weapons from school classrooms. Thankfully this never amounted to anything—the boys got wind of us lying in wait and stayed home. But I was clearly not myself. The group context diluted responsibility and created anonymity. I followed the crowd and let other people do the hard work of making decisions for me. Like the middle-aged and middle-class women who went 'shopping' off-the-rack at abandoned department stores during the 2011 riots, I got carried away with the moment and with my peers. I had no real grievance. I was only partially committed to countercultural norms. As David Matza (1964) said, I was able to 'drift' into delinquency and drift back out again.

Admittedly, my assessment of the riots was largely speculative because at the time there was very little substantive evidence available. But a comprehensive 'reading' of the riots, which encompassed interviews with 270 rioters and was published some months later by the *Guardian* and London School of Economics, agreed that the government had mistaken the role of gangs in the summer disturbances (Lewis et al., 2011). The riots were instead precipitated by hostility toward police, particularly over the use of stop and search, and a deep sense of injustice. A 'citizens' inquiry' into the riots likewise concluded they were caused by a combination of high youth unemployment and basic police incivility (Citizen's UK, 2012). Other studies cited as contributing factors the growing divide between rich and poor and concern over a lack of decent affordable housing.[1]

The riots began when a protest about the police shooting of Tottenham resident Mark Duggan turned violent. After initially claiming that approximately 30 percent of those arrested in London were gang members, the Home Office (2011) revised the figure to 19 percent, a figure that dropped to 13 percent countrywide. But rioters and gang members do share similar profiles. Like gang members, many of the rioters were existing criminals. The Ministry of Justice (2012) reported that 76 percent had a previous caution or conviction, 26 percent had more than ten previous offences, and 26 percent had been in prison before. Like gang members, the rioters were also predominantly young and male. Just under half were aged 18 to 24, with 26 percent aged between 10 and 17 years old—children, in the eyes of the law (Home Office, 2011). A third of them had been excluded from school and the majority had educational difficulties. The racial profile of the rioters also closely resembled the ethnic make-up of the local population. The majority of rioters in London were black or of mixed race, for example, while in Manchester or Liverpool, they were overwhelmingly white; ditto gang members (Metropolitan Police Service, 2007).

Many of themes associated with the riots also overlap with the themes that came out of my research with gangs. This is perhaps to be expected given that the London boroughs most affected by the riots (Croydon, Hackney, Haringey, Lambeth, Lewisham, and Southwark) are the same boroughs in which my fieldwork took place. Rioters identified the same economic (that is, the absence of money, jobs, opportunity) and social (that is, disproportionate treatment, the search for respect and so on) motivations for joining the riots as my interviewees did for joining gangs. Rioters, like my interviewees, described being repeatedly stopped and searched by police. Some rioters, like my interviewees, came from 'troubled families' and 'dysfunctional homes' (Cameron, 2011). But where the rioters and my interviewees differed is that despite what the government first claimed, the rioters on the whole were not as committed to 'criminality' as my interviewees were. My interviewees did not 'drift' between conventional and criminal behavior as I once did (Matza, 1964). The question is, why not?

This chapter explores some of the aforementioned themes in detail, with the aim of better understanding the purpose of gangs and the motivations of gang members. I begin by exploring interviewees' lived experiences of violence within the fieldwork sites.

## Welcome to the neighborhood

Compared to most large American cities, London is relatively safe. Shadow Home Secretary Chris Grayling famously made the mistake of implying otherwise, conflating the estates of London with the street corners of Baltimore, the city portrayed in gritty US television drama *The Wire*—a curious analogy given that the annual murder rate in London is two deaths per 100,000, compared with a staggering 35 per 100,000 in Baltimore (Watt and Oliver, 2009). One criminological axiom, however, is that crime is local and crime rates vary dramatically among neighborhoods in close geographical proximity (Sampson, 2006). Crime continues to trend downward nationally—homicide in particular is at a 30-year low—but for interviewees living in areas with no infrastructure and lots of gang activity, it felt like crime was going up. Approximately 40 percent of the 145 teenage homicides in London occurring between January 2005 and December 2012 were perpetrated within the six fieldwork boroughs (Citizen's Report, 2012). For total homicides overall, Lambeth ranks first, Southwark ranks third, Hackney ranks fourth, Haringey ranks sixth, Croydon ranks eighth, and Croydon ranks tenth out of London's 32 boroughs (Wikipedia, 2012a).

### Under-protected

When I first proposed this study in 2007, the teenage homicide rate in London increased nearly 70 percent from a steady decade average of 16 to 27. When Billy Cox, 15, was gunned down in his bedroom on Valentine's Day that year, he became the third teenage boy shot dead in south London in just 11 days. He followed James Smartt-Ford, 16, killed in front of hundreds of people attending a disco at Streatham ice arena

on February 3, and Michael Dosunmu, 15, shot in the early hours of
February 6, as he lay in bed at home in Peckham. Such murders had a
significant impact upon the community. Said one key informant:

> The game has changed. Gangs will now kill you in public with your
> family and friends watching. They will run up in a man's house and
> assassinate him while he's asleep. The home used to be a sanctuary
> but now nothing is off limits. Kids are sleeping in body armor for fear
> of being shot in their beds. They feel like they can never be alone.
> They must always watch their back because someone's out there
> waiting for them to slip.

The proximate presence of these threats, both real and perceived,
increased support for gangs and enabled them to successfully persuade
others that they belonged to and protected the community. Protection
was indeed one of the primary reasons why interviewees joined gangs—
gang membership was described as rational adaptation to the perennial
threat of violence that was present in the neighborhood.

Many interviewees expected to die not from old age and natural
causes but from interpersonal violence. Every day they were forced to
negotiate environments in which the young were viewed as prey by
various predators. Member 42 said, 'I live in a certain area where gangs
are having fights on that main road. Daily. I live off that main road. I'm
caught up in it.' Member 26 elaborated:

> Drug-dealers trying to sell, crack fiends looking to steal or score, and
> gang members out to make a name for themselves. Fuck Afghanistan,
> we need troops out here. Every time man be leaving his yard he walks
> into the Gladiators' arena. Sometimes it's kill or be killed.

Interviewees regularly made lifestyle changes to manage everyday
threats associated with perceived risk of violent victimization, including, in some cases, making alternative travel plans because of safety
concerns on their way to and from school. They were almost preoccu-
pied with studying the environment for possible threats and often so
attuned to the harassment they faced on the streets—the threats, grop-
ing, suggestive gestures, and lewd comments—they had developed a
repertoire of physical and verbal gymnastics to help defuse it. To project
an image that they are 'not to be fucked with' and best 'left the fuck
alone', said Member 11, youths walked with a 'kind of bop'— that is, a
confident and typically arrogant or aggressive gait—and practiced their

'screw face', which can only be 'described at best as a blank expression' and at worst as 'hostile' scowl or look of distaste (Gunter, 2008, p. 353). As Member 22 said, '[y]ou've gotta look tough, scary, not like one of them Chris Brown niggers, all sweet and shit'.[2]

For some interviewees, violence had become a part of everyday life. They viewed fighting as the best or only way to resolve conflicts and gain respect. When Member 31 was in Year 7 at school, for instance, he got into a fight with a boy who 'wanted to be the badder man [with] more respect'. Member 31 recalled:

> He pulled out a knife. He was brandishing it. I didn't think he'd do it but he actually stabbed me. ... He went for my chest, my neck, but I moved my hand to block it and it hit my wrist. He ran off. I was wearing a black tracksuit ... I lifted up my hand, I saw blood pouring out of my sleeve. ... He'd cut completely through the artery and the tendon in my wrist.

I pick up the relationship between violence and respect in Chapter 3, suffice it to say here that fighting was almost a daily occurrence for interviewees—in some cases they fought so often that it was impossible for them to even quantify. Member 17's best estimate:

> I felt like it was every day. I just wanted to be with my friends but I couldn't because I would see a girl on the bus and she'll come up behind us, she might have a bat in her hand, metal baseball bat, and I mean I have to fight her.

Riding to his friend's house one afternoon, for instance, Member 32 was 'stabbed twice in [the] leg' for refusing to submit his mobile phone and bicycle to 'the group of boys [who] came around to rob anyone in that area'. He explained,

> Someone ran from behind me and pulled my hood over my face ... we was just fighting and I remember, like, someone going for me with a knife. ... I'd been stabbed in the leg. But, [because of] the adrenaline, I didn't realize [until later].

Member 7, a female, recalled an equally gruesome experience:

> I was beaten up ... with a bottle nine times in the back of my head. ... Bottled nine times before it bust on my head, there was a great crack

on my head. Nine times ... because it wasn't cracking on my head
that's the only reason why she carried on, do you see what I'm trying
to say? She bottled me nine times and I actually felt it nine times.
I will never forget it.

Incidents such as these often occurred before interviewees ever associated with gangs. Interviews with young people not affiliated with
gangs but living in the same areas, moreover, confirmed that they too
grappled with similar issues and shared similar experiences, regardless
of membership status. A consistent theme in the gang literature, however, is that youths involved in gangs are disproportionately victimized
compared to youths who are not (Peterson, Taylor, and Esbensen, 2004;
Taylor et al., 2007). The data do not allow me to make general comparisons, but I can report that 19 of the 69 gang member and associate
interviewees had previously been threatened with guns, nine had been
shot at and three actually had been shot; 55 had previously been threatened with knives and other weapons, 28 had been stabbed, and nine
had been injured with other weapons; 41 had been robbed; and one had
been kidnapped. All 69 interviewees also reported that they had family
or friends who had been shot, stabbed, or beaten by gangs, and at least
seven reported that they had family or friends who had died as a result
of gang violence. Member 3 told me, 'I've had one proper deep, like
friend killed and two school friends that I used to go school with killed.
So altogether three school friends dead.'

Only a relatively small number of people are actually involved in the
most serious violence. Trevor Bennett and Katy Holloway (2004, p. 313)
extrapolate, for instance, there are approximately 20,000 active gang
members in Britain, with a confidence level of plus or minus 5000.
This is likely an underestimate given the data is based only on those
gang members aged 17 and above in the arrestee population from 1999
to 2002, but even 50,000 is a drop in the ocean of 62 million people.
A neighborhood can feel very violent even when the actual perpetrators are comparatively few in number, however, not least because the
community often knows the fantastically active offenders by name.
The police also often know them by name, my fieldwork suggests, but
in communities historically 'over-policed and to a large extent under-
protected' (Macpherson, 1999, p. 312), confidence of residents in police
to properly intervene is low:

Police is all about numbers. They're not about anything else. If
there's like a 10 percent decrease in crime on the streets, then they're

all right with that regardless of whether things are actually any safer or not. Out here you're not living under police protection. No matter how many times the police said they'll protect you, they're not going to protect you. So we find our own protection. We protect our own ... 'cus the police ain't doing shit for us, we police ourselves. We equip ourselves with tools to protect ourselves, you understand? We're a phone call away. Where the police? Police just tell you to go file a report.

Member 25

As gatekeepers into the criminal justice system, police provoked the ire of interviewees most, but their frustration certainly extended to the system at large. Member 37 observed:

That's the fear that people are facing out there and that's why so many guns and knives are getting too high out there. The police can't protect you. Because if this person get rid of me, he ain't going to go to jail, he'll ... go into remand for a couple of years but then the case will get shut down because there's not enough evidence, so 'we're going to have to let the person go. We can't keep him too long'. ... The police say to us, 'we'll protect you, just come to court, we'll make you speak behind the glass, no one will know'. They can't protect you for shit. For a young person, from this estate or from this particular place, if you're going to make them do something like that, at least remove them. Remove the whole family, because you know once they go to court and stand there and say 'yeah, he done it', if they go back to the estate, you know exactly, their house is probably burned down or their little sister be getting raped.

Suspicious of outside authority and increasingly tolerant of law breaking as a strategy for getting by, some communities had developed the sort of inward-looking insularity conducive to the emergence of drug markets and gang structures. One Lambeth resident told me, 'As more and more people turn a blind eye, the gangs become more and more blatant. More brazen. Someone can get robbed at knifepoint at a crowded bus stop and simply no one intervenes.' Outsiders may see a 'community', he added, but insiders see something very different: people who have 'invested everything' in the community, such as small business owners, living side-by-side with people who have 'no investment whatsoever in the community', in part because they have come to see the community as part of their oppression.

This community elder went on:

> You ever walk down Brixton Road [in Lambeth]? Get off the tube, walk up the stairs and before you're even out the station door you get asked if you want some Skunk. You can smell it. Then, outside Superdrug and the old Woolworths, it's crack. Keep walking and outside KFC it's cannabis again. Outside Ritzy cinema, then, you can pretty much get anything. Now I know this. You know this. Don't you think every kid around here knows this? They have to run the gauntlet every day just to get to where they're going.

'Would more police on the streets help?' I asked. But herein lay the paradox: some people are comforted by increased police presence, but others feel it makes interactions with the police more vitriolic and full of suspicion.

## Over-policed

There is a long history of assertive policing of London's black communities (Hall et al., 1978). Interviewees said that intense police supervision and frequent stops and searches had created resentment among them, which generated hostile suspects and increased their probability of arrest. Member 45 said:

> If you're black, you're suspicious. If you're black in Brixton, forget about it. The police hassle you. 'Where are you going?' 'What are you doing here?' The same officers stop you time and again. They know your house is just there but they do it anyway because they can. So straight away your back's up, but if you say something they get all aggressive, pushing you up against the wall and shit, humiliating you out in front of your girl. There's only some much you can take.

Interviewees described stop and search as being excessive and disrespectful. For example:

> [Some] things that the police do are totally unnecessary. It's like, you're walking, you're walking, you've just come back from college minding your business and suddenly the bully van pulls up and ten of them jump out all yelling and screaming. You're put up against the wall, they put their hands in your pockets. [They tell you to] jump. I've got my work in my bag, they chuck things out, there's nothing in it. ... Then they just leave it all there on the floor, 'sorry'.
>
> Associate 12

Member 36 even recalled an incident in which he was handcuffed, thrown into a police van, driven to a neighboring borough, and forced to walk back through rival gang territory. He said that the police were fully responsible for the fact that he was robbed of his mobile phone that day en route home, but he never reported it because he knew no one would believe him.

It's easy to dismiss the above as the neurotic musings of a disgruntled gangster, but I've been there when an unmarked car screeches up on a corner and men in plain-clothes jump out demanding compliance from teenagers. It's scary. From the wrong angle it looks like the cops are robbing the robbers. Hence why interviewees would refer to officers of the Met's Territorial Support Group, who are responsible for a lot of stops and searches, as the 'Take, Smash, Grab' or 'boi dem'—a reference to the way in which militaristic police allegedly 'boi' or bully kids into submission. Interviewees cited such behavior as evidence that the state openly discriminated against black people and that conventional protection under the law was either not available or not applicable to them.

First impressions count. If someone's first stop and search is a bad stop and search then that someone will likely resent the police for life. Repeat negative police encounters, moreover, can combine with a perceived lack of attention to the victimization of black young people to validate the notion of joining a gang. For example, Associate 12 said:

> Me personally, I've had a bad experience with the police before as well so it makes you just hate them. It makes you want to do the opposite of what they want. So basically they kind of, like, trigger your desire to be part of this [gang].

Young people in these areas face a double bind as they construct their identities. If they adopt the dress and demeanor of a 'neek' (a portmanteau word from 'nerd' and 'geek'), they face ridicule and violence from some of their peers. If they emulate the dress and swagger of a 'gangster', they face repeated interventions from the police. As Member 37 defiantly stated:

> You're automatically stereotyped. It's like all black people are criminals. [The police] got this policy where, more than three [people in a group], you're considered a gang so you automatically get stopped. ... After a time, you feel like, 'oh we a gang now? Okay, we'll show you gang.'

More than validating the notion of joining a gang, therefore, harsh discipline can embolden the gangs to challenge the police and effectively take them on.[3]

In their defense, law enforcement argued they resorted to a more militaristic style of policing the black community only because they received little cooperation from the black community in the first place. Some police cited cultural barriers with recent immigrants, specifically African refugees, who presumed police in Britain were as unethical as police back home. These were legitimate concerns. As a child, for example, Member 32 witnessed a family member gunned down by police during an armed raid on his village. Experiences such as this forever change people's view of state authority. To further confound matters, local authorities housed rival Somali clans and other warring ethnic groups together in the same social housing estates. As one police officer recalled, 'It's like putting Irish Catholics and Irish Protestants together at the height of the Troubles and expecting them to all get along because they're Irish.'

## A tale of two cities

Interviewees aged amid a soundtrack of barking dogs, domestic disputes, gunshots, and police sirens. They played in dilapidated hallways, poorly illuminated stairwells, and weary elevators peppered with broken glass, crude graffiti, and the stench of urine. 'The perfect set for a post-apocalyptic movie,' one gatekeeper quipped during a routine tour of his estate. Interviewees reported being confined to socio-economically deprived areas of the inner city where access to basic services such as doctors and post offices was limited and opportunities for valued employment and consumption were absent:

> There's no jobs, no opportunities here. Walk down, like, when you came here, what did you see? Bookies, off-license, chicken shop, pub, and ain't no nice pub but some, you know, with bare alcoholics sitting there all day. Dodgy mobile phone shop, pound shop, another chicken shop. I don't even know where the library is right now. This place is almost built like to encourage crime.
>
> Member 13

For Member 26, surroundings such as those described above create the perception among young people of 'two Londons' living side by side; one characterized by wealth and power and the other characterized by poverty and deprivation. Member 26 completed his version of the 'dual city' thesis (Mollenkopf and Castells, 1991) by saying, 'We see those rich people over there and we want what they got. We want our piece. So we'll shot green [cannabis], steal, rob, fight, till we get it.' His sense of relative deprivation was heightened by the fact that his mother was part of the 'working poor' and thus had direct and at times intimate knowledge of the lives of the affluent families she served.

Wealth and poverty sit side by side in London. They always have, but things are different since the sudden deregulation of the London Stock Exchange or 'Big Bang' in October 1986. Seemingly overnight, London became one of the world's critical financial hubs. In 1986, banking, finance, business services and leasing accounted for 15.5 percent of UK GDP. By 2008, the figure for business services and finance alone had almost doubled to 29.2 percent, according to the Office for National Statistics. Explosive growth created a super rich class of traders, investment bankers, and hedge fund managers (Freeland, 2012). Russian oligarchs and other rich foreigners, in turn, were 'drawn to London by the rule of law, a favorable tax regime, a cluster of big houses, vibrant culture, superb private schools and the presence of other rich foreigners' (Economist, 2012a). But the 'average' Londoner lacked the specific human capital necessary to service this new knowledge-based casino economy, which rewarded the gamblers rather than the grafters.

Under the pressures of globalization, deindustrialization, privatization, and drastic cuts in public expenditure, British workers saw real incomes stagnate while the richest saw their share of national wealth surge. Since the 1970s, income inequality among working-age people rose faster in Britain than in any other rich nation. The share of the top 1 percent of income earners doubled from 7 percent to 14 percent today (Organization for Economic Cooperation and Development, 2011). Traditional youth labor markets collapsed. Traditional black jobs in manufacturing and nationalized public services disappeared (Pitts, 2007). Although spending on public services went up, at the same time benefits to the poor were worth less and taxes were less redistributive (Standing, 2011).

We now know that explosive growth in the financial sector also brought greater risks. Pre-Big Bang, banks were constrained by strict capital reserve and liquidity ratios and sensible rules that limited the taking on of excessive risks in mortgage lending. Bankers were equally constrained by fixed-rate commission. Post-Big Bang, all bets were off. The rise of derivatives created a network of products that locked global markets together and increased the threat of contagion. Excess consumer credit and rising technological materialism gave only the appearance of wealth among the middle class. Banks grew too fast, borrowed too much, and became too big both to fail and manage. In 2008, the bubble burst.

Haringey is now the most divided borough in London. Of its 19 wards, four are in the richest 10 percent and five are in the poorest 10 percent. Southwark is the next most divided borough, with two of the richest and four of the poorest wards in each area. Croydon, Hackney, Lambeth, and Lewisham are not far behind (London's Poverty Profile, 2011). Such contrasts in affluence, power, and esteem between different communities were highly visible and resonated with particular force among interviewees, exacerbated by the rhetoric of a celebrity culture that upholds the right of all to accomplish their 'dream'.

Race was the 'principal modality' (Hall et al., 1978, p. 347) through which interviewees sought to comprehend the disadvantage and discrimination they experienced. The implication that some interviewees drew from their social position—and the disproportionate educational exclusion, unemployment, and underemployment that their families and neighbors experienced—was that a dominant 'white' society had impeded all legitimate potential to realize their goals. They did not perceive their experiences as being anything to do with class, but they reported a heightened—even Mertonian (1938)—sense of exclusion from the achievement of legitimate goals and an awareness of crime as an alternative route to success. After describing the poor work rewards of his mother, Member 37 asked:

> So who are you to tell me not to go there? You're going to slave me. You're going to make me work for you and you're going to tax me, you're going take all my money away from me? Basically I'm working for nothing. I'm working and yet my money's just going to go back into your hand?

His use of the word 'slave' as a transitive verb links with Member 48's perspective on how racism is a force that is used against him and so can also be used (by tapping into English folklore) to justify or neutralize offending:

> Being black is nuts, the odds are against us, man. People push us in the corner and force us to do things and then when we do, they go on like they are shocked and better than us. I refuse to go to work to get paid shit and treated like shit. Look at my mum and how hard

she works and it doesn't get her anywhere. Fuck asking, I'm taking. I'm like Robin Hood. Take from the rich to feed the poor.

Member 48

The interviewees above evoke the legacy of black servitude in much the same fashion that Ken Pryce's (1979, p. 56) black research participants did over thirty years ago; considering the menial 'shit work' available to them as 'slave labor'.

The experience of racism is both current and historically reproduced. Member 44 reported on the experience of his grandparents and how this had broadly shaped his expectations about the world, or 'worldview':

My grandparents, when they came here, were less than dogs in the eyes of some white people. No blacks, no dogs.[4] They don't forget that. That get's passed down to their kids. ... My parents were in the [1981 Brixton] riots. They were there. So, it's projected onto us, their own prejudices, their own insecurities, ideas that the system's at fault, the system's racist. They tell us everyday, never trust no one. So, you get this deep hatred, you hate the establishment from day one.

Member 44's statement comes in the context of explaining the violence of his peers. Such violence was justified, by some interviewees, as being of the same order as the violence used by the government:

You got, alright, if you look at the Iraq war, Afghanistan, all these other wars that the Governments are planning, it's like they, they think that us young people we don't, we don't see it or we don't know what they're doing. ... So for a Government, you're telling young people 'don't commit crime, don't do this, don't do that'. But yet you're flying off to other countries and fighting for things that does not belong to you, things that have no rights to do with you. And it's like if you're doing that then how do you expect the young people to behave?

Member 37

Interviewees were highly aware that the British government sees violence as a legitimate means to pursue its own ends. As discussed, they saw violence around them in their everyday lives, but they also saw governmental violence on their television screens. As the 'gangsta' rapper and actor Ice-T once memorably observed, violence is not confined to a culture of the street: 'We do car-jackings, but that's very small when compared to country-jackings, when America goes into Panama and takes out its leader and puts in its own leader' (Julien, 1994).

Arguably such statements are merely 'techniques of neutralization' gang members use to rationalize their behavior after it occurs or when it is called into question (Sykes and Matza, 1957). But the fact remains, violence runs throughout British society, and has done from before the time that some interviewees' ancestors were violently taken from Africa to work as slaves on plantations in the Caribbean and elsewhere.

## Education, education, education

Popular success stories about people who pull themselves up and out of poverty by the bootstraps conceal the realities of life in poverty. They deny the effects of power relations in terms of ethnicity, class or gender on the outcomes of young people—outcomes that are not simply dependent on various individual capacities such as intelligence, ability, appearance, attitude, motivation, self-esteem, and so on (Wyness, 2000). In legitimate markets, wealth and fame do not come easily, and for most young people securing even a modest slice of the action requires months if not years of delayed or deferred gratification through education and training, which, interviewees argued, was a wait too 'long':

> Everything was long. I couldn't even be bothered to sit down and do my GCSEs[5] because it was long. I couldn't even be bothered to sit down and revise because it's long. Couldn't be bothered to go school because it's long.
>
> Associate 1

Work in legitimate markets likewise involves too great a separation of work and play. The unattractive length of the educational preparation for a conventional career could, owing to the presence of gangs in their neighborhoods, easily be compared with alternative pathways to 'success' commercially promoted in the films, music videos, video games and adverts targeted at young people:

> In terms of them aspiring to be someone and someone in life, they don't aspire to be an educated person; they don't aspire to be someone that graduates from university. They aspire to be this. ... 'cus

footballers, musicians, they tend to have flashy cars and nice clothes and they want that luxury and sometimes they don't see themselves getting that luxury through education. They get that luxury from the street.

Member 46

Available work in gang-affected communities is typically law-paid, insecure, and service-oriented. In contrast to conventionally approved routes to success, therefore, gang membership offered the prospect of excitement and edginess. One gang member reported on this life of high-profile consumption of designer clothes and dazzling nightlife:

You just spend money on nonsense, you spend like, a £1000 on a jacket, do you know what I mean? Money just gets spunked on absolutely nothing. You might go out and spend £300, £400, £500 at a club. You know, you go out and buy the most expensive bottle of champagne, you know, instead of buying just shots of drinks, you'll buy the whole bottle. Yeah, they call it 'quick money' 'cus it goes quick.

Member 12

Gang members live financially in the present in part because they do not expect to live at all in the future—living day-to-day, there is little incentive either to defer or delay gratification or to be cautious or careful. Associate 1 even spoke about gang members vying to impregnate young women under the pretense that opportunities to father children later in life are curtailed:

Man dem are saying, 'Yeah I want to breed a girl now. I soon die, so I might as well just breed a girl. At least I got someone to carry on my name innit.'

Britain's recent double-dip recession compounds interviewees' sense of foreshortened future. There are now over one million youth unemployed in Britain, which is one in five of those aged 16 to 24. Breaking these figures down by race, we see that half of young black men available for work in Britain are now out of work (Ball, Milmo, and Ferguson, 2012).[6] The number of young people who have been unemployed for more than a year, moreover, is up a massive 874 percent since 2000, from 6260 to 60,955 (TUC, 2012). And rising unemployment has placed school-leavers in direct competition with more experienced workers in the hunt for jobs, forcing them to become more dependent on their own agency and motivation—personal and social skills that less affluent youths are less likely to develop (Margo et al., 2006).

Interviewees struggled in school in part because they lacked outstanding talent and parental support, but also because they did not fully understand the intensity of the competition and what they needed to do to compete effectively. They described increasing pressure to attend university, but with graduate unemployment at 25 percent and average student loan debt at £26,000 (Power, 2012)—and that's before the scrapping of the Education Maintenance Allowance and the rise in tuition fees from £3000 to £9000 per year—interviewees described higher education as yet another swindle. Recent research suggests that black graduates are three times more likely to be unemployed than white graduates within six months of leaving university (Elevation Networks Trust, 2012). Member 29 observed,

> My cousin went uni[versity], read his books dah, dah, dah. He still can't get a job. Man's in bare debt living off benefits.

At the same time, interviewees bemoaned the creation of bogus GCSE 'equivalency' courses and the low expectations of school personnel based on notions that students were disadvantaged by broken homes and pathological family structures. My fieldwork indeed reintroduced the paradox I first observed as a schoolteacher.

Three out of four black boys fail to reach the basic threshold of five or more good passes at GCSE (Smithers, 2005). When adults talked with me about struggling students they often blamed exogenous variables such as poverty, a lack of parental support, or low cultural capital. Very few held the teachers or the schools responsible. But when interviewees were asked to explain poor educational outcomes, they more often blamed endogenous variables, such as collapsing buildings and chewed-up textbooks; curriculum they described as 'outdated', 'irrelevant', or 'insulting'; and the disapprobation of 'frightened', 'inexperienced', and 'insensitive' teachers who apparently associated restricted language skills with intractable ignorance. Interviewees directly faulted their teachers and their schools, in other words, and believed they could be better students if they had better teachers and attended better schools.

Some interviewees dropped out of school entirely because school made apparent their individual inadequacies. Others fell behind in their studies or suffered fixed-term and permanent exclusions because they failed to *a priori* accept school rules as fair and teachers' authority as legitimate. They instead filled their time in the company of gang members:

> Those times when I was getting suspended [from school]. Three, four, five days. I would hang out with the older boys, the older boys over by red flats. Doing crime and stuff. Being inside the cars that they were stealing and stuff. Joyriding around Clapham. Having a bit of drink. Take two tokes on a spliff and that. Flirting with crime. That's how it started. Petty stuff, low-level crime. Graffiti. Doing what everyone else was doing.
>
> Member 44

Even when interviewees stayed in school, the prevailing culture at the schools they attended simply denigrated the desire for academic achievement:

> W]hen you tell people 'I just did my GCSEs' or 'I'm studying today' or 'Can you come out? No, I'm studying', [the response is] 'Oh man you're moist, you're not on it man, move [out of my way].' Like, people don't wanna be around you 'cus they're like, 'Well, you know what, you're not on my wave so bun you.' People don't find [school] exciting. They don't understand that. ... [Y]ou see neeks that sit down and do their work, they're a joke man. That don't get you no ratings. That don't get no, 'ah, look man's banging out his GCSEs. Yeah, he's sick.' No. No one ain't saying that. Man's saying 'well done, cool for you, anyway back to the gang life'. If they go school, they go home, change their uniform, come back out ... and stay out all night till early hours of the morning.
>
> Associate 1

The schools interviewees attended also suffered from gang-related violence 'spilling over' from the streets and the continued presence of older gang members on campus with their associates. Non-gang interviewees even expressed concerns about encountering gang members while walking to and from school, threats and harassment by gang members in or near school, the presence of weapons in school (one teacher reported confiscating what he thought was a toy gun from a student, only to discover it was a real firearm), and tension and fights between gang members at the end of the school day or in spaces where adults are not always present, such as playgrounds and cafeterias. Zac Olumegbon, 15, for example, was ambushed and murdered by five members of the GAS gang at the gates of Park Campus School in West Norwood, in July 2010 (Press Association, 2011).

## The trouble with families

The government claims there are 120,000 'troubled families' in England, 'characterized by there being no adult in the family working, children not being in school, and family members being involved in crime and anti-social behavior' (Department for Work and Pensions, 2012). Aside from fact the term 'troubled families' (like 'troublesome youth groups') almost deliberately conflates families experiencing multiple deprivation and families that cause trouble (see Levitas, 2012), gang members are often thought to be a product of such 'dysfunctional homes' (Cameron, 2011). This is not a strictly Conservative narrative: Justice Secretary for England and Wales, Jack Straw once blamed the 'continuing problem' of gang violence on 'the absence of fathers who are actively involved in parenting' in black communities (Daily Mail, 2007). This begs the question, what is the relationship between family structure and gang membership? Do broken families 'cause' gangs? Is parental neglect a risk factor for gang membership? Do some families even encourage gang membership? My fieldwork, which included interviews with gang members who are parents and the parents and siblings of gang members, offered some insight.

A small number of interviewees prioritized the social support and peer affirmation gangs offered in the absence of family. Member 3 explained, 'Not everybody has a family, like if you go through the care system [or] your dad's in prison, you never had what it is considered a "normal" family.' Member 14, for example, recalled regular competition with his siblings for scarce resources such as food, clothing, space, and parental attention. He 'never had that direct mentor', he said, and was visibly moved when I asked about his childhood, agreeing to talk about it only in rhyme:

> I think everyone should stay close to their mum,
> Stay close to your mum, like a bullet and a gun,
> 'cus my mum looks at me like I'm not a son,
> So I go out and do something dumb.
> I feel like I haven't got a mum,
> But I got a gun, chilling on my ones as I sit and bun.
> I'm telling you that nobody loves me,
> Nobody hugs me,
> Niggers want to mug me,
> You can't mug me, son, I'm lovely.

Fuck it, take your whole crew out like rugby.
My mum can be a bitch but my dad keeps hitting me,
Never forgiving me, hitting me,
Hating me, hitting me,
But he don't live with me.
My head turning, I started loosing it,
Head started burning, so I burnt it, turned lunatic,
Started cocking guns,
Then I started using it.
Dad said I was dead,
Then I started proving it.

Member 14 was not the only one to describe adverse childhood experiences such as abuse, having a mentally ill parent, domestic violence against a parent, a household member in prison, divorced parents, or a household member with a drug or alcohol problem. Practitioners I met speculated that Member 14 and others like him who had been exposed to one or more traumatic events that threatened or caused great physical harm in childhood suffered from an undiagnosed form of post-traumatic stress disorder (PTSD)—an anxiety affliction that can statistically increase one's propensity for violence (Hosking and Walsh, 2005). One school counselor observed, 'These are angry young men, emotionally numb. They don't care whether they live or die. They have nothing to lose, which is what makes them so dangerous.'

In this context, Member 24 warned, 'If you don't grow your child, someone else is will grow him for you. And we aren't necessarily giving the right ways of teaching.' Member 28's story is illustrative in this regard. After his father walked out, Member 28's contact with adult men was relatively limited. The most readily available source of male approval became the older gang members in the community who 'hung out on the block' and 'flossed' or flaunted their success in the underground economy through conspicuous consumption of designer clothing and ostentatious jewelry. Their ability to give children like him 'pocket money' and to buy expensive consumer items as gifts, Member 28 added, made them attractive to members of the opposite sex, which further enhanced their reputation. He recalled:

People looked a lot older and a lot bigger when you're younger. ...
He looks like, I don't know, he was a black guy, Jamaican, but say he looks like, you know, like a stepdad or an uncle that your mum might know and you hang about with. But he's always surrounded

by younger people. ... He'll take you to go and eat. He'll put money in your pocket.

Member 28 said that the gang eventually became like a family to him:

I started hanging out, like getting calls to go youth club, parties, stuff like that, randomly going out, just hanging on the block really, that's just about it, like just started hanging out.

At the parties he met other older gang members. He danced with their female associates. He smoked his first joint. He drank his first alcoholic beverage. Before long he had seen too much, shared too much, and knew too much about the gang. In his own words, the gang 'filled a void' left by his father. He was 'home'.

Member 28 was not alone in describing his gang as a surrogate 'family' network. Member 25 said he was 'hugging the block' because he had 'no one else' and it was the 'warmest thing' for him. Member 33 said simply,

People out here seems to find more love outside than in their own families, they'll tell you 'the street was my father, yeah, the streets raised me, not my mum or dad'.

But if the gang is a family, my experience leads me to conclude that it is an abusive one—gang love is very much conditional (see Chapters 3 and 5). Despite the weakened condition of the family among interviewees, moreover, the vast majority of them appeared far more committed to their natal families than to their gangs. Life in the gang simply provided a means of contributing to the household. When his father left, for example, Member 37 assumed the role of 'man of the house'. He explained:

I just needed to get more money and help my family. I wanted to buy a house, move my mum off the estate so she didn't have to struggle no more.

During my fieldwork, I met low-income families; families who could not afford a number of food and clothing items; families living in overcrowded housing; families where no parent has any qualifications; families where at least one parent has mental health problems or a longstanding limiting illness, disability or infirmity; but I rarely encountered families for whom all of the above was true, thus challenging the notion they were 'troubled'

(Department for Work and Pensions, 2012). I also rarely encountered a situation in which no parent in the family was in work. Instead, parents were often working multiple jobs to make ends meet. What this created, however, was a lack of supervision because parents could not afford to supplement time away from their children with time in the company of other dedicated adults. This, in turn, presented opportunities for interviewees to associate with gangs. Member 37 noted,

> [Our] parents have enough going on paying council tax, paying rents, paying this, paying that, that ... they haven't got time to be paying for your PlayStation 3.

Hence, '[we] feel they need to go out there and rob'.

Sudhir Venkatesh (1997, p. 95) reminds us that gang affiliation may well be the 'principal public identity' for many gang members, yet much of the social interaction in gang-affected communities occurs in situations where 'gang membership is not marked and where gang members are known by other roles'. As the mother of one gang member told me, 'It's easy to forget sometimes but gang members are just children, they're our sons and daughters.' Gang members do not forsake their families when they join gangs, but some separation between gang life and family life is often necessary, said Member 7:

> If you're young and you're in a gang you cannot let anyone know where you live. You only can meet the people that you're with 24/7 every day, the people you've known the longest, yeah, know where you live. Because when you're young, people like to come to your house. ... But when you're old you can get killed outside the house, that's the difference. They'll probably come out with 10, 15 people and beat you up. And obviously that's distressing your mum. Yeah, if you've got a little sister, that's distressing your little sister. And if you're in a gang and you're high up you can't stay in the house and watch TV. They'll just do whatever they're doing outside the house inside your house. You have to come outside and confront them. ... So you're going to be fighting in front of your mum, your little sister, that's how it is and if you're getting beaten up with a pole, you're getting beaten up with a pole and that's how it is. Do you see what I'm trying to say? That's the reality of it. Yeah, so, you can't let no one know where you live. Yeah, you can't or you'd be in problems, yeah, because if the rival gang finds out where you live, they'll go to your house. And there's nothing that you can do.

Perhaps this is why gang membership was perceived as being largely out of the family's control. Some families were blissfully ignorant of their connection to gangs, even when they benefited from it through financial compensation or local social recognition. Others were in denial and were unwilling to recognize or admit that their child was anything more than peripherally involved in gangs because of the stigma attached to the label. Still others could not see any other alternative. One parent who resided on the Fenwick estate where Billy Cox died, for example, told me:

> It's too dangerous for kids to play outside 'round here. Parents see their children with gang members on the estate but don't say anything because it's better to be on the inside than on the outside. It's better the devil you know than the devil you don't.

Member 47 offered the following insight into why parents might become indifferent or incurious about the gang-related activity of their children:

> You see young boys give their mum money and she knows what they're doing. She knows that they're selling drugs. Do you see what I'm trying to say? Because your parents love you, they keep a blind eye to it. They know what you're doing or they have a slight feeling what you're doing but when a person's in love, they see a person for how they'd like them to be rather than how they really are.

After years of irregular employment and discrimination, some families certainly regarded 'street skills' as more valuable than 'academic skills' (Mayer, 1997, p. 51) and advocated seriously for gang membership as a route to redress and economic advancement. But they were a minority. The majority of families, particularly those who had personally succumb or lost loved ones to gang violence, thought gang membership had a detrimental impact on familial relationships and thus outright condemned it. The parents of gang members, particularly gang members who kill, suffer immensely and struggle to understand how and why their children could act so violently. Their lives, too, are changed forever. In the search for meaning, some first-generation African and Caribbean families conceded that because their British children knew they could not be lawfully disciplined in the manner they once were, parents felt like they had lost control of their children. In some instances they even blamed witchcraft and spirit possession for the 'moral corruption' of their offspring.

Like Elijah Anderson (1999), I found patriarchal fathers, strong-minded single mothers and fiercely assertive grandmothers to be key figures in the cultural struggle for respectability in gang-affected neighborhoods. But, as discussed further in Chapter 5, the children of individuals already associated with gang activity are at risk of becoming obligate gang members, drawn into crime by virtue of familial association. Following one's relatives into crime creates in part the dynastic succession that gives gangs longevity and durability. Member 45's gang career, for example, began with accompanying his father during criminal activity:

> My dad would go debt collecting and make me and my brother beat them up. He told us, "this guy stole our money". He was a drug dealer so it wasn't his money, but we didn't know. "We need that money to eat, rah, rah, rah". And these were grown men, but they couldn't do us nothing 'cus they were scared of my dad and he's standing there watching. So I'm, 13, 14 [years old], beating up grown men, letting out all my frustration, and I'm thinking, this feels good. And my dad's, like, for the first time, he's like proud or something. So it started from there. Beating up grown men.

Unemployment and underemployment in the inner city eliminated the old patriarchal order of male breadwinner and head of household. Sons are now inheriting the legacy of their fathers' 'search for respect' (Bourgois, 1995). They too are taking refuge in the underground economy, becoming second- or third-generation drug dealers. They too are finding dignity and a sense of identity through brute force. At the same time, absent fathers was a recurring theme throughout my research, in part because a period of imprisonment was considered part of the normal life experience by interviewees, their families, and the wider communities they came from. Black prisoners indeed make up 15 percent of the prisoner population compared with approximately 2 percent of the general population (House of Commons Home Affairs Committee, 2007). And once a prison record becomes endemic to a community, said Member 45, 'everyone 'round here knows someone who's done time'.

Member 45 said he knew his father was a criminal from a young age. He recalled,

> People coming into the house all night. I'd smell stuff, you know, I knew it was drugs. I could smell it upstairs, but if I came out of my bedroom or asked questions my dad would shout at me.

Time spent in foster care and group homes, however, offered little reprieve from the criminal life. To the contrary:

> There was crime going on in the care home. The people that was meant to be caring for us, they're committing crime as well. They're involved as well. Telling me to go get this for them, go get that for them. So obviously, I'm a kid, I'm thinking this is normal. Like, that's how it is.

Social learning theory holds that people learn behavior, especially aggression, by observing and imitating others (Bandura, 1977). Interviewees certainly had role models that failed to adequately control their own criminal or violent impulses. The continuous redistribution of neighborhood populations through incarceration, moreover, contributed to an absence of 'capable guardians' (Cohen and Felson, 1979). Violence simply procreates violence in spaces where no one can hear you scream.

## Concluding remarks

To understand why youths join gangs we must first understand the contexts in which they join. There are longstanding problems that the black community faces related to the 'difficult' schools (Debarbieux and Baya, 2008) that interviewees attended and the lack of supervision they received—partly because of the large number of single-parent families or two-career homes where both parents are working—and the attraction of gangs that pervaded their neighborhoods. Gang members clearly have high aspirations to succeed and share with their non-gang counterparts the material expectations encouraged within advanced capitalism. Overt differences in life chances have, however, translated into perceptions of injustice that in turn affect the decisions they make about their life strategies.

If, as Anthony Gunter (2008) argues, we need to add individual choice to the political economic explanation of gang membership, Matza's concept of drift cannot help us. Gang membership is a choice, but a host of social, psychological, economic, and political pressures that accompany the life experiences of contemporary black youth constrain the parameters of that choice. This is a choice that would have much less resonance with young people in gang-affected areas if they saw more evidence that commitment to non-subterranean values among their families and peers actually led to the achievement of valued goals.

However, the choice to pursue a gang career should not be seen as the result of an individual cost-benefit analysis of the utility to be gained from it (Clarke and Cornish, 1986). Rather, this is a 'situated choice' (Laub and Sampson, 2003, pp. 281–2). These young people are not determined to act by a social structure, which produces them as subjects without agency. But neither are they the self-contained agential units of the neo-liberal imagination.

'There is no such thing as society', Margret Thatcher told *Woman's Own* magazine in 1987. Each of us has to look out for ourselves, not expect 'society' to take care of us. Gangs have taken this advice literally. They look after themselves. And who can blame them? One of the main functions of government is the management of capitalism through ensuring legitimacy of the current arrangements. Given the state aided and abetted the cowboy capitalism that led to the 2008 financial melt-down, recent history suggests a failure on the part of government in this regard. In recent years, moreover, the institutions Britons rely on to keep one another in check—Parliament, the police, the press—have all been implicated in a series of scandals undermining public morality, from MPs' expenses and bankers' bonuses to phone hacking and Jimmy Savile, not to mention 'plebgate', Libor rate fixing, corruption in sport, and abuse within the Church. Member 40 said:

> From watching what I'm watching, it seems that the Government's are just like me, out on the street doing what I'm doing. But it's just that they're richer and they're looking after their richer people, which is just a handful of people. … [The] politicians and all these other so-called people that sits in parliament decide what goes on. … So they're a gang as well. Young people see that. I see that. I don't know about you, but I see that.

People obey laws that they consider legitimate. Involuntary police–citizen encounters that are perceived as unfair further detract from that legitimacy. If people feel that society is unfair they are less inclined to play by the rules—rules that interviewees saw as designed to serve the purposes of the social groups who were active in performing the exclusion they experienced. Hence why gangs had replaced many social institutions for interviewees. Gangs make their own rules.

Gang members were not responsible for the 2011 UK riots but examining them in this context is still useful. Interviewees described lives marked by the same violence and intimidation, racial intolerance, economic inequality, intergenerational unemployment and underemployment, and alienation or exclusion from mainstream education as the rioters (Lewis et al., 2011). They resented the perceived rejection of themselves and their families by others. Having absorbed the lessons of the acquisitive world, however, they used gangs to create the life that material deprivation and poor life chances otherwise denied them (Hall and Winlow, 2008). Gangs are not an alternative *to* society, as Thrasher (1927) once argued, but rather a functional reflection *of* society, which gang members only ever symbolically reject.

This alternative social and economic infrastructure incorporates both *public* and *private* sectors. The public sector deals with the gang's delivery of goods and services for its members, including defense, justice, and recreation. And in Chapters 2 and 3, I explore how the private sector, or black market, provides the means for gang members to generate both financial and reputational capital. Suffice it to say, in the communities in which they operate, prominent gang members can, partly due to the fear they inspire, be accorded deference, status, respect, and even a kind of celebrity 'rating':

> You'd get looked after and you can for a short time at least be the man, yeah? That's what kept me entrenched in that lifestyle. I loved it. Loved it. I was getting, people were boosting me up, I got cash in my pocket, and no one could touch me. I'm living in the middle of [gang set space]. I forgot to lock my car. Do you know, I checked the car, it hadn't been touched, yeah? It hadn't been touched at all. My car had, like, a stereo bass and everyone knew this. But the car was untouched. That's the respect I had. It was a long time before I was picked up by the police and I went a long, long time without being even stopped. … I was almost invincible at that point. Your name was chattering in the backgrounds, but people wouldn't dare come to your face and say anything.
>
> Member 50

Such is the result of the evolution of gang life, which is the focus of Chapter 2.

# 2
# Gang Evolution

When Prime Minister David Cameron (2011) launched his 'concerted, all out war on gangs' after the riots he described the enemy combatants in the following emotive terms: 'Territorial, hierarchical and incredibly violent, they are mostly composed of young boys ... [who] earn money through crime, particularly drugs, and are bound together by an imposed loyalty to an authoritarian gang leader.' Critics (see Hallsworth and Brotherton, 2011) argue that Cameron evoked a stereotype of the American 'criminologists gang' (Katz and Jackson-Jacobs, 2004). I have no doubt that he did. The irony, the next two chapters argue, is that Cameron was right. Not about the organization of gangs *in the riots*, but about the organization of gangs *per se*. This is gang life, but not as the British traditionally know it. Gang life has evolved. Here I shall demonstrate how, with emphasis on the natural progression of gangs from recreational neighborhood groups to delinquent collectives to full-scale criminal enterprises to providers of extra-legal governance.

This chapter outlines in detail how gangs start life as purely recreational groups but over time they attain different functions, thus expanding the menu of goods and services they can offer. The four stages of recreation, crime, enterprise, and governance are not mutually exclusive, but rather each stage builds upon the previous. If one were to think of a gang as a house, the 'recreational' stage is the foundation. To continue this metaphor, 'crime' marks the addition of the framing. This is when the house (that is, the gang) starts to look like a house. Next, 'enterprise' corresponds with the installation of the guts of the home. Finally, 'governance' sees the addition of the appropriate exterior and interior finishes.

Of course, without sufficient resources a house cannot be completed. Some fail inspection. Others get foreclosed on. Some burn down. Others get burglarized. The housing metaphor is merely illustrative, but it is true to say that some gangs reach completion while others collapse or stagnate. Of the 12 gangs sampled, for example, not one remains solely recreational but two (Delta and Foxtrot) are still making the transition from crime to enterprise, which reflects in part their shorter life span (less than five years). Five of the 12 gangs (Alfa, Echo, Golf, India, and Lima) present as mature criminal enterprises with tendencies for ordering exchange. The remaining five (Beta, Charlie, Hotel, Juliet, and Kilo) attempt to regulate the production and distribution of one or more given commodities or services unlawfully.

## Stage 1: Recreation

Forming identity and interest groups—what the father of gang research, Frederic Thrasher (1927), refers to as 'ganging'—is normal adolescent peer behavior. It was unsurprising, therefore, to find that the gangs in my sample were born out of familial connections and friendships formed in local schools, communities, and places of worship—the latter catering to devout congregations drawn from different ethnic groups. Some gangs even trace their heritage back to the 1950s and the young blacks that united as a way to protect each other from white-ethnic gangs. As one grandparent living on gang turf told me:

> I couldn't leave the house, couldn't go to the club on a weekend, visit my girl, for fear of being attacked by Teddy Boys out 'nigger hunting'. People would throw a brick at you just for being black. I got called 'fucking coon', a 'monkey'. It was scary. So, we had to always be in a group for protection. It wasn't a gang like nowadays. Yeah, we fought with other groups, but it was about survival. It was about fighting for recognition.

Some 50 years later, ethnic minorities and young immigrants occupying an expatriate identity are once again banding together around a common cultural heritage, shared experiences of cultural estrangement, and in response to repeat, sometimes racist, bullying and victimization at school or on the street. Says Member 37:

> The only thing that's keeping us together in the middle is our situations. That's what brought us together as a group in the first place is our situations. Either a single parent, no dad or no mum, or nobody just don't care about you and you're just out on the street living by

yourself and you feel to have some associations to get ahead. So it's just our situations that brought us together.

With weak family ties in London or, in some cases, no reference group at all because their parents remained abroad, these youngsters formed gangs as a means of social support.

Membership within such gangs is not governed by strict rules and rituals, but rather occurs as a consequence of shared history. Members enjoy similar interests, life trajectories, and experiences, not least the same spaces (schools and neighborhoods). Gang names, in turn, are often derived from these spaces, regardless of whether they are imposed from within or without. As Member 45 explained, 'If you're from Clapham, you're a Clap Town Kid.' Such gangs provide activities and a social life. Their presence (both in neighborhoods and in the cultural products that interviewees consumed) enabled interviewees to learn and transmit ways of creating social lives that they found meaningful and enjoyable. Member 38 outlined the average 'day in the life' of a gang member as follows:

> You sleep through the morning because you are out late and there's nothing to get up for. There's no set time for anything. You wake up, go out, meet your friends in wherever they hanging out, sit on the block. If it's a weekend you'll probably hear about a party, a house party or a party in a hall. You call as many people as you can and that's it, you go.

Interviewees also reported deriving pleasure and being 'up' on the dangerous and forbidden behaviors to which their social networks gave them access. Member 37 said, 'the only way you're laughing is when you're outside doing certain things that you're not supposed to be doing'.

As Mac Klein and Cheryl Maxson (2006, p. 69) point out, 'gang members spend much more time hangin' than bangin''. Regardless of what evolutionary stage a gang is in, the vast majority of gang members' time is indeed spent sitting around listening to music, 'spitting bars' (rapping, see Chapter 4), hustling girls, drinking alcohol, smoking cannabis, and sharing stories—acts indistinguishable from those untaken by many adolescent peer groups. This social role persists over the evolutionary life of the gang, with gangs moving from structured activities back to informal ones. Nevertheless, part of the 'buzz and the hype' of gang membership, said Member 43, was 'travelling to different areas and causing problems ... robbing people, starting fights, taking people's girls'. Member 44 made a similar observation:

> We used to go to parties and stuff. Try and impress the girls and stuff. Hang around. Smoke drugs. Hit on girls. Go party. There's not really no deep conversation with each other. Go to Clapham Junction. Go to New Cross. Have fights against the Ghetto Boys, the [Clapham] Junction Boys. Big chains, big cars, glamorous stuff. That was the only kind of fun I really saw. That was fun to me.

In this first stage, crime is opportunistic and rarely acquisitive. Delinquent 'adventures' or 'exercises', such as fighting or acts of petty vandalism, Member 48 argued, were rewarding in and of themselves because they offered reprieve from boredom and released endorphins in the brain. And the prospect of such adventure was one of the key reasons for spending time with gang members. The natural high brought on by pain, danger, or other forms of stress was supplemented by alcohol and cannabis use. It was 'innocent fun', Member 48 added. But all things must pass.

## Stage 2: Crime

Although gangs begin life as recreational groups, crime and violence can quickly become intrinsic to group identity and practice. Adolescence has long been associated with heightened rates of delinquency. G. Stanley Hall (1904, p. 404), who is widely accredited with bringing the term 'adolescence' into common parlance, argued 'a period of semi-criminality is normal for all healthy [adolescents]'. Hall recognized that culture influences one's expression and experience of adolescent 'storm and stress'. By engaging in criminal acts, interviewees became people of 'respect' in street cultures where respect was everything (Anderson, 1999). Crime was rebellious and exciting. Other youths began to fear them. Girls were suddenly attracted to them. The only problem was that crime also attracted other criminals (both allies and rivals) and law enforcement.

Resulting 'in-group' and 'out-group' favoritism (Tajfel and Turner, 1986) created a fascinating double standard—gang members viewed the traits of their own gang as virtuous but typically perceived those same traits as vices in rival groups. During my fieldwork, insiders would describe aggressive gangs as assertive, for example, whereas outsiders would describe them as callous. External conflict and threats forced gangs to strengthen their internal structures and become both much more violent and cohesive in order to survive. As Member 38 explained:

> We was committing crimes so we sat down together, it was like a meeting, I suppose and we just gave each other names and it started like that. Because it was not like socializing, it was actually going out to commit crime and do stuff. We was premeditating what we was doing before it happened. Planning it up.

Indeed, gangs at this stage often change their names to better reflect their criminal components. Brixton's 'Younger 28s' gang, for example, changed their name to the Peel Dem Crew (PDC), which has its roots in the Jamaican 'peel dem', meaning to 'steal from them', and better described the extent of their activities (Hill, 2007).

The police response to gangs such as PDC inadvertently helped to solidify them. For example, one police officer recalled:

> We were frequently arresting young boys who claimed to be Muslims to garner preferential treatment in the cells. We called them the 'Muslim Boys' because they were quite literally Muslim boys, which obviously stuck because they started calling themselves by the same name.

Some Muslim Boys, a splinter group of PDC, had indeed converted to Islam and, after the September 11, 2001 and July 7, 2005 terrorist attacks, respectively, began posing as Islamists to gain street credibility and trade on false perceptions about links to al Qaeda. Member 9 once similarly described Beta gang as 'more than a gang ... we're a brotherhood, faith is keeping us', adding 'we are Muslims, Allahu Akbar [God is greater], we have guidelines ... does that scare you?' But when questioned, he and his friends appeared unable, at best unwilling, to explain in detail the basic pillars and tenets of Islam.

Following largely unsubstantiated rumors that the Muslim Boys were forcibly converting young men to fundamentalist Islam at gunpoint with help from corrupt Imams, the Mayor of London's senior advisor on policing described the gang as a criminalized front for terrorist extremists and 'as tough to crack as the IRA' (Hill, 2007). Local police similarly over-emphasized the threat of the gang in order to tap into a burgeoning counterterrorism budget and bring state resources to eliminate it. There is precedent for an association between gangs and domestic terrorism. Jeff

Fort, the charismatic one-time leader of Chicago's Black P Stone Nation gang, for example, was controversially convicted in 1987 for plotting to commit terrorist acts on behalf of Col. Muammar el-Qaddafi's Libyan government (Moore and Williams, 2011). But in the absence of real evidence, the association in this case merely enhanced the reputation of the gang; for while the Muslim Boys were certainly responsible for a number of violent crimes, neither they nor PDC, who were incorrectly reported to have over 2500 'members', presented the size or scale of threat that was implied (Hill, 2007). Such 'bad' press was good for business.

For gangs to truly take hold and flourish they must develop a reputation for violence. Violent reputations save on the costs involved with identically reproducing said asset or property; as Thomas Hobbes (1651) once wrote, 'Reputation of power, is Power'. Gang members rely on the reputation of their gangs for making good on their threats. The violence capital of individual gang members may vary, but if a gang holds a reputation for violence established by years of violence displayed by multiple gang members, then every member of that gang benefits from a reputation acquired by the efforts of others. Others impute a high probability of being violent to a new gang member, therefore, not necessarily because he himself has demonstrated violent tendencies, but simply because he is a gang member. The group is an extension of the individual and the individual is an extension of the group.

Gangs in embryo have little or no established collective reputation, thus it is up to the founding members to create one by patrolling territorial boundaries and participating in 'active street duties'. 'We would come together ... literally tooled up—screwdrivers, spanners, cleavers, bats, hammers, whatever we could get our hands on—and police the streets', said Member 35. The aim was to establish bragging rights about who was the 'toughest' gang in town based on peaceful mergers or violent takeovers of other gangs. So began the trend of gangs attaching the postal code of their district to their name and adopting colored clothing, gestures and hand signals, even a variety of allusions and metaphors (see Chapter 4), to cheaply and accurately advertise, communicate, and identify fellow gang members. Early on in my fieldwork, Member 43 educated me on local gang colors:

Densley:      So if your gang has colors, how do you show your colors?

Member 43:   Bandannas and clothes. It really is like America. It's blue, red, green, black, yellow, purple, white, girls in pink or whatever.

Densley:      And those colors, the ones you just mentioned there, in what sort of geographical space are we talking about? Is that just in one area of south London or is that across ...

Member 43:   All of them colors, all of them colors are all in south London. All of them colors [are] just in southwest London, not southeast, just southwest. ... Purple and green are basically the same crew, just like different ... it's like a crew in a crew. But say you was wearing purple and you went to a red neighborhood. Problem. Red went to a green neighborhood? Problem. If you're wearing yellow and you went into any other neighborhood? Big problem.

Within some London boroughs, multiple gang 'sets' even started identifying with one particular color. Some gangs went so far as to design and manufacture their own branded clothing items, including belts, or belt buckles, which could be used as weapons because, unlike other classes of offensive weapons, young people did not need to account for being in possession of them.

Young people soon began purposefully hanging out with their friends in places where action was likely to happen, such as on the 'frontline' between perceived gang territories:

> If you're posting on the strip, certain times you're waiting there to see 'something' happen. Either you're waiting for a fight, or you're waiting for something bad to happen basically. Waiting for the police to come and ask you to move so can make up issues, make up problems or just do something silly, like go rob a shop, rob the policeman. ... On frontline your trying to like, you know, impress, sort of, kind of, show that, 'rah, this is your end' so if anything's going down or if it's popping off you'll be there to back it, basically.
>
> Associate 1

Frontline was defended down to the curbstone. The act of someone from a rival position 'caught slipping' (crossing the threshold) was interpreted as an affront to the gang's power and reputation:

> This is my house. These are my ends. Would you let someone break into your house? That's disrespect. You disrespect my ends, I'll come down on you hard. This is my house, my rules. Everyone 'round here knows if you cross this one road, it is death. Your life is on the line.
>
> Member 4

In this context, Jack Katz (1988, p. 141) has argued that once an attack by another group becomes public knowledge, 'a failure to respond threatens to make retrospectively ridiculous the pretensions of all in the attacked group'. But retaliation leads only to more retaliation, not least because it feeds the myth of the righteous kill. 'According to the inescapable pragmatism of all action, force and the threat of force inevitably breed more force', said Max Weber (1978 [1915]). London's 'postcode war' began in earnest.

Gang membership is about 'taking no shit from nobody', Associate 17 told me. But, as Katz (1988) also observed, the pursuit of physical pleasure and awareness, reinforced by constructing and perfecting a gang member identity, provides strong motivation for young people. 'Posting on the strip', as defending the neighborhood from incursions by outsiders is known, generated feelings of intense joy, liberation, and power among interviewees. It also redefined existing territorial rivalries along London's sheer number of schools, postcode areas, and natural geographical boundaries; to the extent that the new generation of gang members has no idea why they fight: 'It's just always been this way', said Member 27.

Monetary gain from street crime and wanton violence was minimal. Interviewees, such as Member 20, argued that the proceeds were barely enough to obtain the necessary accouterments, such as jewelry and trainers, which kept them ahead of their peers in the competition for social esteem:

> You rob a phone it's cash straight up. But you get five pound here, ten pound there. And what, these shoes [cost] £100, this jacket [cost] £300. That's a lot of phones.

The risks inherent in such overt criminal displays were further cause for concern, said Member 50:

> Back in the day when I first started, that was the thing; you gotta [sic] rob someone for a nice phone or like a fiver or, or stuff like that. Now robbing people for that will just get you sent to jail for, for nothing.

And yet, street crime was common among interviewees and, in order to gain the reputation sought through its perpetration, it was often violent. My findings thus confirm John Pitts's (2008) assessment that respect and recognition are far greater incentives for the more overt criminal activity of gang members in London than monetary gain.

As the first generation of gang members matured out of adolescence, however, 'bank balance' and the pursuit of material wealth supplanted their desire for 'street credit':

> When I first joined we weren't really on the making money thing, we were just like getting our name around, going around different areas going yeah, we're [gang name], don't fuck with us. But then as we got older we just started getting more organized, just working on money, like dealing drugs and stuff, just, we just wanted to make money, that was it.
>
> Member 46

To make ends meet, interviewees first engaged in what Sánchez-Jankowski (1991, p. 132) describes as 'crude economic activity'. They sold stolen or counterfeit goods—that is, until streaming content over the Internet curtailed demand for pirated CDs and DVDs—and burglarized multi-occupancy student flats, taking laptop computers and mobile phones—items that are high value, portable, and easily jettisoned. Over time, syndicated aggravated burglaries and street robberies became a means not only to enhance individual and collective gang reputations, but also to generate a 'preliminary accumulation of funds' to be invested back into criminal commodities such as drugs and guns (Ruggiero, 2000, p. 51). Some gang members travelled together on double-decker buses to commit crime because it created difficulties for police in terms of containment, effective use of stop and search, and dispersal on the street. Others robbed local drug dealers of their 'cash and stash', Member 36 said, safe in the knowledge that drug dealers 'stockpile' and are in no position to call the police to settle their disputes.

Still others would rush or 'steam' into train carriages, Member 44 explained, to 'klep' passengers at knifepoint or attack high-value 'gaming machines' in bookmakers and betting shops with crowbars and screwdrivers. They robbed commercial premises, taking the cash register and whatever else they could find, or cash-in-transit from drivers as they replenished automated teller machines with cash cassettes at retailers, banks, and petrol stations. Some of these high-risk high-reward ventures were opportunistic but most of them were calculated. Gang members would work in teams with a designated driver and 'look out', tailing Group 4 Securicor vans from depots in Vauxhall using stolen, 'pool' (that is, shared vehicles registered under the name of a 'clean' gang affiliate), or hire cars (for example, see Daily Mail, 2010). Either way, enterprise was the name of the game.

## Stage 3: Enterprise

In the recreational and criminal stages, gangs are like start-up companies with limited operating histories and narrow employee benefits. The founding members sustain such gangs. The value of each gang is based entirely on intangible assets, or what is known as 'intellectual property' in legitimate markets. The first recruits enter at the ground floor and essentially receive the equivalent of pre-Initial Public Offering stock options. They join, in other words, because they see high potential return on their investment, but their investment is extremely high-risk because if the gang ceases being competitive and goes bankrupt, all stock options become worthless.

Only when a gang 'goes public' are the original investors rewarded. The overall forecast for the gang changes, however, because the gang stops dealing in hypotheticals and counterfactuals and starts dealing in tangible goods and services (access to suppliers, greater prestige, more deferential treatment and so on). Recruits, in turn, may no longer be investors willing to defer gratification, but rather consumers seeking immediate gratification without any of the costs. For the first time, people go to the gang as opposed to the gang going to the people. The gang, in turn, begins to display less personal orientation and more goal orientation—specifically a commitment to financial goals with crime as a means not an end. Member 40 posited: 'We've got a common goal which is like you try and grow the reputation and you try and make money … economics is a very, very important part of it.' Rejecting the notion of gangs as benign recreational groups, fellow gang member Member 37 quipped: 'If you want to hang out and play PlayStation, join a youth club.'

Simon Hallsworth and Tara Young (2004) argue that what separates gang members from organized criminals is the latter view crime as their 'occupation' whereas the former do not. Approximately 80 percent of the gang members I interviewed, however, explicitly characterized their gangs as remunerative drugs 'businesses'. For example:

> It's organized crime. We had an aim, an aim being money, yeah, an aim being to generate capital for the big man. … We are in competition as a business with other businesses, that is, other gangs, other businesses for products, for opening hours, for size, for price, you understand? We are the competition, for security, for all of those things.
>
> Member 50

Once you have the money to buy the drugs and distribute it, you are doing business. That's how I see it. ... If it's drug dealing, it's business ... you have to be there, you have to be there on the spot, come correct every time ... you have to start from the ground, it's hard. Just like working in Tescos [supermarket], stacking shelf and wanting to become a manager, working your way up. That's how it is. ... You got to put in the time, the effort, everything. Everything, just like how you do it in a 9 to 5 job. You have to be consistent, just like any other job.

Member 37

The involvement of British gangs in the drugs business is well documented. Pitts (2008), for example, describes drug dealing as the major preoccupation of gangs in London. According to Judith Aldridge and Juanjo Medina (2008, p. 19), 'most' gang members in research city 'were involved to some degree in [drug] dealing'. Existing police intelligence also shows that approximately 80 percent of London's 250 gangs participate in street-level drug dealing, and individuals who have links to gangs are believed to be responsible for 16 percent of London's total drug supply (Metropolitan Police Service, 2012a).[1]

The organizational and structural features of gangs are typically seen in the area of drug sales (Mieczkowski, 1986; Skolnick et al., 1988; Taylor, 1990; Sánchez-Jankowski, 1991; Padilla, 1992; Levitt and Venkatesh, 2000). The drugs business within London gangs very much resembles the multi-level marketing structure of direct-selling companies such as Amway and Avon.[2] Gangs essentially stop recruiting their peers and begin recruiting subordinates, resulting in the incorporation of approximately three levels of power and decision-making authority: (1) a higher level, or 'inner circle'; (2) a middle level of decision-makers, or 'elders', that develop gang organization by generating sales and building an active customer base; and (3) a lower level of 'youngers' who are directed by their elders and thus accountable, punishable, or capable of being rewarded by them.[3] As these names imply, some degree of organizational evolution is age-graded and at times reflects the chronological age-grading system built into the British education system, which inherently determines children's friendship patterns and access to significant adult figures. I elaborate upon these ideas in Chapter 3.

### The drugs business

Gangs rarely manage or control drug distribution systems at the organizational level, focusing instead on the street-level. Drug networks follow immigrant flows (Ruggiero and South, 1995). Drugs do not emanate from gang-affected areas, but rather end up there because gang-affected areas are a target market. As the Matrix Knowledge Group (2007) observes, heroin arrives from Afghanistan through Albanian, Turkish, and South Asian (predominantly Pakistani) networks based in the UK. Cannabis resin (hashish) is mostly imported from Morocco, Pakistan, Lebanon, and Afghanistan. Herbal cannabis, which is usually not as strong as the resin form, is imported from Africa, South America, Thailand, and the West Indies—although some particularly strong herbal forms with high levels of tetrahydrocannabinol, known as 'skunk', are cultivated in Holland and Britain. And cocaine comes from Central America through British expats based in Spain and Colombians living in south London. Displaced by the ubiquitous 'war on drugs', moreover, Jamaican 'Yardies' exported their own violent trade in crack cocaine from the garrison communities of Kingston to the Caribbean settlements of Britain. They modeled a ruthlessly violent gang culture for local youths, the remnants of which can still be observed in gang members' use of military terminology and the presence of Jamaican gang subsidiaries in London, such as the Shower Posse and Shower Chicks in Peckham (Pitts, 2008).

As John Pitts (2008) argues, globalization has changed the business model of traditional organized crime in London to incorporate youth gangs. One interviewee reflected upon their interactions with adult business criminals as follows:

> I wouldn't say I knew exactly where the stock [of drugs] was coming from. I knew sort of like, some of the people that we had to meet were at the top, like, you have some of the Turkish mafia who you go and get like your heroin from. … They're grownups. Yeah, they're serious organized crime. We dealt as well with … the Adams family. Yet again, they're very, very serious organized crime. You know, they're the modern day Krays, do you know what I mean? … You got some of the Russian mafia as well like, or you get Eastern Europeans now. You meet them down in the docks, you get stuff down there. … They might have containers on the docks, I ask no questions, get told no lies, you know what I mean? You know, when it comes to some of the drugs, like, you go and meet some of these old white dudes in the country that's grown it and he comes and shows you, 'Here's my, you know, greenhouse full of bloody skunk weed.'
>
> Member 12

Member 50 also observed how adult business criminals contracted 'muscle' from local gangs as additional manpower to murder informants and competitors. He and others were even enlisted to serve as couriers in a simple cocaine market structure that involved direct importation from the Caribbean—'secreting it in body passages' and swallowing it in grape-sized latex rubber packages:

> Every time he paid us, he'd only pay us half, though. So we'd get the money for the end the last job and half for the next. The idea was he wanted to keep us on. ... There was a job that came up ... it was to bring some drugs back, drugs about my person, yeah, so from St Lucia. ... He gave us a proper little shack ... a terraced house in the hills ... we had a swimming pool, a Jacuzzi. ... We had drivers, if we wanted to go anywhere. ... We went to the clubs. ... There was one strip club we went in called Solid Gold and like the queue in that place was unreal. We just walked straight past them all.

Member 50 never made it past Customs and Immigration at Heathrow airport. He served eight years in prison for trafficking two kilos of cocaine.

For him and others, however, imprisonment merely facilitated social interaction with other career criminals. 'When I was 16, I got a five and a half [year sentence], came out when I was 20, more clued up about how to make this money than when I went in', said Member 8. 'In prison you are constantly around goons, every kind of criminal. Everything that went on outside the jail went on inside and more', Member 47 recalled. Because drug prices in prison are 'heavily inflated'—'a point two [gram bag] of brown in there is £50; out here, it's like £10', Member 8 explained—and corrupt prison guards will 'facilitate' transactions as a means to 'placate inmates', he added, the 'guys who deal ... in prison ... come out very rich'. And the boundaries between gangs and organized crime become increasingly blurred.

Elders purchase drugs on demand from their inner circle, either working alone or pooling their resources to make larger initial buys. As Member 38 explained, the inner circle 'make their living selling guns or selling big pieces ... of drugs ... on credit with strings attached'. Elders, in turn, proactively build and mentor their own 'downline' (in direct-selling parlance) of younger distributors, who in time build their own distinct customer bases, thereby expanding the overall gang organization. Member 50 explained, 'People know who you work for and you've got your own rep [and] your own people working for you.'

Elders supply their youngers through a series of 'blind drops' in which drugs quotas are wrapped in plastic bags and strategically placed in advance into loose masonry, overflow pipes, toilet tanks, receptacle chambers, car wheel arches, and so on:

> [The elders] just drop off what they need to drop off and then they're off to whatever they're doing. Everything is hand delivered. They use 'pay as you go' phones with no contract. They don't use text messages. They don't come on the street with the lower ground dealers.
>
> Psylocke

> The older ones … don't stay on frontline because that's hot. They don't wanna get caught selling, [doing] whatever they're doing. … They'll pass through frontline make sure everything's going good or whatever but they're not really posting on the frontline to do their drugs cart. That's just hot. That's just stupid. That's just basically saying to yourself, 'I wanna get caught. I'm selling drugs over here.'
>
> Associate 1

Elders rarely handle the contraband in which they deal. Directions are later sent via Blackberry's encrypted instant-message service, or, in the case of one gang, instructions recorded on MP3 players. Economic transactions are arranged in person or by telephone, but mobile handsets are routinely changed in order to combat police surveillance (a trick some interviewees said they learned by watching the hit television series, *The Wire*). Messages are also often coded. Firearms may be endowed with female names, such as 'Loretta' the Beretta handgun or 'Tanisha' the TEC-9 submachine pistol, for instance, so that when gang members speak of 'going out' or 'looking after' a particular weapon it sounds to outsiders as though they are either embarking on a romantic date or caring for a sick relative.

Most youngers are employed by their elders to work what was known colloquially as the 'drugs line', although some are sent out 'on assignment', Member 13 told me, to explore 'new markets' in areas where they are unknown to police; notably commuter cities with vibrant night-time economies. Youngers also serve as couriers, making deliveries by bicycle or moped, which are ideal for negotiating the alleyways and back streets of estates. The 'line' refers to the client list, which is unique to each individual gang member. Complete lists of trusted users are stored on mobile phone SIM cards akin to the Rolodexes of business executives. In this context, SIM cards can become a commodity—a big 'line' equates to thousands of pounds worth of business that can be sold to the highest bidder. This explains in part why gang members often maintain multiple telephone numbers: one for family and friends, one for other gang members, and one for clients.

Drug sales are fundamentally an individual or small-group activity, not coordinated by the collective gang. The gang instead provides the reputational and criminogenic resources to sustain the enterprise. Elders earn income both from the retail mark-up on any drugs they sell personally and the sales volume they and their downline generate. Youngers, in turn, receive a small wage or cut of the profits:

> When the elders start a drug line business they get people to work on it and just pay them like £100 a week just to sit there and sell their drugs. That's it. They're 14 and they're getting £100 a week for nothing. ... So they're coming to school with the freshest trainers every week, they don't care. One hundred pounds is a lot to a little kid. For standing round giving, like, a fiend, what, two little rocks? That's it. Easy money.
>
> Member 32

Income variation between elders and youngers thus appears 'highly skewed', perhaps even similar in proportion to the wage disparity found in legal franchises and Levitt and Venkatesh's (2000, p. 786) 'drug selling gang'. For example:

> [As an elder] you can more sit back and make money. You've got everyone else running about for you. And even if you're not doing something you're taking a cut out of something else, you know what I mean? You go out there and earn money trying to stay as much below the radar as possible. You're literally putting bits on people to say, 'Ok, well, I need you to go out and, you know, you've built up a line.' You know, you've got cats phoning that line, 'all right, here's the line, you go out, you sell the drugs. I'll give you the drugs, just go out and sell it. Yeah? This is what you're getting for a week', yeah? So they've got a weekly wage, which might be something like £500, but they're making five, six grand ... for you. ... Yeah, they're getting, like, a 10 percent cut out of it. You know, or there's a percentage that they get out of what's made. Peanuts compared to what, you know, you're taking home for yourself. ... Those are the kids you like because they're entrepreneurs. Sometimes they don't even know that they're working for me or working for me second or third hand. All

you're doing is literally, now and again you come, you meet them, you drop the bits on them and you're in, you're out. The best way to put it to you is like the director or CEO of a company. Or like a General in the Army. He doesn't need to be out there on the front line but he still has the troops doing the work.

Member 12

Elders typically deal within lower-risk private networks. Buyers and sellers know each other and routinely cooperate in arranging illegal transactions that occur inside private (for example, hotel rooms, homes, cars) or semi-private (for example, bars, nightclubs, stores, motorway service stations) spaces.

By contrast, gang youngers usually work within higher-risk public networks, making sales to buyers in public settings such as streets and parks or in hallways and common areas of buildings. They sell only a few drugs 'wraps' or 'rocks' at a time, sometimes carrying them in their mouths so that if the police arrive the evidence can be swallowed. Earnings are contingent upon a large number of transactions because people who use drugs typically do not have the resources to buy in bulk. In one more elaborate scheme, however, members of the Golf gang sold drugs out of an unmanned launderette, concealing small quantities of product in their laundry and behind tumble driers and change machines.

On average interviewees estimated that heroin sells for £33,000 a kilo at wholesale and £45 a gram on the street. Hashish costs around £80 per ounce or £16 for an eighth of an ounce. Herbal cannabis costs anything from £70 per ounce to £140 for strong strains such as skunk. Heavy and regular cannabis users consume approximately one eighth of an ounce per day. But cocaine is where the real money is, in part because the drug caters to diverse lifestyles and attracts a variety of social groups. Cocaine sells for approximately £25,000 per kilo or £6000 for a nine ounce bar at wholesale but tends to sell for £45 a gram or £25 a half gram on the street. High-quality 'Peruvian' cocaine (50 percent-plus purity) can sell for up to £60 per gram and low-quality 'budget' cocaine (under 20 percent purity) retails at as little as £25 per gram. A gram of cocaine makes between 10 and 20 lines for snorting, which will last two people anything from a couple of hours to a whole night, depending on the strength of the drug and the users' appetite and tolerance for it, says Drugscope (2012). The average price per line thus is around £3. Profits are considerably enlarged when gang members cut with cheaper agents to increase their volume or 'wash up' the cocaine to make 'free base' crack. A single 'rock' of crack the size of a raisin and weighing about 0.2 grams, for instance, retails at around £20 (equivalent to £100,000 per kilo).

Success in the drugs business depends on acquiring the funds to make bigger drugs purchases:

> The more you buy the less the mark-up, and that comes down more with time when your supplier trusts you. It still comes down to money. Money is power. If you can dead the connect [buy the entire drugs supply], then people start to have to come to you. You become the man.
>
> Member 20

Things are rarely so uniform, however, not least because gang members may consume drugs supplies before they are sold or accept other forms of payment such as consumer goods, firearms, even sex. People who walk around with large quantities of product on them also become priority robbery targets, as Member 40 observed:

> The minute someone starts getting rich off of shotting, they buy a bigger bag [of drugs], and they buy a bigger gun to protect the bigger bag ... when you getting that type of money, there's consequences that come with it. Like Biggie [the late American rapper The Notorious B.I.G.] says, 'more money, more problems'.

To avoid a reputation as someone always in possession, but also to remind others of their role in a bigger organization, gang members will instead tell new and unfamiliar customers that they first need to go visit a 'friend' in order to fulfill their order.

Interviewees typically overestimated the scale of their drug dealing operations, as the following analogy demonstrates:

> We're entrepreneurs, we work hard for it bruv. Youngers be making a grand a week shotting. Do you even earn a grand a week? Getting them out of the game is like telling someone working at Merrill Lynch [investment bank] to quit and go work at Sainsbury's [supermarket].
>
> Associate 4

Gang members were eager to pull thick rolls of banknotes out of their trouser pockets to illustrate a typical 'night's work', but amounts quoted often refer to revenue rather than income. They also struggled to transform cash into wealth. The highest individual net worth I recall during my fieldwork was £40,000 in cash hidden in shoeboxes under a bed. Admittedly, this was a lot of money for a kid with no qualifications and little employment prospects—it would easily eclipse my student loan. But very few gang members had the human and social capital to launder profits through casinos, pawnbrokers, money couriers, small bank deposits, and remittances transferred using hawalas and money service businesses such as Western Union. One interviewee resorted to depositing cash into the bank account of a wealthy private school girl he had known since primary school. Another interviewee laundered money buying stored value 'gift' cards. In one high-profile case, gang members used ticket machines at train stations to launder dye-stained banknotes obtained through cash-in-transit robberies. They purchased cheap fares, paid with high denomination stolen cash, and pocketed the 'clean change' (Daily Mail, 2010).

Despite the pursuit of mythologized riches that gang life entails, the reality was often the reproduction of menial, low-status and poorly paid work. Reminiscent of Levitt and Venkatesh's (2000) assessment of why drug dealers still live at home with their mothers, Associate 1, for example, described the less-than-glamorous reality of gang life:

> We think if you've got a couple of grand you're balling. You're making it big. You're making money. That's big time. … But hold on … after them couple bags are gone what are you gonna do then? … How much money are you making? Like most of the dealers I know live in hostels. … They don't have houses or flats. They live in hostels. Man's got a 125 [cc] motorbike or a moped. 'Yes, I'm balling.' You're not balling. You live in a hostel. … you [live off] benefits. … and you drive a [Renault] Clio.

Associate 1 argued that the misperception that such individuals are 'balling' stems from the mythology of gangs and a failure to appreciate the pyramid form of drug distribution networks, with a broad base of low-status retail dealers at the bottom:

> What we live around now, like the people that we see now, they're petty drug dealers. But we don't know this 'cus, we think rah, they got bags so they must be making gwop, innit.

So the occupation of drug dealing, in the reality of most young people who enter gangs, does not provide the hoped-for escape from the economic constraints imposed by their class position and racial marginalization. Associate 2 said with irony that when 'you go out the area [to the country], drug dealing and that ... people think that's the high life'.

During my fieldwork, I sat in bedrooms adorned with large flat-screen televisions and stacked ceiling high with boxes of Nike shoes, but these reasonably expensive items were incongruous with the threadbare carpets, broken fittings, and mattress on the floor to sleep on. Gang life is about keeping up appearances. Hence why when I asked Member 9 about the carets conspicuously wrapped around his wrist and neck, he replied: 'The bling bling is all just show; I heard you [were] coming so I wore it.'

## Stage 4: Governance

Gangs in the enterprise stage are comprised of individuals for whom involvement in crime is for personal gain. By some margins, therefore, such gangs would already constitute organized crime (see Marshall, Webb, and Tilley, 2005, p. 6). Some gangs, however, evolve to an even higher state of being and thus meet more robust standards of definition. Not only are they suppliers of illegal goods and services, for example, but they aspire to be the sole suppliers of them in a given domain (Varese, 2010).

Some argue that 'turf' is what separates gangs from organized crime (for example, Decker and Pyrooz, 2011b), but in reality territory is a primary resource of organized crime (Varese, 2011). Members of the Hotel gang, for instance, distribute drugs in and around the brick-built quad-shaped flats of a labyrinthine social housing estate, which is comprised of nearly 900 apartments. Gang members have ripped out security cameras, smashed lights, and tampered with electromagnetic locks and intercom systems on communal doors to help conceal and expedite their nocturnal deals in the alcoves and stairwells. They have also modified attic and floor spaces, electrical boxes, emergency access ladders, and service cupboards in communal areas in order to hide sealed plastic bags which contain drugs, knives, and other contraband, and to make these items difficult to attribute to any one specific gang member.

The Hotel gang has monopolized the distribution of drugs and firearms in the area, but also is engaged in a violent campaign to reduce competition and govern neighboring markets. They even extort small business owners who operate on their turf (a barber, café owner, and newsagent, respectively). Gangs in the governance stage indeed have both will and mechanism to use violence in furtherance of group goals. And perhaps the most potent symbol of violence is a gun.

'Do you know how easy it is to get a gun in Brixton?' a streetwise teenage girl once asked me, rhetorically. Turns out, not as easy as she would have myself and others believe. As Member 50 explained, 'From the age of 10 or 11 upwards, kids have gotten access to a gun', but because Britain still has some of the 'tightest gun control legislation in the world', the country is certainly not 'flooded'.[4] Guns are a scarce commodity, to the extent that they are typically pooled among gang members. Member 43 recalled,

> All the older lot had at least, from what I know, they had at least four guns. There was one point where I saw a black bag full of guns, I mean from pistols to shotguns and semi-autos all in one big black bag that they shared out when needed.

Some rival gangs are even forced to use the same weapons, which they lease from a common source for between £50 and £250 per day. When multiple gang members in close proximity claim access to a firearm they are indeed often referring to the same-shared gun. In other words, people you would not expect to be allies can use one single gun on a given estate, which may be linked to multiple offenses.

Most gang members resort to using 'rebore' replica firearms and 'homemade' bullets (ammunition has a limited shelf life thus is as rare as the gun that fires it). For example, my fieldwork introduced me to a Bruni Olympic .38 starter pistol doctored to fire low-velocity ball bearings down a smoothbore barrel and an Airsoft assault rifle, with a magazine capable of firing upwards of 50-rounds, converted to shoot one single shotgun cartridge. Despite the novelty of such items, conversion imitation firearms often misfire. According to unpublished statistics, 75 percent of all firearms recovered by the MPS in 2006–7 were not even capable of firing. I even heard about one gang member who blew off three of his own fingers in a botched point-blank assassination attempt.

New 'clean' weapons without a criminal or forensic history are expensive and difficult to procure. Shotguns are the domain of gypsy traveller communities, for instance, who typically do not do business with outsiders. Ready access to firearms is thus what separates gangs in the governance stage from gangs in earlier stages of development.

Gangs that govern do not need to share with others because they have 'armorers' at their disposal:

> Yeah, it's young black boys carrying the guns and using them, but it's old white men, businessmen, Essex boys, Russians, Lithuanians, supplying and converting them. We don't do that. You need special lathes and tools to replace the pin, drill through the barrel etcetera. These are professionals, guys who know how a gun works, its components and that.
>
> Member 42

Former army sergeant Paul Alexander, for example, was jailed indefinitely in 2009 for supplying 'assassination kits' and other weapons to street gangs (Cobain and Siddique, 2009). His military background was perhaps no coincidence:

> This country is highly secured, yeah. You can't get nothing through this country unless you got someone working on the inside ... like at the airport side of things. Because there ain't no way on this earth, yeah, someone like myself or a gang member like myself is going to travel to a country to pick up a gun and get it through the system here. When I used to go and get whatever ... it's Army soldiers, people that have been through war and, or people that have got their connections to them things. ... You can go to them and buy them, buy off them. Because guns, yeah, come in fresh box. There ain't no way in this country you're going to get a gun in a fresh box with bullets fresh. ... The amount of things that I've seen, it's ridiculous.
>
> Member 38

> When it comes to guns and that, even from the Army. Very, very easy. ... High-ranking officers as well. High-ranking officers have got me in their houses. ... You've got to remember last year [the military] lost quite a few arms.
>
> Member 12

Just after these quotes were obtained, Shane Pleasant and Ben Whitfield, two former soldiers of the Third Battalion, Yorkshire Regiment, went on record that weapons could easily be obtained in Iraq or Afghanistan, either by buying or stealing from locals and foreign police, and the practice was common in the British army. The two men were among seven soldiers from the Yorkshire Regiment who were found guilty of being involved in an international gun smuggling ring (BBC News, 2008a).

Vladimir Lenin once said, 'One man with a gun can control 100 without one.' For gangs in the governance stage, violence is instrumental more than expressive:

> This ain't no thing where we stand here like we own this piece of concrete and kill you just because you live five minutes this way or that. But if you come violate what we've created ... what we doing here ... the thing we got going on here, then there's trouble.
>
> Member 11

Violence is used both to protect drug markets when they are threatened and prevent others from setting up in competition with established drug dealers. Member 9 explained: 'We don't just go around shooting people. This is about money. It's all about money. Stack paper and maintain.' Likewise, Member 50 described one gang's response to someone trying to cheat him and go at it alone:

> He took the money that I was supposed to have been owed and rather than give it to my sister to help her pay the rent and whatever else, he tried to set himself up with a cocaine dealer. But, of course, the people that run the area didn't like the idea that this little kid was going to try and, and also he had no one to have his back, now, did he? So apparently he got beaten up quite savagely and they took the drugs back and the cash anyway. What an idiot.

There is no external mechanism such as an oversight committee to ensure honesty in the drugs trade. Gangs thus become self-enforcing, based on reputation considerations. For gangs caught in ongoing cycles of violent retaliation, a significant reduction in harm is often only achievable once one gang secures a monopoly over a particular market or territory (thus reducing the incentive to aggressively police borders), or if profit potential from cooperation outweighs traditional gang loyalties (Starbuck, Howell, and Lindquist, 2001). Suffice it to say, while individuals can and do enter the drugs market, it is much less risky to do so as part of a gang.

Another feature of governance is gangs moving into legitimate business. Ex-gang leader Elijah Kerr, for example, argues that PDC is no longer a gang but a 'street movement' entitled 'Poverty Driven

Children', which encapsulates an underground record label ('PDC Entertainments'), a clothing line ('Public Demand Cartel'), a barber-shop ('Pristine Designer Cuts'), a youth engagement project ('Code 7'), and investments in the local night-time economy (see http://pdcent.com/profile/). There is precedent for this model. Chicago's infamous Gangster Disciples once published a 120-page 'blueprint' that rebranded the gang as a legitimate community organization interested in the 'Growth and Development' of young black men, albeit underwritten by the drug economy (see Papachristos, 2001).

One can only speculate how a group that is 'poverty driven' can so afford to pay for its business premises and to produce and promote its work; suffice it to say that revenue generated from music record sales and live performances in this age of digital media cannot cover it alone. Indeed, Kerr alludes to 'taxing' drug dealers on the Angell Town estate where PDC operates (Hill, 2007), thus implicating himself in the business of organized crime.

Another sign of governance is when the benefits gangs bestow extend beyond the immediate membership of the gang. Some gangs in London, for instance, protect community residents from violence and exploitation, provide them with financial sustenance, organize recreational activities, and otherwise 'serve' the community, not unlike certain larger American gangs (Sánchez-Jankowski, 1991; Venkatesh, 1997; Patillo, 1998; Sobel and Osoba, 2009). Gangs are not conventionally restrained from taking action, which is advantageous not only in illegal markets, but also in community settings that may not have reliable access to official or bureaucratic state means of action (as a result of history, money, and social standing). Some people want to cooperate with police but feel like they can't because they fear retaliation or have involvement in the case that exposes them to other charges. So they bypass the police and go to the gangs. As Member 11 explained, gangs can dispense 'quick justice' upon those that unduly prey upon 'innocent people'.

In Chapter 3 I demonstrate how gangs develop rudimentary structures, systems for issuing orders, rules that govern member interaction, and continuity over time, to ensure their effectiveness as suppliers of goods and services. To regulate the distribution of goods and services, however, gangs must also invest in the 'resources' of violence, territory, secrecy, and intelligence (Gambetta, 1993). The latter two deserve additional explanation.

Gangs require an informational advantage to stay one step ahead of rivals and the law. I recall once standing on the corner talking with a group of gang members—incidentally joking about the parallels between life in the gang and life in the academy in terms of 'reputation management'—when one of them received a telephone call from a 'lookout' positioned at the window of an adjacent building: he had watched our entire conversation and demanded to know who I was and what I was doing there. Gang members likewise listen in on police scanners and conduct research on the Internet regarding basic police surveillance techniques, the function of different police units, and the meaning of police shoulder boards and identification numbers. On one occasion, Member 27 showed me a record of officer shift patterns and the make, model, and registration number of supposedly 'unmarked' police cars. He described updating these data as part of his 'job'.

A gang's capacity for information gathering is part of its reputation. A gang's reputation, in turn, is intricately tied to its control and influence within the local and larger community. During my fieldwork, I learned about gangs paying local residents to act as 'sentinels' and gangs corrupting police and local authority employees so they turn a blind eye to certain activities and provide early warning of new suppression efforts. In some communities, 'clean skins' above suspicion provided personal alibis, safe houses, and stash houses for gang members. In others, gang members had befriended nightclub door staff through local gyms and sports clubs in order to obtain valuable information and ensure clemency during personal security checks. Beta gang even provided nightclub security in return for *carte blanche* to deal drugs on the premises. Bottom line: gangs were beginning to encroach upon and 'govern' all aspects of life in the neighborhood.

## Concluding remarks

This chapter has argued recreation, crime, enterprise, and governance represent not distinct gang business *categories*, but rather actualization *stages* through which gangs progress. Each stage builds upon the previous—it transcends and includes its predecessor. Gangs evolve from relatively disorganized neighborhood groups into more corporate entities in response to powerful incentives and a commitment to financial goals. Those that aspire to govern territories or markets thus do so to reduce the uncertainty that characterizes the environment in which illegal entrepreneurs operate. Once gangs reach their highest stage of development, therefore, they come to resemble not just 'crime that is organized' but something altogether more sinister and difficult to deter: 'organized crime'.

Are London's gangs unique in this evolutionary process? Such is a fundamental question for future research. Having here helped to validate some of Pitts's (2008) findings in London, my short answer is, 'not necessarily'. Manchester's Gooch gang, for example, started life as a teenage 'posse' embroiled in turf wars with rivals the Doddington gang and Old Trafford Cripz, but quickly graduated from petty violence and theft to murder and large-scale drugs distribution (Jenkins, 2009). As a truly 'global city', however, socio-economic and spatial polarization is perhaps greater in London than in any other UK jurisdiction (Sassen, 2007). The history and diversity of London, moreover, presents greater organized crime influences and opportunities (Decker, Van Gemert, and Pyrooz, 2009), from Afghani and Pakistani heroin traffickers to Turkish and Albanian heroin distributors, Columbian cocaine suppliers to Cambodian cannabis growers, and Jamaican 'Yardies' to Lithuanian small arms dealers (Ruggiero, 2000; Ruggiero and South, 1995). Member 20 noted, 'Things that you shouldn't have, like guns, drugs, are there regardless. Someone's gonna use them.'

Demonstrating the extent to which gangs and organized crime intersect in London, the Adams family crime syndicate even allegedly put a price on the heads of the three youths convicted for the 2008 murder of schoolboy Ben Kinsella because, in the words of Prosecutor Nicholas Hilliard QC, 'they weren't happy with a killing on the streets of their area' (Kelly, 2009). Organized crime in London thus is not 'abstract phenomenon'—'the drugs are dealt, firearms used and acquisitive crime committed in local neighborhoods' (Murphy, 2009). Perhaps such is why ethnographic research in comparable cosmopolitan cities finds evidence of gangs as organized crime (see Decker, Bynum, and Weisel, 1998). Which brings me to my next topic: the organization of organized crime.

# 3
# Gang Organization

'The trouble with organizing a thing', says Laura Ingalls Wilder (1941) in the classic novel *Little Town on the Prairie*, 'is that pretty soon folks get to paying more attention to the organization than to what they're organized for'. These few short words perfectly capture everything that is wrong with gang research. Instead of investigating gang processes, which research tells us are actually important (see McGloin and Decker, 2010), there is a tendency among scholars to want to revise articulated gang typologies and put gangs in neat little boxes (see Sheldon, Tracy, and Brown, 2004, pp. 42–3). This chapter attempts to bring the gang back into gang research by examining group size and (sub)group inter-action, hierarchy and leadership, organizational mobility, incentives, rules, and sanctions for violating the rules: measures implicated in prior research for understanding the nature and extent of gang organiza-tion (Decker and Van Winkle, 1996; Decker, Bynum, and Weisel, 1998; Decker, Katz, and Webb, 2008).

Buddy Howell's (2012, p. 70) review of the key elements of gang definitions concludes that after criminal activity, 'The organizational structure of the gang is the second most frequently specific aspect of gangs.' But delinquent group structure in Britain is traditionally 'more fluid and less tangible' than in the United States (Downes, 1966, p. 122). Low levels of gang organization are found throughout the British context (Aldridge and Medina, 2008; Bennett and Holloway, 2004; Bradshaw, 2005; Mares, 2001), except in London. John Pitts's (2008) research is indeed something of an empirical outlier in Britain, show-ing gangs that are much more organized (and evolving exclusively toward organization), which begs the question: are such findings shaped by Pitts's approach to fieldwork (never clearly articulated, but in all likelihood guided strongly by criminal justice agency accounts), or by the different real-world context of London gangs compared to those found in other large British cities? The answer, it seems, is the latter.

## Gang size and interaction

As discussed in Chapter 2, gangs invariably start life as small recreational groups of friends. The number of functioning members in the group can be reasonably flexible between five and ten, with a few hangers on. As group size grows, however, there are greater opportunities for potential interactions, but also more formality and less intimacy (Simmel, 1950). With each new gang member connections among gang members multiply. In a gang of five, for example, there are 10 possible interactions. Gang members can stay in the same room and hold a single conversation. In a gang of 10, by contrast, there are 45 different relationships—too many open channels to follow. Space becomes a commodity. Inclusive conversation becomes impossible. Members thus retreat into smaller and safer subgroups. I observed this pattern of behavior first hand at countless gang assemblies and parties, although it is of course not unique to gangs: families undergo similar processes at large reunions, as do students at college bops.

The size of a gang thus affects its ability to cooperate in a task. All 52 gang members reported the existence of subgroups within his or her gangs. These subgroups are not discordant factions (group loyalty still exists), but rather they are instrumental outlets for gang enterprise. Gang activities are much more likely to originate from within these subsets than from the entire gang acting as a unit. Gang subgroups ('crews', 'batches' or 'cliques' in gang parlance) were typically defined or determined by age with and without affiliations to each other in an overarching gang structure:

> There's a lot of little crews, but they all go, go back to one big, big crew. … The younger ones they have, 'cus they hang about themselves they have their own little crews, that's their own little crew. This is our little crew and then there's the elders' little crew. … But when we go to like parties, we all come together. Or when we hang out or we go youth club we all come together right, and everyone knows each other like that. But usually when we just hang out on the street, it used to be like the youngers by themselves, maybe with a couple of

us or us with a couple of youngers and a couple of elders, but usually it's just every little group by themselves. ... People were just rolling in twos or fours and only coming together in parties.

Member 43

Larger gangs may even formally incorporate separate auxiliary gangs or 'sets' for their younger members. Gangs typically denote these younger sets with a prefix, such as 'younger' or 'tiny'. In Southwark, for example, the 'Young Peckham Boys', 'Younger Peckham Boys', and 'Peckham Kids', are all age-defined sets belonging to the older 'Peckham Boys' gang; although such names have since been replaced with more ominous-sounding acronyms such as DFA (Don't Fuck Around), PYG (Peckham Young Gunners), and SN1 (Spare No One). The reason is that small groups accomplish more in less time than large groups do. They also attract far less scrutiny from law enforcement and rival groups.

Gangs must not be viewed in isolation, to the extent that many of them are almost defined by their proximity to other gangs. As Member 39 said, 'How can you be a gang without a rival gang?' This rhetorical question speaks to Thrasher's (1927, p. 46) classic notion that gangs are 'integrated through conflict'. But there is also a number of natural loose alliances and groupings among disparate gangs. Small gangs, for instance, cluster around large gangs to gain better access to the wholesaler suppliers of criminal commodities. Borough allegiances also often transcend local gang affiliations. Rival gangs in the 'blue borough' of Lewisham, for instance, are known to call a truce and amalgamate during periods of inter-borough rivalry with the 'black borough' gangs of Southwark or the 'green borough' gangs of Bromley.[1] Member 27 explained,

It's a gang with your area. When another gang like invades that area or someone from a different area invades that area, all the gangs come together as one. No matter if they like each other, all the gangs come together to defend that area.

Once a dispute subsides, however, local rivalries typically resume as per the 'postcode wars' touted in the media.

Gangs also coordinate via incidental contacts made in schools, prisons, or young offenders' institutions. Alliances formed in schools between disparate gangs or gang members are surprisingly common because school catchments regularly cross territorial boundaries. Many children indeed travel out of borough to go to school because their local authority simply cannot accommodate them. Member 46 explained:

> You go to school, you've got tons of different people from tons of different areas. It's not just because you go to school in Lewisham that means that everyone there is from Lewisham. You get people from Peckham, you get people from Croydon and, you know, if they're involved in something where they are, do you know what I mean? You get to know what they're involved in, they get to know what you're involved in and there becomes those ties because if I want something done down there or if I'm going down there and someone tries to stop me and go, 'Right, who do you know around here?' ... For me it's like when you go to those different areas, it's about who you meet.

Interviewees likewise described the way in which they used time spent in prison to forge important strategic alliances with members of opposing gangs, often along the lines of business interests:

> At Feltham [young offender institution] you almost, like, knew everyone and everyone would know who you was, you knew who they were or knew something about their crew and it was easy like that. ... So when it comes to setting up, like, different links with different people from different boroughs and all the rest of it, I'd turn around and go, 'Well, yeah, I know north London and I know the Archway lot and know the Holloway lot.' But, you know, when you're doing crime and you're doing, say for instance, you're doing fraud, you want as many different links as possible because, you know, there's many different opportunities to get this thing up and running. So you want to have as many different people from many different areas knowing what it is you're doing.
>
> Member 12

Gang-related disputes can carry over into custody, but the logical need for prisoners to band together with people from the same home area, or with similar cultural reference points, particularity when held some distance from their homes, means that disputes can be put aside. Bonds between members of allied gangs may be further solidified by the decision of prison authorities to suppress violence by separating prisoners according to their gang affiliations:

> It was a joke. ... I went to jail only to link up with man that went in a week or a month before me. When I went to Feltham [young

offender institution] and saw [gang member], the first thing he said and did was laugh, spud me, and say 'they got you too'? ... The gangs continued in jail and within that, all the little cliques came together. People from your own circle that you didn't really know or get along with on the outside, they would stick with you in jail. They would introduce their man so it went on. The gang got bigger, got stronger.

Member 49

Prison thus becomes a space for the expanded business and territorial organization of gangs. Prison helps solidify the group and clarify its direction by providing a link between the system and the street. The so-called Northern Line, for example, are a connection of gang members from opposing north London gangs—primarily in Haringey, Enfield, and Islington—who initially came together around the in-prison drugs trade but continue to work together after release.

As gangs expand in size and evolve in stature they tend to develop more formal structures to ensure longevity. No longer can gang members assume that other gang members are 'insiders' in sympathy with what they say or do. Now they must take the larger audience of gang members into consideration and implement quality management techniques designed to break down individual identity and mold recruits into full group members (see Chapter 5). Overall gang organization, in turn, starts to rely less on personal attachments and more on established rules and regulations.

During the recreation and crime stages, gangs operate without specific aims and are characterized by loose structures and fluid memberships. As gangs grow, however, first generation gang members become *de facto* elders (and a few among them, the inner circle). This is related to tenure more than anything, with roles and responsibilities allocated according to talents and interests. With size, then, gangs become more stable and capable of withstanding the loss of one or more members, which is crucial given the risks of injury and incarceration inherent to gang life. Much as corporations expand and contract during periods of boom and bust, respectively, gang rosters may swell in times of crisis, such as impending gang violence or to protect turf or drug markets when they are threatened.

Gangs cannot continue to grow *ad infinitum*, however, because in the underworld common organizational problems of asymmetric information, imperfect monitoring, and opportunistic behavior are exacerbated (see Gambetta, 2009b). Overseeing gang business is a challenge at the best of times. In Member 3's words, 'you don't write much down 'cus it's all evidence if you get caught'.[2] More gang members mean more problems because there are more gang members to monitor.

Gangs mitigate their agency problems in part by keeping agency chains reasonably short. Indeed, although the number of members varied, the gangs I encountered were never very large. Average gang size was around 40 members with a 'set space' (Tita, Cohen, and Endberg, 2005) limited to areas in and around one social housing estate. As Member 43 outlined:

> There's about 30 people that are in it properly and then there was other people that are associated with it 'cus they live around or they know people or they're family. But there's like the people that made it, like the older lot [the inner circle], then there's our lot [the elders] and then there's the younger ones. But they came afterwards because [the inner circle] added all the people that were associated with it as youngers, so it worked like that.

Bigger gangs comprised no more than 140 members across multiple sets and enjoyed territorial claims of less than one square mile. A large gang thus would barely qualify as a mid-sized legitimate business, which encompasses between 50 and 250 employees, according to the Small Business Act for Europe. The largest show of strength by any one gang during my fieldwork was en route to the 2008 Lambeth Country Show, a large outdoor festival, where police rounded up approximately 80 gang members onto a red double-decker bus.

## Hierarchy and roles

Gangs further address agency problems by arranging their members in a vertical ranking. The gangs I observed were organized around a small tight-knit group of seven or so gang members who shared roughly equal authority over all other members. This 'inner circle' is made up of first-generation gang members now aged in their mid to late twenties and above, thus old enough to have built some solid criminal credentials. Inner circle gang members had in most cases grown up together in and around gang turf or otherwise knew each other as relatives and old school friends. The inner circles of at least seven gangs I engaged with, for instance, were comprised in part of cousins and siblings:

> Looking back now, there's only a few people I'd say, 'Yeah, boom', they have my back. They were like brothers to me. They were like,

they were like blood and still are. ... Like, some of them are my cousins and I know that they would ride or die for me, do you know what I mean, like? Others are like people that I've grown up with since I've come here, like. One of my friends, I've only been in this country since, what, 1990, we met each other in '91. So, I met some of these guys, like, the year after I come here. We've been brothers from then, do you know what I mean? ... I think it's probably the longevity of the relationship that made that close-knit crew. ... Even though I'm almost like, I'm like the head; there are a lot of people that don't know my real name or where I live. So it's like, it's like a tiered system. You've got people that just hang around with you when you're out and about, you've got, you know, other people who are a bit closer but they still don't know you; you know, you'd, like, meet them in certain places and you congregate and you have different bits and pieces with them. And you've got other people who are your close, close, close friends, your inner circle who might even come to your house and see your mum ... you trust them to a very, very deep extent. You know if anything goes wrong, you can count on them.

Member 12

In a world where trust is fragile, these established connections were key to the daily operations of the group.

Tacit status hierarchies unchanged since the group first came together generally dictate the internal dynamics of a gang's inner circle. The group invariably possesses one dominant or 'charismatic' (in a Weberian sense) personality who is, for all intents and purposes, the *primus inter pares*:

| | |
|---|---|
| Densley: | So, who's in charge of the gang? |
| Member 43: | The boss. The top dog, like some guy ... |
| Densley: | Is it really just one guy at the top? I mean there's a lot of elders and stuff ... |
| Member 43: | Yeah, there's elders and then in the elders there's one guy. |
| Densley: | And he's at the top? |
| Member 43: | Who came up with the name, who came up with the contacts, whatever and he's at the top. |
| Densley: | Who does he answer to? Anyone? |
| Member 43: | His mum. |
| [Laughter] | |
| Member 43: | No. He don't answer to no one. Seriously. |

The person described is the gang's unofficial or hidden leader, but to reduce the appearance of dictatorship within the gang and appease its members he is neither endowed with such a title nor assigned with written formal duties. The first among equals is not elected but rather asserts himself through exceptional achievement in crime, proficient stewardship of enterprise, and, above all, a reputation for violence. I know one gang leader, for example, who served under warlords and militiamen as a child-soldier in a civil war that killed tens of thousands and was characterized by such brutal behaviors as mutilation, rape, torture, and murder. He's 'remorseless', said one police officer, 'life is cheap [to him]. He's been inured to violence. Violence comes easy.'

Randall Collins (2008, p. 20) argues, 'Those individuals who are good at violence are those who have found a way to circumvent confrontational tension/fear, by turning the emotional situation to their own advantage and to the disadvantage of their opponent.' It seems the aforementioned gang leader turned his lack of empathy into an advantage. Member 45 was likewise good at violence because violence was, in his words, 'kind of a release'. He explained: 'I would always be the first to offer to fight, innit, 'cus I was angry. I was mad. I didn't care who it was, it could be the biggest guy, I would just fight.' Violence assertion is one route to *obtaining* leadership during the recreation and crime stages:

> Once you commit murder and you get away with it, you straight away, your mentality is I'm a leader because I've done murder, other kids ain't got the heart to do that and I've got, second of all I got away with it. I'm back on the street, I can do it again. So then that's when people are scared of you. So then you become a leader because every time you're walking down the street people are looking down, 'cus they're scared to look in your face. Now you're a murderer. Now people are thinking twice to talk to you in a certain way because they might think they're going to get the same thing, do you see what I'm trying to say? 'If you touch me I'll murder you, straight. I've done it before, I'll do it again.' So that's when you become a leader. You rule through fear.
>
> Member 8

Violence is also key to *maintaining* leadership during the enterprise stage. But a penchant for violence alone is of course not enough. The leadership must also display a certain degree of entrepreneurial acumen because without a strategy for growth, the a gang stagnates and its members defect. At the end of the day, the gang needs to keep its underlings scared, but satisfied.

The first among equals is essentially the gang's instrumental leader, which developed out of his being a ringleader back in the embryonic stages of the gang. Such an individual is typically credited with coining the name of his gang and the form of some of its key symbols. He focuses on getting things done, from illegal transactions to organized raids on rival turf, typically through the adoption of an authoritarian or autocratic style that demands obedience. As Member 30 explained, 'If someone doesn't want to do something, it's like "you think you've got a fucking choice? You think this is a democracy, bruv?"' Yet, like a true Weberian (1978) bureaucracy, responsibility is distributed across the inner circle which means that gangs are able to sustain operations even when key individuals are removed.

Given that leaders within gangs assert themselves, there is no agreed form of succession planning, in which those higher up in the gang designate a successor to take over operations upon their imprisonment, retirement, or death. Instead, inner circle gang members typically assume certain roles and responsibilities based on a claim to some expertise. During my fieldwork, I encountered senior gang members that specialized in aspects of the drug business or in planning cash-in-transit robberies. Others focused solely on the modification and supply of firearms. Still others became expressive leaders who concentrated on internal dispute resolution and gang members' well-being. Either way, since leadership makes others more conscious of a person, inner circle gang members can have a huge target on their backs. The irony is that their gangs would likely collapse without their creative input.

For example, inner circle gang members are not as tied to geography as their comrades. As a result, they are free to travel far outside traditional territorial boundaries to socialize and meet. Sometimes the objective is to seek out neutral territory where the risk of encounters with other gangs is low, often it is to visit venues where confrontations are more likely (notably nightclubs and 'pay parties'), and thereby initiate symbolic and actual shows of strength. Visits out of borough are also used to cement networks developed through contact in school or prison that contribute to gang cooperation.

Inner circle gang members are typically the most senior gang members, based upon age and longevity of gang involvement, but also acquired violence and financial capital. Below them lie the elders, a mix of first- and second-generation gang members, aged between 17 and 24 on average, and the youngers, second- and third-generation gang members, typically aged between 11 and 16. Gangs achieve their reputations from the inner circle, but such individuals tend to distance themselves from the gang name and symbolism once it is established, in part to conceal the level of gang organization from outsiders. Member 38 elaborated using the following popular culture reference:

> The people that make the most money in these gangs like from drugs and that, they're not seen. They're somewhere else. They're playing God somewhere. You will not see them. They're affiliated with the gang, they're running the gang, but they don't really partake in any gang activities. ... Those that are good at what they do don't even come into contact with the police. A thing that you should watch is *The Wire*. I don't know if you've seen that. ... There are a lot of Stringer Bells in this world, really there are. They start with a platform that's illegal and they build on that with something that's legal. They be modest with their spending. Might start a car business or might own a couple of cars, then from that he starts doing number plates. So whenever someone comes to ask them to account for their money, they be like, they have the documents there already. So, you're the smart person, you're the plan behind the business. You're the one calling the shots. You don't want to get your hands dirty so you're going to get somebody else who's stupid enough. That's proper gangster.

Elders are therefore responsible for advancing or, at the very least, sustaining the 'street legacy' of the inner circle gang members.

Elders handle day-to-day decision-making and the more physical or violently predisposed among them serve as 'muscle' or contract 'gunmen' for the inner circle. Member 43 described them simply as, 'the people that you would call when you want someone gone, to shoot somebody ... they move quietly, like an assassin'. Such individuals are often implicated in unsolved murders and benefit from gang mythology:

> You just hear stories about them. You see them and they look mean, like they just look like they don't care, like, or they're always wearing something that you know that they've got [a weapon] on them like black leather gloves. ... They're big in the gang. They are like the hardest person in the gang. They're like on the levels of the top elders, the insiders.
>
> Member 34

Member 34 implies that gunmen are easily to spot because they wear a leather glove on one hand. The glove is meant to protect against forensic evidence and signal to others that one is 'strapped'. Such a cheap signal is, however, easily mimicked. Like the classic Dr Seuss (1961) children's story, star-bellied Sneetches feel superior to plain-bellied Sneetches until someone finds a way to put stars on all the Sneetches and Sneetches can no longer tell each other apart. Alas, countless young people within and without gangs now wear one glove in an effort to deter potential assailants, but the signal is meaningless.

Real gunmen really only carry weapons about their person in the minutes before they intend to use them, which confounds police investigations. As one officer told me,

> We know who the gunmen are and what they're doing, but they're like David fucking Copperfield [a magician]. A call comes in or you swear you've just seen them with something, but when you stop and search them, they're clean, it's gone. It just vanished into thin air.

The best gunmen are skilled in the arts of deception and counter-surveillance. One Hotel gang member, for example, instructs his subordinates to dress like him and form a phalanx around him when walking in the community. He travels deliberately complex routes and has strategically hidden dustbin-liners full of clothes around his home estate to facilitate Superman-esque quick changes. 'He just does everything smart. He'll do something and disappear', Member 36 said.

Elders support their youngers in all aspects of gang business, as Member 7 explained:

> That's how the younger ones are getting their protection. That's how the younger ones are getting their guns, getting ... their money and how they make money selling weed or selling cocaine or selling heroin such like that. Their elder, yeah, that's how they do it. Because they couldn't get it otherwise. Anytime a little younger stabbed someone or does something to someone the elder probably is there and influencing. And if he didn't want it to happen, it wouldn't happen.

The youngers are essentially left to make reputations for themselves, but also to assume the risks that the achievement of such notoriety involves. Says Member 39,

> If they get in trouble, if they get arrested, that's them, nothing to do with us. Worse thing is if they get arrested with the drugs or gun or whatever, they owe, they owe us if you know what I'm saying.

Some might say that youngers are primarily concerned with creating attention for themselves and diverting police attention away from the true business purpose of gangs—the petty crime of the youngers is a 'smokescreen' for the organized, for-profit criminal activity of the gang elders, said one police officer. He added that a relatively small number of young adults were simply 'taking advantage' of the 'chaotic lives' and social formations of children living in deprived neighborhoods.

## Girls and gangs

Of all those associated with gangs, girls play perhaps the most diverse role. The vast majority of female gang members are associate or auxiliary members of male gangs. They are 'groupies', Associate 8 said, attracted to that they naïvely think are harmless 'social rewards'. Although a few may rise to be independent of male authority, girls are typically lower status and subservient to male gang members. Girls are treated with little respect, and as Member 26 described, they are easily replaceable: 'When a girl gets caught the boys will find another one to do it, to take their place.' Nonetheless, girls are 'useful', Member 26 explained, because they 'do the dirty things that boys don't want to do or that puts the boys at risk like holding the weapon ... or holding the drugs in the house or a lot of money in the house'.

Since law enforcement are less likely to search or suspect females, girls perform integral gang duties, such as couriering contraband or information, laundering cash, luring rivals for ambushes, liaising between gangs and gang members or between the street and prison, and providing alibis, logistical, or domestic support. Some girls even find strategic employment, infiltrating local government agencies to secure intelligence on gang members. The irony of girls' subservient role in gangs, Associate 7 told me, is that through the 'pillow talk' they engage in when sleeping with gang members, they become privy to the gang's most secretive and sensitive information. I have written elsewhere about the sexual role of girls in gangs (see Densley, Davis, and Mason, 2013), suffice it to say that girls and gang members typically 'bond through a relationship, or a friendship, or whatever', no matter now abusive (Associate 7). And, bearing in mind that the vast majority of gang members are teenagers, the relationships they have with women are the source of the vast majority of intra-gang and inter-gang conflicts.

## Mobility

Multi-level marketing is a system of business that puts more emphasis upon the recruitment of distributors than on the selling of products. As Member 50 explained:

> The reality of the situation is the gang is a triangle. The triangle is the business, just like any other thing. Got people at the top, people at the middle, people on the lower level although now the bottom level could be really, really wide because you're recruiting numbers all the time.

Member 50 describes the gang as a triangle, but it is in reality a pyramid. Multi-level marketing is intrinsically flawed, yet it appeals because it sells the dream of material wealth and independence and appears to be outside the mainstream of business as usual. Avon's (n.d.) website, for example, champions the ideal of a 'flexible' business whereby you 'make your own hours' but enjoy 'unlimited earning potential'. This sounds very much like the sales pitch street gangs use when recruiting for the illicit economy. What both groups fail to advertise is that the system benefits the few over the many. For every gang younger who makes a decent living or even a decent supplementary income from drug dealing, there are countless others who do little more than break even. If the basic idea is for sellers to recruit more sales persons then rather than expanding the client base, they are increasing internal competition. Only those who control the gang and supply the drugs at the top profit by having more youngers trying to out-sell each other. For those at the bottom, the gang becomes survival of the fittest.

Internal processes betray the true relations of forces between elders and youngers and the real state of affairs regarding the purpose of gangs. Elders spoke quite openly about the exploitative nature of elder–younger relationships, with youngers seen merely as a tool for gang business:

> Elders normally use these people to do their dirty work. Do you see what I'm trying to say? Like, hold this in your house or give them something to do outside the streets. They just use the young people because ... police wouldn't really stop a younger person. So an elder will say, you know, 'you go and take care of this for me'. They do it, and that'll bring up [the younger's] rating. And they want to do it because obviously they want to be like these people more than anybody else. ... Like I said, you do our dirty work basically.
>
> Member 37

Youngers' 'false consciousness' is a result of control that they either do not know they are under because of the non-pecuniary benefits associated with gang membership or which they disregard with a view to their own possibility of upward mobility within the gang. Youngers are still in the 'reasons to join a gang' phase, whereas elders occupy a 'reasons to stay in a gang' phase, which is far more selfish.

In their dreams of entering at the ground floor and expecting to climb to the penthouse over time, youngers have been fooled by history. During the recreation and crime stages, participation in gangs was a rite of passage, meaning that as gang members got older they dropped out and the younger generation stepped in to take their place. As gangs became enterprises, however, they provided such powerful economic incentives that gang elders were loath to retire. Instead, they put measures in place to ensure the gravy train never ended. Gang structure served a purpose: the rich got richer.

## Incentives: The ratings game

Gang members often talk about living life at the 'end' of a 'road'. Life on road is a literal description in as much that gangs are street-oriented groups, but more precisely life on road is a metaphorical description of a career-like journey, in which a gang member's 'stripes' or 'ratings' (literally, peer respect) measure both how far in they are and how much they deserve to be taken to the next level. As Member 7 explained:

> You have to build up your stripes because if you don't build up your stripes, who are you? You'd be sorry to say, what have you done? So you have to build up your stripes like because no one will respect you. You see what I'm trying to say? If no one knows you for nothing bad no one's going to respect you. Who are you? But they know you if you disrespected a person or beated [sic] up this person or robbed this. You see what I'm trying to say?

Life on road thus is best understood as a game or tournament of the most committed. In some cases the game is entrepreneurial and youths use ratings to build their own personal brand or business, but the true players are gang members because it is gangs who establish the rules and keep score. Member 7 added:

> You had the rankings. Like, you had top people ... in the gang. Then there was the middle and then you had the low ... if you're at the bottom it's for a reason. Some people just stay there because they're

nice there. That's their position [and] they really don't want to go any further. The people at the bottom normally come out of the gang first ... because they know this ain't for them, they just done it to do it because of their friends or because they're scared and need protection. It's a social thing. The people at the top, they have to do it or they want to do it. ... For them it's a money thing. But people at the bottom, they know really and truly they don't want this lifestyle. They know in their hearts that they're not really cut out for it, you see what I'm saying? ... The people in the middle stick by the people at the top. They want to be at the top. ... They don't want to come out the game. ... They want to be like you.

Member 7 said there are no true 'free riders'. Member 12 observed:

If you're reaping the profits and whatever else it is that we're doing ... you know, we know all the bouncers on the club doors and you're getting in there for free or whatever, then you got to contribute. You think you're on the fringe so you're forgiven? It does work like that. Once you're in, you're not going to be on the fringes, you get involved.

Gangs also offer a controlled territory in which to play and, as discussed, a host of economic and other incentives.

The object of the tournament, Associate 1 argued, is to become a 'known' figure, albeit within the narrow confines of one school or social housing estate:

You wanna be higher up because ... you get more ratings innit if you're higher up in the game. If you get higher up, you're somebody bigger. ... Certain people know who you are more. People know about you more. Like, certain people you could say something 'Oh d'ya know about this person?' and they'll say 'yeah man know about him. Der, der, der. But other people.' You'll be like 'Do you know about them?' 'No I don't know them.'

Gang members who are actively competing for ratings occupy a quasi-celebrity status in some jurisdictions and maintain a very public persona. As one police officer remarked:

There are celebrities who try not to get papped [photographed by the paparazzi] and celebrities who do. You know, celebrities like [media personality and former glamor model] Katie Price, who is famous just for being famous. The same is true of gang members. The serious guys, those with the real talent, stay hidden. Those with something to prove hang around the school gates trying to get their faces known. On the street it's all about being known. Image and perception are everything and some of these elders literally have celebrity status. A few days ago I saw two of them hanging outside the [local] school gates. You could see from the reaction of the kids walking home that they knew who they were. No shit, they were acting as if they had spotted [professional footballer] David Beckham or something. They were all excited. After a while these two guys walked over to one of the teachers, hugged him, you know like half-hug half-handshake as they do, and talked. They knew the teacher as a volunteer youth worker. But how does that look to those impressionable young people? I tell you, it looks like the teachers answer to the gang.

For this reason, gang members can often identify exactly when and where someone first 'bust' out on to the scene and became a true player:

[N]o one knew who they were and then [it's] like ... Man bust in '03. ... That's when everyone knew about you. You stepped up your game, you started doing bigger things, feel me? So that's what happens when you start progressing in the game you start doing certain things.

Associate 1

Youths punch in to the game via a landmark event that is typically violent, such as a schoolyard fight or an impressive display of courage against the odds. Further ratings are earned via participation in illegal activities or demonstration of deviant behaviors esteemed by gangs, such as sexual conquest. As Associate 8 noted, the 'more stuff you do the more ratings you get'. Member 41 elaborated:

He'll start doing stuff where he gets his rep, like he'll go and stab someone or go shoot at someone or go rob a big dealer from another area or do whatever. He'll just start getting ranked up like, he'll earn respect by doing that.

Some girls associated with gangs are willing to equal or best the level of violence perpetrated by the boys to build ratings in a slightly different competition: the competition to be recognized as the one true *female* gang member. Member 38 gave the following example:

I've known some girls who do stabbings within the gangs. ... Some girls will do it because they see themselves as boys. You know, so you have the little tomboyish one who will just, who sees herself as a boy, who dresses like a boy and everything and you know, trousers down and everything and will do what boys will do and they will want to do. ... They will hold a knife and they will get the call 'You need to bring this knife down to whichever part I'm at if I need it' and they're the ones, that's the ones that will do that for the gang.

Fighting is integral to such girls' sense of identity, in part because violence is seen as their only means to achieve 'real respect' from the boys:

> Them girls would get real respect 'cus ... they used to rob other girls and beat up other girls and do, like, if the boy don't want to hit the girl then he use her to beat up other girls. She's thinking like a boy. Like, I just want to beat up people, hurt people, she's hard-core. Hard body chicks. She gets respect.
>
> Member 28

Girls with hard-earned 'real respect' thus typically look down upon others who 'prostitute' themselves to the gang for the same ends:

> There's more reputation as well because you're known, you're respected by boys and that's a lot. When you're respected by a boy and not in a sexual manner or that, boys enhance your reputation. It's not 'yeah, we went out with each other, yeah, she sucked my dick, I respect her so much'. No, boys respect you because you done the street, because you fucked some girl up for talking shit about you. When a boy is talking highly of you, yeah, and they say, 'Do you know what she's done?', you get more rating from people. More respect. That's how it is.
>
> Member 7

But Member 7 is the exception not the rule—girls in gangs typically do not obtain ratings through *what* they do, but rather *whom* they do. By 'touching skin' with a gang boy, girls appropriate some of his 'hood celebrity' and likewise become somebody 'known':

> They try to get like, fame off knowing boys. Saying 'yeah I know this person, I know that person'. ... They start having sex with gangbangers. ... They sit down, making status claims. Like, writing 'yeah, I belong to this gang, I belong to that gang, you lot can't do nothing about it'.
>
> Associate 1

Partha Dasgupta (1988, p. 62) observes, 'Reputation is a capital asset. One can build it up by pursuing certain courses of action, or destroy it by pursuing certain others.' Interviewees were clear that serious violence was the fastest way to rise to the top. Member 33 mused, 'One week you can be the boy that everyone thinks is a nerd then you can do like three shootings in that week and everyone thinks he's changed now so then he's fierce.' Likewise, Member 10 said, 'If you shank someone then you pretty much shoot to the top.' Member 8 added that within gang territory, news of violence travels fast: 'If you go out there now and kill someone and stab them quickly, people that are young and who are there are going to know that you've killed this person ... your ratings are going to go up.'

With the above said, an equilibrium must be achieved that balances enough violence to enhance individual and gang reputations but not so much that gang business is threatened. A dead body, for instance, leaves corroborating forensic evidence and invites the full weight of police investigatory resources. The scars and stories of the survivors of gang violence often better corroborate one's ratings. As Member 2 elaborated, 'Most people don't stab people to kill them, just to send a message ... "you know what will happen next, I let you off with a lick".' When knifes are around, however, pushing and shoving can escalate into 'shanking'. The fact that gang members use knives to deliberately 'make a mark' implies that some fatal stabbings are merely a 'scratching' gone wrong.

'Guns for show, knives for a pro', is a throwaway line from Guy Ritchie's (1998) *Lock, Stock and Two Smoking Barrels*. But it may have some utility in explaining gang violence. As discussed in Chapter 2, the symbolism of firearms typically exceeds their frequency of use. A gun is a ranged weapon. It can be used to project violence even when unused—showing the 'bulge' is often enough to gain the respect of rivals—while in robberies, brandishing the weapon typically suffices because people do not wait for proof that it works. The physical distance gained by using a gun also implies a certain amount of mental distancing. As the hitman in Michael Mann's (2005) *Collateral* quips, 'I shot him. The bullets and the fall killed him.' But a knife is an intensely personal weapon and means of dispatch. Knife crime is a high culpability crime. Member 8 explained:

> Knifes don't jam or run out of bullets. You actually feel the knife go in. You're there. You have to look into man's eyes. Feel him as he falls to the floor. Blood pouring everywhere. People screaming. It's real. No doubt about it.

Only a small number of individuals have what it takes to stab some-body without serious justification or provocation. They are those who Member 12 terms, 'hyped cats':

> The hyped cats … they're always very hyperactive … they always want to be at the forefront, yeah. Which means that you don't need to be at the forefront. … They're always going to flare up and some-times you want that person that's going to flare up and you just go to them, 'I'm going to put something here for you, go and use it.' Because as far as they see it they need to prove themselves to me, do you know what I mean, like? So if they need to prove themselves to me, I can put anything on them.

Research suggests youths will set aside their moral standards if by doing so they will be accepted by a chosen group (Emler and Reicher, 1995). But as Member 12 explains, the agency problem for gangs lies with the fact that so-called hyped cats are prone to 'go out and do crazy shit' either because they enjoy it or they desire advancement within gangs. The fact that such violent people are 'a bit slower in the head … basically unwired', Member 12 added, is a 'double-edged sword' for gangs:

> You're an asset because I can use you. So you can be used for whatever I want you to be used for, because you're trying to prove yourself to me, yeah? But you're also a liability because you can go out and do something wrong and not finish the job and then who are they com-ing back to? They're coming back to the whole crew. You are affiliated with this crew, so if you go and do something against another crew because you had to prove yourself, you become a liability because you become, you know, people put X's on our heads because of what you've just gone out and done. We've all got a bit of that in us, but most of us got control with it. See, I get to a certain point where I see red and if I see red there's no going back but there's some of these kids who, it's almost like they don't see that red but they create it. You know, it's like a waving a flag to a bull. And if you're one of these peo-ple who just creates the feeling yourself you're almost, you're an asset but also a liability. … A lot of these hyped cats think that because they become so hyped that they can become the face, yeah? And if you can become the face everyone knows you and you're the most powerful, yeah? But it doesn't always work like that. That's not always the way the system works. The hyped cats are there for a reason. They're there to get hyped, they're there to get taken down. If the police want to

take you down, 'cus you want to get hyped, you go ahead. You know what I mean? There's always someone else who will take over.

Member 12

To ensure violence is used appropriately in line with gang goals and not individual goals, gangs use incentives; that is, they give ratings not only for spectacular acts of violence, but also for following directions. Levitt and Venkatesh (2000, p. 781) observe, 'a willingness to engage in limited violence increases the likelihood of promotion to the rank of officer, those who engage in wanton violence do not advance'. Member 38 agreed, 'I mean they could be sending you out to go and rob somebody or to go and stab up somebody. It depends on what they ask you to do and if you go and do it that's how you can get your status built up a bit more.' And such ratings matter because they translate into financial opportunities:

We do look out for people that are good at it ... if someone's working for me and they're working extra hard and they're getting everything done by the time that I tell them to yeah, and every time they come into me they get it done, I'm going to have to promote them. ... I can keep encouraging them. ... Because you know one day they might come with £10 short, they might come with £20 short, which is really minor until you get to the 100s and 200s. Ten, 20, if you're coming with that obviously you're making mistakes so I'm not really going to bring you high up because if you come higher you're going to make more mistakes.

Member 37

Gang elders indeed use the possibility of internal promotion and material wealth, no matter now slim, as an incentive system to address agency issues and retain gang members. Member 44 said simply, 'It's the same as a company. You might start at the bottom, but you work your way up to the top. Once you get to the top, you know, you've made it. Your role changes ... your role on the street itself decreases.' And only those gang members who demonstrate obedience, commitment, strong sales skills, and product knowledge position themselves to gain access to more valuable drug lines and ascend in a structure that by definition is not a meritocracy.

From their 'clock in' date forward, gang members have a finite amount of time to amass ratings in the game. Many more fail than do succeed. Youngers typically remain positive about their chances to advance within gangs in spite of low promotion rates partly because they look around and see other youths making no greater headway than they are. Like soldiers in elite units, gang youngers form a subjective sense of well-being by looking inward and comparing themselves to other gang youngers (Stouffer et al., 1949). They climb the hierarchy in competition with their peers rather than their elders; thus they feel less deprived than they probably should because neither their colleagues nor themselves are being promoted. Gangs are self-referential, an 'echo chamber' or enclosed space for the reverberation of peer affirmation.

Some youngers grow tired of waiting to be acknowledged, which precipitates what John Hagedorn (1988, p. 5) describes as the 'natural splintering process' of gangs over time into smaller, more cohesive units. As Member 40 observed:

> I don't know, the elder might have not shown [the younger] love and respect and show them ratings like what they should be getting. It's all up to how the young person is feeling. If he feels to stay by the elder, then he will stay. But if he can't get to do what he wants to do with you because you're top in your gang, if he feels to leave then he will just make up his own name and move on. ... If he feels that he's made enough name for himself and now he can leave, he can do his own independent stuff.

Deference among gang youngers toward their elders has declined, said some gang members:

> Nowadays the younger lot or the hype lot don't like to listen to no one. They're their own boss, if you get what I'm saying. Their respect level has dropped a lot from the elders to like everyone else, it's dropped a lot.

Member 39

Some interviewees attributed this shift to the increased availability of 'the great equalizer', firearms:

> Everyone's got a weapon now basically. No one fights with fists, everyone fights with weapons. It's either a gun or a knife. So people aren't scared of no one no more. Even the weakest person ... can get a gun like that. So if you trouble him or he remembers you from school, he can go get his gun, he's going to shoot you. No one's scared of no one because he's got a gun.

Member 44

But as noted in Chapter 2, guns are nowhere near as available as gang members would like others to think. Youngers still depend upon their elders for access to criminal commodities, 'even if the youngers are causing more noise', Member 20 said. And the younger generation is certainly making enough noise, lamented Member 43:

> They're like peoples' cousins, little cousins, little brothers. They're just young, like people that are still in school, like first, year seven and like that age. They're just running around screaming blah, blah, blah, we rep blah, blah, blah, I'm younger, whatever, I'm this guy's cousin, I'm this guy's little brother. ... These young ones are running around screaming everyone's name to be feared in school. ... You'll walk down the street and you'll see people screaming [gang name] that you've never seen before. Never seen. And you ask them 'who are you?', [they say] 'I'm thingy's cousin, I'm thingy's friend.' Everyone's got a cousin. And the people they're saying aren't even involved.

When elders perceive threats to their status within gangs, however, they typically resort to uncustomary levels of aggression or encourage it in others—a finding consistent with Jim Short and Fred Strodtbeck's (1965) seminal work on gang processes. I heard about one gang member, for example, who upon his release from prison stabbed his own younger in order to regain the role that he had encouraged his younger to occupy in his absence.

The prospect of rising up through the internal hierarchy, to a position where social status is higher and earnings are far more than what would be attainable in legitimate markets, remains their primary motivation for gang members even as they age and move into different roles within gangs. But as Member 28 aptly stated, this is a 'young man's' game. Gang members in their 20s still playing in the 'little leagues' are extremely vulnerable to the 'up and coming' boys around them who seek to earn ratings at their expense:

> Look, you're my elder and I'm your younger. You was once bad, now you're not no more. I'm doing bad things and people are realizing. They notice that I'm bad, I'm worse than the worst. I used to get more reputation on the street through your name. Now it's my name that's out there. People see me and they're looking to the floor. Shook. I don't need you no more, you gets me? So I just leave you. All of the people out on the streets are scared of me so I could have my own little crew made up that can come for you. I've got certain connections inside it,

'cus now, I'm the next top guy, you're not. I rebel against you, literally stab you in your back.

Member 37

As in conventional walks of life, if someone in their mid-20s is still living at home, 'hustling' to make ends meet, and hanging around on street corners with prepubescent teenagers, they begin to lose their appeal. Youths looking for role models don't respect them and girls looking for stable partners don't desire them. Such gang members are essentially past their 'best-before' date. Life on road thus has a short expectancy aside from the risks of injury, imprisonment, and early death.

## Rules

Each of the 12 gangs I studied had oral traditions and expected norms of conduct, both of which were enforced by older disciplinarians within the gang. None of the gangs had a set of formal written rules, but they all had a fairly consistent set of informal unwritten (and in some cases, unspoken) rules. Some rules, such as deference to one's elders and respect for the symbols of the gang, have already been discussed, but the following warrant further explanation.

### Disciplined violence

On the one hand, violence (or the convincing threat of violence) ensures the maintenance and expansion of gang business that, because it is illegal, cannot be protected by law. On the other hand, violence upsets the community, attracts police attention, and increases the probability of arrest. As such, gang members may want to be associated with psychopathy or an atavistic capacity for brutalizing acts of violence—indeed, I know them to weave extravagant myths around such acts to further humiliate one's victims—but there are limits to violent behavior and sanctions for going beyond them.

Member 46 told me about a former colleague, for example, who kicked his victim so many times in the face that he stained his new white shoes with blood. At the bequest of the watching gang, he finally stopped kicking, only to look down at the now claret leather, and scream at his target, 'Fuck! Look what *you've* done. *You've* ruined my new shoes.' He then proceeded to 'punish' his victim further, kicking him until he his head 'exploded' over the concrete. This person could not be controlled so he became surplus to requirements. Not only did this person not advance within his gang but also he was apparently 'taken out' from within because, in the eyes of the gang's inner circle, he had proven himself a liability. In Member 46's words, such 'gratuitous violence wasn't cool with the elders'.

As discussed previously, violence can earn youth respect and recognition, which are prized. Indeed, some youths have so little to feel proud of in their lives that 'respect', which Anderson (1999, p. 33) defines as being 'treated right or granted the deference one deserves', is all that matters. With such an overdeveloped sense of personal pride, youths become hypersensitive to single, often minor, acts of perceived disrespect. When Member 31 was jokingly 'dissed' by a member of his own gang, for instance, he recalled thinking:

> He's disrespected me. I've never really been able to deal with my emotions properly. [I felt] just anger. Angry. I've always been aware. That mentality, it stems from the roads. My anger at that time was to throw this boy off the back of the bus. Top deck. I didn't care. You get trapped in the mentality that you've got to show off to your friends, show off to the girl sitting next to you, you've got to do this, wet someone up, unless no one will respect you in a ways.

Member 31 actually showed restraint in this instant. But in another incident on a bus, Member 36 learned that disrespect, no matter how slight, could be a cardinal sin:

> This group of boys and girls came on the bus, making noise, acting up. And one guy decided to sit next to me and he was asking me questions about where I lived and who do I know around the area, such and such. And I was like, 'I'm not gonna answer you these questions. I don't know you.' He was like, 'rah, you giving me lip'. He was a lot younger than I was. He started to act up. He leaned on me, so I'm like, 'why you leaning on me, are you gay or something?' He's like, 'no, no' and everyone started laughing at him. He obviously didn't like that. He got up and was like 'this guy, this guy'. ... He reached underneath the bus seat and smashed a glass bottle ... [and] hit me on my right, right side of my neck. I felt a sharp pain. I'm thinking, 'what the heck this guy do?'. The wound just opened up, it started spraying out the blood. It was coming out in big glops. Dripping all over my shirt.
>
> Member 36

For most people, shame is a psychically annihilating event. When we feel shame, it is not uncommon to wish the earth would open beneath our feet and swallow us up (Campbell, 1994). Pre-eminent psychologist and psychoanalyst Erik Erikson (1977, p. 227) views these reactions of shame as expressions of rage turned against the self: 'He who is ashamed would like to force the world not to look at him, not to notice his exposure. He would like to destroy the eyes of the world. Instead he must wish for his own invisibility.' The problem is that when one is shamed, or 'disrespected' in the claustrophobic world of the gang, invisibility is not an option. Instead, youths use violence to project the feeling of shame or humiliation onto others and 'replace it with its opposite, the feeling of pride' (Gilligan, 1997, p. 111). For otherwise dispossessed youth, violence is their only remaining resource.

Alas, we can account for the spate of recent teenage homicides in London attributed to minor insults or provocations, such as brandishing a 'dirty look' or hailing the wrong person in the street. These murders, much like the 2011 UK riots, evince 'gang member' activity (in which individuals in gangs undertake violence and criminality as independent agents) not 'gang-related' activity (in which individuals in gangs act as agents, or in furtherance, of the organization; for a discussion, see Sánchez-Jankowski, 2003). Gangs heavily scrutinize 'gang member' activity. Gang norms that support the administration of violence and diffusion of criminal responsibility conceal this reality from outsiders. The guy in the white shoes, for example, was reprimanded because he did not appreciate the evolutionary stage of the gang he was in. During the enterprise and governance stages, violence is a means not an end—violence must be used appropriately in line with gang goals not individual goals.

## Silence

Gangs violate many if not most of the Biblical Ten Commandants (Exodus 20:1–17), but there is one Old Testament passage, 'He that keepeth his mouth keepeth his life: but he that openeth wide his lips shall have destruction' (Proverbs 13:3), that resonates deeply with gang members. Silence is scrupulously observed among gang members because secrecy furthers business and ensures longevity for gangs. Gang members, one police officer quipped, practice a 'teenage omertà', that is, a mafia-inspired 'code of silence', which guarantees protection from prosecution or conviction. Member 6 agreed that all gang members must 'keep schtumm' and maintain a 'wall of silence' around the gang.

Even the youngest gang members, Member 6 added, are experts at intimidating witnesses, delaying identity parades, and finding ways to postpone court hearings (from asking for medical reports on their own fitness to plead to simply failing to show up). Each of these actions, in turn, reinforces the image of gang members as people who refuse to give evidence to the authorities and use whatever means necessary to 'bust case' (beat the justice system). A simple 'no comment' response during a police interview can increase the likelihood of a longer prison sentence, but as Member 1 best articulated,

> When people get arrested, then you see who your friends are. Whoever blabs in like, in the interview room, you never trust again. Me, myself, I don't like snitches. Snitching is suicide.

Gang members' aversion to 'snitching' is perhaps best understood in the context of the 'Stop Snitching' website, which, until it was taken down in January 2011, offered help to people who did not want to cooperate with authorities and controversially posted flyers around a south London estate, urging people not to give information to the police after a 17-year-old was shot dead (Davey, 2011). It is unclear whether the site was linked to a campaign of the same name that first gained national attention in late 2004 when an eponymous DVD including footage of a number of men claiming to be drug dealers threatening violence toward anyone who reported what he or she knew about their crimes to the authorities (especially those who inform on others to get a lighter sentence for their own crimes) began to circulate the troubled American city of Baltimore.

The 'Stop Snitching' slogan later became mainstream in the hip-hop community as many rappers expressed support for this mantra. Entire songs were devoted to warning others about the violent repercussions of snitching and testifying (Kubrin, 2005). Once word spread, corresponding accessories became popular in urban youth fashion, particularly t-shirts of a stop sign emblazoned with the words 'Stop Snitching'. Some interviewees indeed owned this shirt, doctored with fake bullet holes, implying that snitches should (or will) be shot for their actions.

## Sobriety

Gang members smoke a lot of weed, but they rarely get high on their own supply. Drug use beyond recreational levels is prohibited in gangs not only because it reduces profit margins, but also because the pharmacological effects of drugs on the user can reinforce the already paranoiac culture of gangs and chaotic nature of gang violence:

> He was sniffing crack and that. Sniffing cocaine and that. I don't want that around me. If you deal, you don't use. That's the rule.

I even hate weed. Can't stand it, trust me. My brother, that's how he died, do you know what I mean? What skunkweed does is it induces psychosis, yeah? And once it induces that psychosis, there's no way back … once you hit that deep psychosis, you can't really do anything for me.

> Member 12

Drug intoxication runs contrary to the instrumental orientation of entrepreneurial gangs. Much like Short and Strodtbeck (1965) discovered some 50 years ago, gangs shun 'crazy acting' members who exhibit severe pathology related to drug addiction because they attract miscellaneous conflict within and without the gang:

Some people are just mentally lost. They just want to do sick things. They'll tell you, 'I don't care about money, I don't care about my life. I'm only here to take souls like the rest. I'm gonna keep on doing it until I die. I'm only here to take souls.' How can you work with that?

> Member 39

The bottom line is that gang members must act rationally. Irrational behavior implies that one cannot be controlled through conventional means. And if one cannot be controlled then one cannot be a gang member.

## Sanctions

When a particularly strong norm is violated, there is little discretion in sanctioning. Excommunication happens when a gang member is found to be a 'snake' or 'snitch', as Member 43 explained:

The elders can stop people from being involved. Like they can say you're de-recruited, 'I don't want to see your face.' If anyone seen this guy, something will happen. So they can do that … [if] you just do stuff that's unnecessary, like really unnecessary. If you stab someone in your crew for no reason then you're going to get de-recruited. Then you're going to get beat up by everyone. If you … snitch on someone, you're going to get de-recruited. If you get de-recruited that is a completely total loss of respect, you have no one who likes you … [you] just fade away.

Enforced separation, typically accompanied by serious violence, is the most severe sanction because proximity is a key feature of gang membership (see Chapters 5 and 6). Yet elders use serious violence, including non-fatal stabbings and slashing to the legs and buttocks, to punish even mid-level infractions—from an unwillingness to conform with group norms to a failure to comply with instructions:

> [You do] whatever your elder or the elders on the block tell you [to] do to get your name higher. So, say for example, if they tell you, 'rah go rob that boy's phone' or 'go do this' or 'go do that', if you don't do it then, you just get punched up if you know what I mean. ... [If you say no] your face will get taken off your shoulders. Like, you wouldn't be you no more, like, you wouldn't have legs left, like, I'm being serious like. ... You can't turn around and tell them 'no' because there's not no 'no' in the game.
>
> Associate 2

When a younger questioned Member 14's orders, for example, Member 14 'slapped him around a bit' and 'stabbed him in the buttocks' so that 'every time he sat down he remembered what he done'. The accumulation of mid-level offenses, moreover, can result in a major sanction tantamount to torture, such as 'jugging' (that is, being dowsed with jugs of boiling hot water), 'keying' (that is, being scratched and temporarily 'marked' with a key, which shows other gang members that this person is a 'traitor' to the gang), or 'branding' (that is, like keying, but with an electric iron).

Economic violations, such as missed payments, typically result in economic sanctions, but they can be accompanied by violent action, particularly when gang members try to protest:

> One of my friends was selling [drugs] for someone else like. ... He got stopped by the police but he didn't have the stuff on him. See, he'd lost it somewhere along the journey. Now he's gone back to his elder and told him, 'You know what? I got stopped by the feds but I didn't have the things on me so its okay.' Well, it wasn't okay. All of a sudden now you've got to work off that money. ... They had an argument, and the older guy ... just pulled out his knife and slashed up his face. And he had to pay it off. That was his punishment. It humbled him for a while.
>
> Member 12

Sanctions for minor or verbal offences, such as insulting one's elders, are applied without hesitation. For example:

> When you say, 'rah, I wanna be your younger', yeah, it's a commitment innit? So how you turning around, after a couple of weeks and saying, 'oh no this is too much for me?' And saying 'I don't even wanna do it no more?' That's a violation. Basically you're violating your elder. You're saying, rah, 'well obviously, I don't respect your name. I think you're moist innit.' So what's [the elder] gonna do about it? So then [the younger] takes a beating. Simple.
>
> Associate 2

For serious violations, a major sanction may immediately follow in a clear case or it may be applied following an investigation. Either way, gang members expect rule violations to be punished and punishments to be consistently applied in their complete knowledge. Hence why so many sanctions incorporate a public 'shaming' element. Gang elders cut out the cane row of one gang younger, for example, forcing him to walk around for weeks with a strip of hair missing.

Elders primarily use violence or the threat of violence to regulate the behavior of their youngers. But interviewees also worryingly disclosed examples whereby *sexual* violence was used as a means to address the supposed transgressions of women. I have written about this elsewhere (see Densley, Davis, and Mason, 2013), but in one case, brought to my attention by a Sexual Offences Investigation Trained (SOIT) police officer, a girl was viciously raped and assaulted because she misplaced her boyfriend's drugs at a house party. Her boyfriend, a gang elder, first demanded that the girl perform oral sex on a 'line-up' of his friends to compensate them for lost earnings, but when she refused, she was held down and raped by four gang members, while two others, including an old school friend, stood guard at the door. I also heard about male gang elders subverting the homophobic nature of gang culture (see Bourgois, 1995) by raping and thus emasculating male gang youngers as punishment. Both issues require further research.

Gangs' use of violent sanctions of course has serious 'drawbacks' (Gambetta, 2009b, p. 35). First, violence draws attention to gang members and increases the possibility of arrest. Second, physical force is costly to reproduce in terms of time and resources and creates countless unintended consequences, particularly when dispensed at a level such that it affects already violent people (Reuter, 1983). Third, and related, violence transfers all the costs of solving the problem of trust (see Chapter 5) to the gang because the impetus is on the gang to prove that its threat of violence is credible, not the other way around (Gambetta, 2009b). Fourth, internal gang violence contradicts any given gang's claims to protect its members, which in turn may reduce support for the gang and deter future applicants. For all these reason, gangs try to prevent problems from occurring in the first place with the careful screening and selection of their members. This process is the topic of Chapter 5.

## Concluding remarks

This chapter argued that gangs exhibit a degree of organizational rationality, whereby gang members develop systems for issuing orders and rules that govern member interaction in order to maintain their social and economic infrastructure. Gangs are not groups of persons that form randomly for the immediate commission of a single offense. They require organizing to maximize efficiency in the provision of illegal goods and services. Thus it pays to look beyond the organization of gangs toward what it is gangs are organized for. Organized and disorganized are not mutually exclusive gang types, as is argued by some, but rather complementary chapters in the evolutionary story of gangs. Evolved gangs have strong identities and highly competitive, hierarchical structures that provide some level of exclusivity. Much of the activity within gangs is age-graded, lest we confuse subgroups with separate gangs. At the same time gangs are not remote islands, regardless of their local orientation. Their external organization means gangs cooperate and compete with each other regularly and routinely. Small gangs gravitate toward big gangs. Established gangs spawn emerging gangs. Global interests transcend local issues. Gang organization, in other words, reflects gang business. And business is only as good as the people who run it, which is the focus of Chapter 5. But first, I explore how media and technology further influence the organization of London's street gangs.

# 4

# Gangs, Media, and Technology

While the government exaggerated the role of social media in the 2011 UK riots—to the extent that the same politicians who criticized Arab rulers for attempting to block digital communications during anti-government uprisings in the Middle East contemplated banning instant messaging during incidents of civil unrest in Britain (Halliday, 2011)—the importance of media and technology in the lives of gang members cannot be overstated. The global transmission of popular culture, the narrowing of the digital divide, and enhanced technologies made possible through a more user-created and user-friendly 'Web 2.0' are changing the ways in which gangs work and gang members communicate. This chapter explores how.

## Smart phones and social media

Many gang members are what Marc Prensky (2001) describes as 'digital natives'. They were 'born digital', thus perfectly accustomed to using new, digital ways to express themselves (Palfrey and Gasser, 2008). My interviewees were highly connected. Smart phones were appendages. Instant and short messages were the currency of conversation. Their virtual worlds and physical worlds appeared synchronous. They simply did not remember a world without social media and where 'going viral' was not a positive thing.

Gang members are not unique in this regard, but they are in their regular use of gang-related websites and online social networking pages, even in school classrooms and IT suites. MySpace was the social network of choice when my fieldwork first began, but, as in polite society, Facebook is now the most popular social networking site among gang members (a finding consistent with research in the United States, see Decker and

Pyrooz, 2011a). The 2010 murder of Sofyen Belamouadden, 15, in the ticket hall of Victoria underground station was actually organized on Facebook (Laville, 2011). Mustafa Gurpinar, 15, stabbed and killed Leroy James, 14, during a 2011 fight also arranged on Facebook, and was later convicted based on footage of the fight recorded on Leroy's mobile phone (BBC News, 2012). But as gang members recognize police are increasingly monitoring and culling social network sites for evidence (to the extent that gang members now refer to Facebook as 'Fedbook'), they are moving back to MySpace and forward to other lesser-known social networks.

Gang members, like regular young people, use smart phones and social media for entertainment and communication with friends. But gang members also utilize technology for criminal ends. They use basic steganography to hide information within image and audio files and applications that allow users to send private messages that, like Mission Impossible, literally self-destruct in seconds. They exchange illegal goods and services via online auction sites and PayPal accounts. And they share information via virtual gaming worlds, chat rooms, and synchronous conferencing protocols. New police radio scanner and real-time GPS tracking 'find my friend' smart phone applications further enable gangs to monitor the movements of law enforcement and gang members, respectively.

Gang members also use Blackberry's encrypted PIN-to-PIN messaging service (BBM) and Twitter feeds to plot 'flash robs', a criminal incarnation of the 'flash mob' phenomenon in which participants use social media to organize impromptu gatherings such as dances in shopping malls (Google search 'Flashmob' for thousands of examples). During a 'flash rob', gang members descend upon retailers en masse and steal merchandise or break off into smaller groups to spontaneously victimize anyone who happens to be in the wrong place at the wrong time. Police suspect that flash robs are sometimes strategically organized to divert their attention from more significant gang-related crime.

Perhaps most importantly, however, gang members have turned the immediacy of social networking into a way to promote individual and collective reputations and to instigate violence between rivals. Social media ensures that information reaches an audience larger than could ever be achieved through word-of-mouth alone. To get credit for their sexual conquests, for example, gang members use social media to 'expose' their sexual partners. Exposing entails sharing or distributing sexually revealing or compromising photographs without the sender's permission, such as by posting them to a default profile or display picture on BBM. Bystanders, in turn, can easily and inadvertently become perpetrators by redistributing images or videos to others.

Gang members are also posting their gang-related exploits on YouTube for posterity. For the first time in history a (video) camera goes anywhere and everywhere. The theoretical implications of this are discussed in Chapter 5, suffice it to say, there are thousands of home videos disseminated online that celebrate gang-related activity—from the most serious violence to being able to walk through the turf of another gang, deface their street signs, and escape unharmed. Member 26 noted:

> Like Peckham youths will come through Brixton, like 'yeah we can walk through Brixton' or Brixton used to go to Peckham and say 'yeah we can walk through Peckham' and it's like this is basically the boroughs will find a disrespect for and then they'll do something about it.

Gang members freely admit their affiliation in their online Bebo, Facebook, or MySpace profiles and post pictures of themselves wearing gang colors and brandishing weapons. Bespoke web pages decorated with emblems ripped from designer clothing and premium liquor brands and aspirational images of marijuana leaves, stacks of dollar bills, automatic weapons, and scantily-clad women, enable gangs to broadcast criminal achievements, threaten rivals, honor incarcerated members, even mourn 'fallen soldiers' lost to gang violence. Associate 15 observed,

> there ain't a single gang on MySpace that won't say 'shout out' or 'big up' this one, whatever … bringing up all the names … drawing attention to themselves.

Gang members 'tag' social media sites through posts and pictures just as they would 'tag' exposed walls in the community with graffiti—to mark territory and advertise their presence, 'roll call' the names of gang members, and show disrespect or defiance (by covering the graffiti of rivals). Bigger 'tags', in high visibility areas, give gang members bragging rights within their gang. Exclusive gang websites operate as virtual turf and are policed in much the same way as physical turf. A single disrespectful comment typed, at a distance, to a rival gang member can escalate into real violence on the streets. Since social networking is instantaneous and mobile, an insult can be posted, read, and responded to in real time, which adds immediacy and impulsiveness to conflicts and retaliations. This is why interviewees described being suspicious, even fearful, of mobile phones in use during miscellaneous conflict—such typically indicates a call is being made for back up.

There is little room for context in 140-character communication. When one gang member was admitted to hospital for treatment of minor injuries after being doused with C.S. incapacitant spray, 'within minutes', said Member 7, people posted online the victim had stumbled into the road and was hit by a car, was blind, and was in treatment for a combination of permanent facial scarring and psychological trauma. None of which was true. News travels fast and in this digital age of perfect remembering, insults appear accessible and permanent, which means what were once minor annoyances for gang members become major public relations disasters. There is no time to reflect and cool off.

The Internet has been identified as a means for radicalized individuals to find one another in a community and mobilize for extremist activity (Decker and Pyrooz, 2011b; Sageman, 2008). Gangs differ from radical and extremist groups in their use of technology, however, because gangs typically intend to reach an audience of rivals rather than recruits. A film removed from MySpace in 2008, for example, showed a bloodied boy being slapped around and forced to strip by members of Croydon's DSN (Don't Say Nothing) gang. The boy was then told to identify himself and repeat the name 'DSN' (Thompson, 2010). As Associate 16 explained, many gang members have an online presence and use social networking tools to attract 'followers' and intimidate rivals by showcasing 'strength in numbers'. The practice is tantamount to the way in which people collect 'friends' on Facebook to build self-esteem and exaggerate their popularity. One police officer explained:

> Imagine your gang has 50 'friends' on Facebook but your closest rival has 1000. Would you go down there and start a fight with them? And for young people not already affiliated, which gang do you think they're most likely to join? It's a popularity contest.

Some gang websites even run online surveys inviting visitors to rank local gangs based on their reputation for 'running the south' or to vote on which gang members have 'shanked up the most p[eo]pl[e]'. This all speaks to Marcus Felson's (2006) 'big gang theory' in which gang size is correlated with gang strength in the minds of young people.

Social media is one of the most effective conduits for gang mythmaking because it transcends territorial boundaries. But conventional media can also unintentionally contribute to gang mythology. PDC's Elijah Kerr, for example, has featured on television shows dedicated to exploring the lives of Britain's 'deadliest men' and is often described in the press as the most 'notorious' gang member in London (Wikipedia, 2012b). These claims provide Kerr and his gang with an exaggerated kudos or status, which during the gang's transition from Younger 28s to PDC also saved on the reproduction costs of having to announce leadership succession.

When gangs post content online, typically the only people who notice are police and other gang members—it's a closed feedback loop. When the mainstream media comments publicly on specific content, therefore, it risks increasing curiosity about it and driving traffic to the gang. Associate 15 said it best: 'The news helps gang members. It's marketing. If your name's in the paper, if you're on *Crimewatch*, your ratings go up.' She added that the reputation of the Peckham Boys, for instance, grew exponentially following reports that the teenagers arrested for the high-profile manslaughter of 10-year-old Damilola Taylor in 2000 were members. Police have learned their lesson—they typically no longer name gangs during press interviews, thus starving them of the oxygen of publicity. But the mainstream media is not the most powerful 'gangs marketing tool', Associate 15 described. Such an honor belongs to 'grime'—a genre of urban music that evolved primarily out of British garage, Caribbean dancehall, and American hip-hop—and its relentlessly nihilistic cousin, 'road rap'.

## The sound of the underground

Gang researcher John Hagedorn (2008, p. xxviii) argues, 'To understand the culture of gangs, first of all, means understanding their music.' Grime originated in some of the most deprived inner city boroughs of east London, particularly Tower Hamlets, Newham, Waltham Forest, and Hackney, and is often hailed for 'giving voice to the voiceless' young people growing up in multicultural Britain (Hancox, 2009). Grime artists indeed often mix autobiographical details about crime and violence with emotional honesty. Member 14, who in Chapter 1 rhymed about his chaotic family upbringing, offered this little *a cappella* freestyle as an example:

> Hold tight gangbanger, standard of living large,
> Cock the latch of the hammer, feel the banger blast,
> Give me the thing and I'll bang it fast,
> So long as I'm camouflaged,
> Two leather gloves, a hat, and a balaclav,
> Pull it in your face and blow your face into planet mars.

Grime's emergence is intrinsically connected to local pirate radio (which incidentally is used by gang members to send coded messages out over the airwaves), with many performers honing their skills out of improvised bedroom studios and achieving 'underground' success before approaching the mainstream. Grime is carried by words recited rapidly and rhythmically over a pre-recorded—typically electronic—instrumental backing. Sasha Frere-Jones (2005) once wrote for the *New Yorker* that grime 'sounds as if it had been made for a boxing gym, one where the fighters have a lot of punching to do but not much room to move'.

The grime scene flourished at street level in Peckham, Brixton, and Hackney via YouTube videos and self-produced CD 'mixtapes'. It gave rise to artists such as Nathan 'Giggs' Thompson, who is now signed to XL Recordings, the label of best-selling artists such as Adele and Radiohead. His breakout hit, Track 9 freestyle, describes a world in which 'everyone's suit [is] the same color as Batman's'—a reference to the black uniform of SN1, the branch of the Peckham Boys that Giggs ran in his teens and early 20s. Giggs went to prison in 2003 for firearms offences and was charged with possession with intent to endanger life in 2012 after police found in his car a loaded semi-automatic Browning gun with a bullet in the breach, the safety off and six rounds in the magazine (Knight, 2012). He was later acquitted. Giggs claims now to have left the gang life behind him, but he continues to upload songs, announce shows, promote albums, and interact with fans via webpages linked to gangs and is often accompanied on songs with adlibs from gang members. The SN1 gang even has its own commercial website (http://sn1giggs.com/) and a shop in Peckham Market that sells Giggs's music and gang paraphernalia, including 'SN1 wear' branded clothing.

Giggs is not alone. YouTube footage suggests that Sneakbo, whose debut single 'The Wave' made the UK Top 40, is associated with the members of Lambeth's GAS gang responsible for the murder of 15-year-old schoolboy Zac Olumegbon (Pappzd, 2012). Local lyricists affiliate with gangs in part because gangs control access to community resources, record labels, recording studios, and performance venues. Gangs also have the capital to invest in studio time, video production, and local record promotion. Member 41 explained:

> That's how it goes because you get the ones that do music, they'll say, 'ah you know what, I haven't even got the money for studio time so I'm going to join these guys and I'm going to do this'. Before they know it they're one of them hanging on road hustling all day.

In the field, I encountered a number of gang members who were in the process of reinventing themselves as grime music producers, deejays, and emcees in an attempt to achieve their dream of material wealth. I also met with a police officer who worked a high-profile case in which gang members bought their own music on iTunes and Amazon websites using stolen credit cards in order to profit from the royalties (Smith, 2009). Suffice it to say, it is often difficult to see where the gang ends and the music 'business' begins. Member 41 observed,

> It all boils down to business, it all boils down to money. The people actually making the tracks, making the music, they see it as a way out of the hood by actually representing the hood.

The path from gangster to icon is well trodden. Rapper Jay-Z went from selling crack on the New York strip to an estimate net worth of $500 million (Chang, 2007). Much like American gangster rappers, grime artists understandably draw upon life on road in their records. Eazy-E who performed with Dr Dre and Ice Cube in the seminal hip-hop group Niggaz With Attitude (NWA), once boasted on the 2003 videotape *Beef I*:

> Some rappers try to rap about shit out here but they can't do it because they don't live it. They was not around it, but we can because we have been around it, and doing it all of our lives, killin', robbery, murders, thieving, gambling, dope dealing ... everything you hear on our records is true.

Some artists, 'studio gangsters' in gang parlance, embellish their messages but the most successful adhere to the old adage 'write what you know'. As Associate 15 noted,

> if you're rapping about it and you're not actually putting yourself in that situation ... then you're a fake already. ... You have to have lived it to be able to put yourself in.

Conflict between rival gangs can therefore be integrated through music because the lyrics typically refer to real-life confrontations. Lyrical battling is a prominent part of hip-hop and grime culture, but as the violent deaths of two of hip-hop's most enduring icons, Tupac Shakur and The Notorious B. I. G., remind us, it can escalate. Sixteen-year-old Iyke Nmezu, for instance, was killed in February 2008 in a row over rap lyrics posted on the Internet (BBC News, 2008b).

Verbal agility is a valuable asset for gangs: by unloading an eloquent tirade of abuse upon their rivals, emcees raise the overall profile of the group and provide a dynamic source of entertainment for its members. Music videos are typically made up of raw footage recorded on video camera or mobile phone and crudely produced on personal computer. The content is rarely anything more than half-naked boys and girls throwing gang signs, taunting rival gangs, and evoking lines and scenes from popular culture. But the music serves a purpose: to deliberately disrespect rival gang members, to aim threatening and antagonistic slants, and to attack personal credibility. While older gang members may tolerate these signs of disrespect and respond with a record, younger members looking to make a name for themselves are likely to respond with violence (Stevens et al., 2009). Art imitates life, but at the same time life also imitates art.

## Reference points

The So Solid Crew, pioneers of commercially viable British urban music who famously reached number one in the UK with the single '21 Seconds' (a clever concept whereby each of the group's ten vocalists was given '21 seconds' on the microphone), are forever associated with several violent incidents involving members of the group or their fans; notable was a shooting in the crowd at one band member's 21st birthday party that 'resulted in a virtual nationwide ban on live performance' (Batey, 2010). When asked about the violent legacy of urban music, interviewees said that live music events turned violent so often because they brought groups of bellicose young men together in hot, crowed conditions. When temperatures rise, and alcohol is consumed, tempers get shorter. They denied that the music itself was responsible. This is important because then Leader of the Opposition, David Cameron, among others, famously criticized urban music for 'glamorizing' gangs and 'encouraging people to carry guns and knives' (Summers, 2007). In the wake of the 2011 UK riots, commentators similarly accused grime music of inciting violence and promoting a 'culture of entitlement' (Hancox, 2011).

This is a familiar narrative; lest we forget the tabloid press blamed 'video nasties' such as *Child's Play 3* for inspiring the 1993 murder of two-year-old James Bulger (Kirby and Foster, 1993). But after the suspect in the 2012 mass shooting at a midnight screening of the film *The Dark Knight Rises* in Aurora, Colorado, reportedly dyed his hair red and claimed to be Batman's nemesis 'the Joker', there is renewed interest in the intersection between media fantasy and violent reality

(Sanchez, Hughes, and Allen, 2012). The Beatles' *White Album* is still associated with the 1969 Manson family murders, for instance, after prosecutor Vincent Bugliosi (with Curt Gentry, 1974) wrote about Charles Manson's supposed obsession with the record. Then followed Martin Scorsese's (1976) *Taxi Driver* and its role in John Hinckley, Jr's 1981 attempt to assassinate US President Ronald Reagan (Hickey, 2012). And finally, there is the theory that first-person shooter video games and Marilyn Manson rock songs may have led Eric Harris and Dylan Klebold to depersonalization, and eventually, the 1999 massacre of 12 students and one teacher at Columbine High School (for a discussion, see Langman, 2009).

Since psychologist Albert Bandura (1977) first argued that media in general, and television in particular, provide a power source of models for aggressive conduct, a large number of studies have shown how popular culture teaches violent behavior (Murray, 2008). My own research leads me to conclude that it is premature to suggest violent movies, video games, and rap lyrics are *causal* factors in gang-related violence—not least because gangs preceded the invention of such mediums, and purveyors of Shakespeare's plays and Puccini's operas, which are plenty violent, appear on the whole to be pacifists. Violent media merely acts as a 'facilitator' for people already prone to violence (Hickey, 2012). As Peter Langman (2009), in his study of school shooters, explains: 'These are not ordinary kids who played too many video games. ... These are simply *not ordinary kids*. These are kids with serious psychological problems.'

In a lost chapter entitled 'The Movie and the Dime Novel', Frederic Thrasher (1927, p. 102) observed that gang members were often voraciously consumed by film, which he described as 'a cheap and easy escape from reality'.[1] Thrasher argued that gang members would predictably gravitate toward action films and 'hair-raising' scenes from which they would pick up certain 'patterns' of behavior (p. 108). My interviewees also picked up some bad habits from the media. Police say the reason why gang members make 'poor marksmen', for example, is because they imitate their Hollywood heroes and hold firearms 'gangster style' or sideways, which compensates less for weapon recoil than the traditional upright method. On a more serious note, the Internet has led to an explosion of sexual content and interviewees admitted using hard-core pornography, which is laced with sexual violence (Gossett and Byrne, 2002), to learn about sex and relationships and thus pick up potentially dangerous attitudes and behaviors toward women (for more information, see Malamuth, Addison, and Koss, 2000).

If popular culture does not *cause* gang membership, therefore, it certainly provides a style for how gang membership is performed and a lens through which gang members interpret their lives. As discussed in the **Introduction**, when we think of gangs, we think of America. So too do gang members. Indeed, interviewees presented a constant conflation of the British and American experience, particularly with regard to race, to the extent that many described Ku Klux Klan rallies, the Civil Rights movement under Martin Luther King, Jr, the Rodney King incident, and so on, as British phenomena. They bemoaned living in the 'ghetto' despite there being no black 'ghettos' in Britain, in the sense of large areas of the city, composed from three-quarters to a hundred percent of black people (Peach, 1996).

There are no public or educational resources to teach how to set up a gang the way there are classes to set up a small business. Gangs thus use structural templates derived from American popular media sources to help shape their organization. In April 2010, *The Sun* in typical sensational style ran the headline 'LA gangs take over UK streets', implying that the infamous Bloods and Crips gangs of Los Angeles had taken up shop in London (Wheeler and Brooks, 2010). But in reality nobody from Los Angeles appeared as a recruiting agent. Instead, by looking at gang culture popularized in the media and adapting styles to local conditions, gangs in London took on affiliations with the Bloods and Crips, which were more imagined than real. Conflict between Bloods and Crips in London 'appears primarily to be a re-labeling of local rivalries that already existed' (Sullivan, 2005, p. 182), much like in other cases of gang migration (Van Gemert, 2001).

For obvious reasons, gangs cannot post vacancies or advertise their services in the classified section of the newspaper. To advertise in plain sight, therefore, gangs rationally seek association with elements of popular culture that help promote their image—borrowing 'conventional' or symbolic signals, so called because meaning is based entirely upon 'convention' or societal forces (Guilford and Stamp Dawkins, 1991), which best convey reputation and achieve intimidation (Felson, 2006, refers to this process as the 'street gang strategy'). As discussed, gangs cannot always outwardly proclaim organization. The Bloods and Crips brands hold real value as dangerous and ubiquitous entities. As Member 1 suggests, the brands can even directly reduce the production of real violence:

> In terms of like wearing colors, like repping [representing] your gang's colors, it's all that, should I, for example, be from another gang, as soon as I see you I'm like 'oh, you're from Crips gang so I'm not going to touch you because Crips gang are hard'.

The Italian-American mafia provide another reference point for gangs. When asked who they aspired to be or from whom they drew inspiration, interviewees invariably cited famous mob bosses, including Al Capone, John Gotti, and Lucky Luciano. As Sánchez-Jankowski (1991, p. 70) found with gangs in New York, moreover, I found London gangs not only trying to organize themselves to imitate what they think the mafia looks like, but also gangs copying certain mafia leadership categories. Gang members used the terms 'younger' and 'soldier' interchangeably, for instance, and one interviewee even described himself to me as 'consigliere' (counselor) based on the mafia model. Elijah Kerr even ironically describes himself as 'the boss of bosses' in a nod to the *capo di tutti capi* of La Cosa Nostra.

Just as the layperson's knowledge of the mafia is derived from such stylized narratives as *The Godfather* (Venkatesh and Levitt, 2000, p. 447), the stylistic features of gang life in London are profoundly influenced by 'expressive black Atlantic diasporic popular cultures' (Gunter, 2008, p. 352). Gang members talk in a street patois shaped by American rap lyrics (for example, referring to police as 'Feds' or '5–0' when there are in fact no federal agents in Britain), use *noms de guerre* that are derivatives of or variations on the names of infamous or fictional gangsters (I met a 'Scarface' who was neither Al Pacino nor Paul Muni during my fieldwork), and choose such icons as Stringer Bell, Vito Corleone, Frank Lucas, Tony Montana, Tony Soprano, Li'l Zé, and the cast of Martin Scorsese's (1990) *Goodfellas* as their avatars on social media sites. This is very much an Americanized world co-constructed in the minds of teenage boys, many of whom have less than five good GCSEs.

But popular culture serves to enhance the reputation of real gangs. Diego Gambetta (2009b) observes how real Mafiosi borrow mannerisms and lines from movies (and popular culture in general) in order to better intimidate their victims. Gang members indulge in similar practices: they invoke fiction to make people believe they are real. Peckham youths described growing up in 'Pecknam' (as in Vietnam) and referred to the Old Kent Road as 'Brooklyn', paying homage to New York City's retail heroin and crack cocaine distribution center. The Streatham-based PIF (Paid In Full) gang takes its name from the title of a 2002 film about crack dealers in New York. The neighboring ABM (All 'Bout Money) gang similarly draws its name from that of the fictional Philadelphia gang portrayed in the straight-to-DVD movie, *State Property*, starring rappers Beanie Sigel and Jay-Z. The list goes on.

## Concluding remarks

From Gutenberg's printing press to Colt's revolver and Edison's incandescent lamp to Ford's moving assembly line, technology is and has always been a catalyst for change. Pitts (2007, p. 21) argues that the installation of sophisticated antitheft technologies in banks and transit vehicles, such as closed-circuit television cameras and digital time-delay locks, for example, partly forced traditional organized criminals to give up on the heists and 'one-off blags' that once defined them and pick up instead on the less hazardous and infinitely more profitable 'business' of illicit drugs. Technology thus laid the foundation for the exchange of goods and services between traditional crime firms and street gangs. One retired east end gangster, who now works in gang intervention, explained this to me in no uncertain terms:

> It ain't easy being a criminal nowadays. Look around, there's CCTV everywhere. Increased security, surveillance, forensic analysis, CSI shit. I paid a check into the bank yesterday and it took 15 minutes to fill out all the fucking paperwork. The world has changed. It ain't like the old days. Big Brother's watching. That's why drugs are so appealing. If you're smart there's no need to get your hands dirty.

As the worlds of gangs and organized crime converge, technology will continue to play a pivotal role. As discussed in Chapter 2, gangs evolve. The use of technology by gangs is in its infancy. During my fieldwork, I started to hear about gang members 'skimming' to steal account numbers from ATMs or retail card readers. It won't be long before gangs utilize technology for other criminal ends, including computer hacking, cyber attacks, and phishing schemes, which are used to illegally acquire personal information such as usernames, passwords, and credit card information. Besides the attractive profits from bank and credit card fraud and identity theft, criminal penalties are also often less stringent for cyber criminals, at least compared with violent and acquisitive crime. 'A typical smart phone has more computing power than Apollo 11 when it landed a man on the moon', writes Nancy Gibbs (2012) for *Time Magazine*. Suffice it to say that unless law enforcement better understands the relationship between gangs, media, and technology, gang members will continue to push the new criminal frontier. Asking Twitter users to re-tweet the hash-tag '#stopgangcrime' and 'create a virtual stand against gangs' is not deterrent enough (Metropolitan Police Service, 2012c).

# 5
# Gang Recruitment

What do street gangs, organized criminals, rebel insurgents, and radical and extremist groups have in common? The answer is an organizational problem: the need to find trustworthy, loyal, and competent members under the conditions of illegality, the use of violence, and risk of infiltration (Pizzini-Gambetta and Hamill, 2011). Existing scholarship generally accounts for the profiles and motivations of recruits into extra-legal groups, but a question that remains is: why do only some and not all of those who share the same 'risk factors' and motivations join? Indeed, the vast majority of young black males living in low-income or marginal areas are not gang members—this is known as the Robins (1978, p. 611) paradox. The reason, this chapter argues, is that people do not only choose gangs, but gangs also choose people.

Risk factors and motivations are crude facts often presented as profound truths that lend no insight into gang processes. 'Many are called but few are chosen'—to borrow from the Gospel of Matthew (22:11–14)—because gangs suffer from serious trust issues. By virtue of growing up in low trust environments (see Chapter 1), it is instilled in children and young people that they cannot have confidence in others, who will always put themselves first, and that any assistance from anyone has immanent costs (Sánchez-Jankowski, 1991). As Member 44 explained,

> We would walk down the street and my dad would put his hood up and say 'keep your head down son, walk fast, don't stop for no one. Don't trust no one. Trust only family.' You learn it early.

Interviewees indeed learned not to become too attached to others, for this only ever results in anguish. Member 37 articulated this notion as follows:

> It's the mentality that you grow up with because everybody else around you have let you down so many times, that is, family, parents,

local authorities or people that just come around and promise you things and just don't do it. It just brings down your trust and it's like you just don't trust no one. You just don't trust no one. Because one thing that you grow up with is yeah, it's good to trust, trust people, dah, dah, dah, dah, but once you start trusting people they start letting you down then you're thinking why am I trusting you? ... When I was growing up I didn't like myself, so why am I going to like you? Who are you for me to like? If I don't like myself, why do I like you?

Gang members appreciate deeply that you cannot inherently trust what people say or do to persuade you that they can be trusted. They must calculate trust because, as Member 24 observed, 'It's too dangerous out there. Anyone can be a snake. Anyone can be the guy in the grass spying.' Gang members are indeed constrained by illegality and secrecy, which provide both opportunities and obligations to renege on their promises (Gambetta, 2009b; van Duyne et al., 2001). People who tend toward criminality, moreover, are unlikely 'to be reliable, trustworthy, or cooperative' (Gottfredson and Hirschi, 1990, p. 213). This begs the question, how do gang members identify and trust similarly inclined individuals in order to engage in sustainable cooperative endeavors?

## Problems of trust

Sociologists typically portray trust as a three-part relationship between (A) the 'trustor', (B) the 'trustee', and (X) the object or result toward which trust is directed. Based on the conditions outlined by Michael Bacharach and Diego Gambetta (2001, p. 150), for example, we might say that gang member A 'trusts' gang member B to do X if gang member A acts on the expectation that gang member B will do it, when both know that two conditions exist: (1) if gang member B fails to do X then gang member A would have done better to act otherwise; and (2) gang member A acting in the way he does gives gang member B a selfish reason not to do X.

In the gang context, X may be to beat someone up, collect a debt, give early warning of police raid, deliver a message, or hide a murder weapon. If gang member B does X under the above conditions he is considered 'trustworthy'. If gang member B is unable or unwilling to fulfill X then he is considered 'untrustworthy'. Trust, therefore, incorporates elements of vulnerability and risk. The risk for gang member A is that gang member B can always gain by being untrustworthy. Gang member

A, in turn, should only expose himself to opportunism if he has reason to believe that gang member B is trustworthy.

As Nesse (2001) argues, there are intrinsic (for example, burning bridges or being bound to a mast—see Elster, 1979, 2000), contractual (Schelling, 1960), reputational (Dasgupta, 1988; Good, 1988), even emotional (Frank, 1988; Hirshleifer, 1987) means to enforce and increase confidence in a commitment. The problem, however, is that these examples of 'trust-warranting properties' (that is, factors that transform the trustee's raw payoffs, thus influencing them in such a way that they do not defect) are seldom directly observable (Bacharach and Gambetta, 2001, p. 153). For this reason, the truster (gang member A, for example) must look for 'signs' of the relevant trust-warranting properties, and the trustee (gang member B, for example), in turn, must take appropriate steps to reveal or 'signal' them.

The above scenario only solves the problem of primary trust. The problem of secondary trust is that sometimes the signs themselves are unreliable and cannot be trusted (Bacharach and Gambetta, 2001). Gang member B, for example, could well be an adventure-seeker ('wannabe' in gang parlance) or police informant mimicking the trust-warranting signs simply to infiltrate the gang and later exploit the trust of gang member A. For example, there once was a boy who wore a reversible jacket—Blood-red exterior with Crip-blue lining—to negotiate the risks inherent in walking between rival Bloods and Crips neighborhoods in South Central Los Angeles. When he grew up, this boy learned and fraudulently adopted the signals necessary to deceive the Crips into recruiting him, only to turn informant for the Federal Bureau of Investigation. Through intelligence, surveillance, wires, and detailed records, he helped incarcerate over 130 fellow gang members (see Lawson, 2008).

In my previous life as a school teacher, moreover, one of my students once permanently scarred his left cheek with a butter knife from the cafeteria because he desired a 'battle scar' to display as a signal of dangerousness to expedite his acceptance among older gang members. The school faculty (the unintended audience) viewed this episode of deliberate self-harm as a signal that the student was afflicted with mental illness. The other students (the intended audience) read the act simply as a signal that, in Gambetta's (2009b, p. 119) words, 'If I am crazy enough to do this to myself, imagine what I can do to you.' The scar thus attracted the gang's attention, but after some due diligence on their part they exposed the boy for the fraud he really was. The implication is that the observable features are sometimes not enough: some signals are counterfeit.

Mimicry occurs when the cost of emitting a signal for being trust-worthy is smaller than the benefit one can expect from appearing to be trustworthy (Maynard Smith and Harper, 2003). Common motivations for mimics include revenge, eliminating competitive criminal enter-prises, consideration in a criminal case, altruism, affection for police, eccentric thrill seeking, even monetary compensation (Forbes, 2008, p. 125). The MPS paid a total £1,863,074 to people with information on criminal activity in the financial year 2008–9. Most informants earned between £50 and £2000 for vital intelligence leading to an arrest, although a disclosure leading to recovery of a firearm was worth £10,000 or more, paid in installments or in gifts valued at commen-surate amounts to avoid suspicion (BBC News, 2009).[1] Covert human intelligence sources can 'earn more per annum than senior Met officers', one police source handler told me.

For all these reasons, before deciding to trust gang member B and recruit them into the gang, gang member A must first screen gang member B by looking for *reliable* signals of trust- (or distrust-) war-ranting properties that are difficult or impossible for gang member B to fake. Gang member B must either volunteer these signals to gang member A or gang member A must probe gang member B to elicit them. This chapter examines this communicative exchange in the context of gang recruitment where the need for trust stems from a lack of detailed knowledge among recruiters about the abilities and motivations of volunteers.

The 'game' of gang recruitment meets the necessary conditions for the occurrence of a genuine signaling episode (Bliege Bird and Smith, 2005). First, there is an informational asymmetry. Volunteers hold hidden information, which may for the gang result in mistaken selec-tion and is costly and in some cases impossible for the gang to obtain. Second, the gang can benefit from reliable information about within-group variance in such unobservable properties. The benefits to the receiver are of course that they recruit a new member of high quality and not a new member of low quality or nefarious intent.

Third, higher-quality signalers can benefit from accurately broadcast-ing this information, but lower-quality signalers have the potential to achieve benefits at the expense of recipients through deception. The reputation of the gang (and its recourse to violence as an alternative to official or bureaucratic state means of action) is of course a common asset, which benefits all members. Other 'selective incentives' (Olson, 1965) the signaler accrues by successfully gaining entry into the gang include: the provision of criminogenic resources; a surreptitious source of income; power to delegate status and rank; and opportunities for recreation, rebellion, and excitement (for a review, see Howell, 2012).

Finally, the cost or benefit to the signaler of sending the signal is correlated with the signaler's quality. As will be observed, gangs will 'not be erratic in the signs they watch for or easily satisfied by cheaply mimickable ones' (Gambetta and Hamill, 2005, p. 11). The knowledge required to interpret and evaluate a signal in this context is itself 'hard-to-fake'. Gang members, by virtue of being gang members, have successfully negotiated the recruitment process and appreciate that in life signals are rarely 'separating' in the sense of a perfect Bayesian equilibrium (Cho and Kreps, 1987). Instead, they look for clusters of 'semi-sorting' signals that, if pointing in the same direction, may together come close to discriminating between 'right' and 'wrong' types (Gambetta, 2009a).

## The recruitment process

Gang recruitment is not a single event, but rather a gradual and lengthy process. The steps in this process are outlined below. My unit of analysis is the process, not individual gangs or gang members.

### Automatic cues

Trust in family, friends, and co-ethnics rests on familiarity and conformity (Misztal, 1996). Gang members really only extended their confidence to a narrow set of in-groups—to family, friends, and others like themselves, but seldom beyond. Member 47 gave the following example:

> I had people all at the top with me but I grew up with them and I've known them for the longest, do you see what I'm trying to say? I've known one since I was in year four of primary school and one was at my christening and lived on the same road as me since I was a baby. My aunt used to look after them so these people I know I can trust. ... They're not just at secondary school or since, since I moved into my hostel or something like that because those sorts of people you can't trust, especially when you're in a gang because you don't know who they're talking to. You don't know who they know ... and who they're close with more than you, you see what I'm trying to say? You don't just give out trust and you only trust the ones that you know, that you can bring them to your mum's house and eat with them at someone's table. Do you see what I'm trying to say?

Member 47, like many black gang members, also told me, 'Being white you would need to prove yourself more than if you was black and trying to get into the gang.' Part of the reason was that, as presented in Chapter 1, white people, as visible representatives of the state and old colonial powers, had become a symbol of black people's exclusion from mainstream cultural and institutional life. White people were perceived as attached to the 'mainstream', said Member 29, and by default 'working for the government'. In black neighborhoods, moreover, white people stood out to the extent that during my fieldwork a white member of a predominately black gang was arrested simply because law enforcement recognized him as 'the only white guy' brandishing a firearm in a group photograph posted on the Internet.

Entry to gangs was also often restricted to individuals who had prior connections to active gang members. Gangs reduce the risk of infiltration and partially solve the problem of mistaken selection by embedding agency relationships in an ongoing structure of personal relationships. Some interviewees even considered gang membership a 'family tradition' to the extent that they actively encouraged their relatives to join, much like university-educated parents encourage their children to attend their alma maters:

> For some people it's just like, it's like for the family ties as well. If you're family, you're part and parcel of it. You've already proved yourself because you're part of that bloodline. Do you know what I mean? Like, if you came through me, you're automatically known, 'Oh well, that's [Member 12's] cousin', do you know what I mean? Or, 'That's his cousin', or that you're someone's cousin, you're someone's brother. And that in itself makes a difference. That in itself puts you steps ahead of someone who might have been around three or four years longer than the next guy.
>
> Member 12

Kinship and friendship ties overlap and increase information about an individual, thus reducing uncertainty. In simple terms, family and friends have track records and reputations, which later afford a rich array of sanctions for the errant gang member (Shapiro, 2005).

### Narrowing the pool

For the recruitment process to begin, recruiters and volunteers must find themselves in situations where the exchange of signals is possible. Gang recruitment typically occurs in local settings where people already know each other and can 'check each other out in the natural course of their daily interactions' (Gambetta, 2009b, p. 9). Exposure to gang members was routine for many interviewees, which often led to curiosity and resulted in observation, approximation, and fascination. As Member 43 observed, 'if you go out into some of these neighborhoods you're almost destined to be introduced to a gang or a gang member, *if you allow yourself*' (my emphasis). Prospective gang members, it seems, must 'allow' themselves to be identified and targeted for gang membership, which means spending time on the streets where gang members hang out and signaling intent to join them:

> It's just like the way people act shows you who wants to be in a gang and who doesn't. You see them and can pick them out, very, very easy ... you know the people that disengage from education, you can see them, when they're out on the street when they shouldn't be out on the street ... we'll ask them questions, you know, 'What are you up to?' 'Nothing'. Sometimes you see what they're up to. And if what they're up to is something that you can tap into, then you do.
>
> Member 12

Neighborhoods are essential recruiting pools for gangs—as they are for insurgents (Gould, 1995) and organized criminals (Lombardo, 1994; Whyte, 1943)—because they are close-knit selective environments. Such environments facilitate information gathering and extended monitoring of volunteer behavior. Member 48 said, 'One thing you must realize about black people is that we notice other black people on road. We size them up, try to figure out what they're about. Are they real? We really see them.'

Gang members typically instigate the information gathering process with a simple question: 'Where are you from?' Separated by boundaries often invisible to oblivious adults, gangs use this question to interrogate unfamiliar faces. The question is 'one of the central practices for demonstrating a gang identity and forcing the respondent to make an identity claim in terms of gangs' (Garot, 2007, p. 50). As Associate 4 explained: 'It's like, people come up to me and go to me 'where you from, blood?' And I say where I live and they come back, 'oh you're this gang' or 'you're that gang' just 'cus of my ends'. London's gangs are highly territorial, which means that living in neighborhoods or attending schools with active gang members produces the expectation that, in Associate 9's words, 'every area has a gang or is affiliated with a gang'. Residence thus becomes a sign 'synonymous with [gang] affiliation' (Pitts, 2008, p. 103).

Like families, local communities produce trust through familiarity and conformity (Luhmann, 1988). In so-called 'defended neighborhoods' (Suttles, 1972, p. 21)—that is, local areas defined by mutual opposition to another area—insiders by definition are somewhat trustworthy while outsiders are either superfluous or threatening. Outsiders, in turn, are limited in their efforts to devise credible signs of trustworthiness. Member 37, for example, explained that if someone from Peckham desires gang membership in Brixton they are unlikely to succeed because Peckham and Brixton are fierce rivals: 'A young person in Brixton ... on these streets, he will grow up to hate Peckham ... [he will appreciate] the Peckhamese cannot be trusted.' A preference hierarchy for recruitment even exists within the territorial jurisdiction of a gang. Member 47 observed:

[My gang] was based out of New Cross but I was actually from Bellingham [approximately 3 miles away]. I went to school with them, but I had some of the [gang members] from New Cross telling me I had to extra prove myself because I wasn't official. I wasn't from where it all began.

Online communities further enable gangs to monitor the places people come from and the company they keep:

A lot goes on MySpace. ... You can't just be any random person and come and put yourself on MySpace. You have to have had some sort of impact on street level already ... it's difficult to fake that because if you say like, 'I'm from this estate', someone who lives in that estate is going to check.

Associate 15

The amateur music videos of prospective gang members posted on YouTube, for example, can reveal where one lives down to the postcode and block; where one hangs out down to the street and park bench; the nearest transportation hubs and amenities, including the hospital one might attend if victimized; perceived no-go areas; even a means of contact via Blackberry Messenger or Facebook. Such signs of local knowledge and proximity are hard-to-fake, but also attract police scrutiny and rival predation.

Locality is not only a sign of eligibility for gang membership, but also a risk factor for becoming a victim or perpetrator of violence (Thornberry, 1998). The ability to accept bloodshed 'is not a subcultural characteristic but a specific skill which, like more pacific skills, can be transmitted from one generation to the next' (Gambetta, 1993, p. 35). As such, gangs treat locality as a proximity measure of a volunteer's violence potential. Member 39, for example, argued:

> You say you from Brixton or Hackney, I'll take notice. You've lived this thing. You say you from Westminster, I'll think you're an idiot. What do you know about this gang thing? What do you know about getting robbed? Getting shanked? Boxing someone?

Likewise, a number of interviewees described instances in which exposure to violence at home, often in the form of physical discipline, or in their community, had primed them for a life of violence in gangs:

> I had violence in my background. ... I saw my mum get smashed in every day when I was little so I was used to violence in my house, domestic violence, and that so fighting and doing stuff on the street wasn't anything new.
>
> Member 7

Gang members also correlated violence propensity with prior experience in war-afflicted areas. Interviewees observed, for instance, how African refugees appeared on the whole to be better acclimated to violence and less fearful of death than native-born gang members, which was considered advantageous for them within what Fagan and Wilkinson (1998, p. 138) describe as the gang 'war zone'. As Member 37 explained: 'It used to be about fists 'round here, then all of a sudden it was machetes, axes, swords, guns. People getting bodied. ... Them African boys don't fuck about.'

### Signaling violence potential

Indices such as those described above help gangs narrow the field of candidates to those with the basic characteristics required to be trustworthy. Next, gangs must determine whether or not volunteers are capable of performing the basic duties of a gang member. Violence is central to gang life, as Member 32 explained:

> The whole gang life is fighting, trying to stab someone, trying to protect a certain area, your business there. It's inevitable. You wouldn't be in a gang if there wasn't other gangs coming to trouble you in the first place. You're always likely to get in a fight where there's gonna be your whole group against another group of people.

As a consequence, gang members need to know whether or not a potential member can fight because if they are ever 'caught in a situation where they are required to fight, they want to feel confident that everyone can carry his or her own responsibility. ... If someone cannot fight well and is overcome quickly, everyone's back will be exposed and everyone become vulnerable' (Sánchez-Jankowski, 1991, p. 49). As Member 29 argued, 'You got to be ... a good fighter as well as just willing to shoot someone because if you haven't got a gun [on you] then you're gonna get kicked in.' In other words, violence potential constitutes a trust-warranting property within the gang context.

Member 43 was one gang member recruited specifically for his fighting abilities. He recalled:

> I got into a fight with another boy who was well known, had a lot of rep ... he got pretty messed up. People heard what I done and [the gang elders] were like, 'yeah you're big, you're big, I want you to be involved'.

Intuitively, the bigger the player one takes out, the larger the pay off; but an even greater part of Member 43's appeal was his altruistic use of violence:

> I was helping people that I didn't know so they thought all right he's got heart. ... The leader told me 'yeah I heard what you did today' and, like, 'man I want you to be involved. You're not just out for yourself. I want you to be part of our little gang'.

Indeed, Member 43 had demonstrated he was capable of administering violence on behalf of others, or as an 'agent of the organization' (Sánchez-Jankowski, 2003, p. 208). In defending others, Member 43 reliably and simultaneously signaled his physical prowess, commitment to an ongoing relationship (Smith and Bliege Bird, 2005), and ability to provide private benefits such as protection to allies in the future (Gintis, Smith, and Bowles, 2001). This, in turn, attracted a larger audience of gang members.

Gang members, then, are keen to recruit individuals with established reputations as good fighters. Recruiting good fighters also has the added benefit of enhancing the gang's collective reputation for violence, which, as discussed in Chapter 2, reduces the production of real violence. Honest signals of fighting ability reduce the number of actual battles, which are destructive to all participants. People who fight frequently, for example, typically develop a certain posture or accrue visible scars and repeated fractures:

> You can see it in their face ... [the] shape of their face. See, if you were like a boxer yeah, you could see that you could break someone's face. ... People that are beefing a lot, they have hard-body faces, unbreakable faces. ... In their eyes, you can see if they feel confident, if they feel untouchable.
>
> Member 2

Signs such as these are honest because they are permanent and hard-to-fake. During my fieldwork, I saw many signs of violent histories, but interviewees usually had to lift their shirts to signal them; which is fine during an interview scenario but impractical in daily life. To transform signs into signals, therefore, prospective gang members must cultivate activities that reveal their violent histories.

In the terminology of Randall Collins (2009, p. 11), some youths 'attack the weak' or participate in 'audience-oriented staged and controlled fair fights', which can be quickly dispersed by teachers and passers-by. Member 6 also described the way in which violent reputations are often enhanced through deliberate occupation of other 'physical worlds', such as boxing clubs and weight rooms, where nakedness and public displays of strength are encouraged. However, physical size and muscle tone are not direct correlates of individual fighting ability. People spend hours in the gym simply to compensate for inadequate fighting prowess or the lack of the 'killer instinct'. Member 6 joked, 'This ain't Las Vegas. Out here, some of them tiny guys, like, they might not be much with their fists but they might be good with a knife or might be good with a gun.'

Signaling displays fail when there is little time to enact them or a deficit exists in accumulated 'violence capital' (Gambetta, 2009b, p. 82). Given that volunteers are predominantly young people, they are often not old enough to have acquired extensive fighting records and the physical signs of having been violent. Recent immigrants and school transfers in particular lack *local* fighting records. When displays fail for prospective gang members, therefore, there is nothing left to do but fight:

> I went to secondary school there and the boys there obviously me coming from Africa they wanted to show off, they wanted to see if they can do certain things or because I don't talk their language and

I speak a certain way they might try and make joke of me so I took the offensive and I started doing things like fighting people. With the fighting came the reputation. 'Cus once no one couldn't take me then it's like I really become scared of you and they want to be your friend. So that's how it started. I could fight any man. Basically I would fight anyone.

Member 37

It is difficult to gain a reputation for toughness unless the skills involved are tested. Member 37 here reminds me of a young Mike Tyson who was repeatedly caught fighting those who ridiculed his high-pitched voice and lisp. School bullies read Tyson's speech impediment as a sign that he was weak or effeminate. By fighting them, Tyson reliably signaled just how wrong they were. Tyson grew up to become undisputed heavyweight boxing champion, winning an unprecedented 12 of his first 19 professional bouts by first round knockout.

Collins (2008, p. 20) observes that despite what we see in movies and on television, 'violence is difficult to carry out, not easy'. Gang members appreciate this thus they deliberately test the toughness of volunteers, such as by picking a fight with them or robbing them in public to observe the response. On the streets there are 'two types of people', said Member 22: those who 'stand up' and 'take care of business' and those who 'lie down' and let others 'get over on them'. Member 39 elaborated:

If you on your ones and someone comes up to you, 'What you got for me bruv?', you look at them in the eye, talk to them straight in the eye, stand your ground. ... don't take nothing from no one. 'You can't rob me fam because I won't let no one rob me.' If you don't react, they'll think you moist.

During the courtship period, moreover, gang members will invariably talk with aspirant members about 'backing them' in a tough situation or fight. This proffered loyalty to the volunteer demands reciprocation because they will be required to back up the gang when the situation calls for it. Member 52 explained, 'You've got to show that you're down to beat people up. ... If someone says "oh I don't like that boy", you'll be one of the first people to say "can we rush him?"' Member 29 added:

When something goes down and you're there, you have to act. You have to go the full road with us. And that's where you find ... there might be 20 guys and everyone's got to get a stamp in to show that they're a part of it. Do you understand that? Some of these kids getting killed because ... you've got 20 guys trying to see who can give you the heaviest thump on your head. They're, saying, 'you know, we are a part of this, we're in it with you'.

One of the gang members found guilty of chasing down and killing schoolboy Sofyen Belamouadden at Victoria tube station indeed told the court he joined in the violence simply because 'everyone else was doing it' (Laville, 2011). Violence proficiency thus appears at times irrelevant. Member 5 argued simply a willingness to 'participate' in 'the madness' (as an attack or gang fight is known), thereby signaling one's bravery and commitment, is enough. Associate 5 once 'hesitated' to hurt someone during a collective street robbery, for instance, and his so-called friends in the gang branded him a 'pussyhole' and shut him out.

## Signaling criminality

Aside from peaceable association, gang members engage in illegal activities together that are integral to group identity and practice (Klein and Maxson, 2006). Indeed, some might say that the criminal or delinquent component is what separates gangs from conventional peer groups (Hallsworth and Young, 2004). During the recruitment process, therefore, gangs look for criminal potential that they can use in the future for the good of the gang. The best sign of criminal potential is past criminal behavior (Ouellette and Wood, 1998). Some interviewees had extensive criminal profiles:

> I was really deep in it. I was in the deep end of the deepest that you could get; knives, gun crime, everything, right. Carrying guns, going on, going on moves with big men, like, to rob places and everything like that. I was in deep. I was shotting ... drugs, I was selling class As. Burglary, stolen vehicles and whatever. You name it, I done it.
>
> Member 39

The full offending history of the 69 gang member and associate interviewees is not known, but what is clear from my fieldwork is that they had committed many more offences than they had been apprehended for or charged with. Only 19 interviewees had been inside, but those who had also spent large portions of time as active and free offenders. Information gathered during the interviews indicates that at least 55 interviewees had committed some form of violence against the person, including assault of a police officer, common assault, actual bodily harm, grievous bodily harm, indictable firearms offences, and threat or conspiracy to murder; 49 had been involved in robberies; and 44 had possessed illegal drugs with the intent to supply. Other crimes included domestic burglary, fraud and forgery, theft and handling stolen goods, vehicle theft and unauthorized taking, motoring offences, affray, and violent disorder.

The above is of course all self-reported crime data, which is notoriously unreliable (Hughes, 2005). Past criminal behavior is best inferred from a prison or offender record. Gang members agree. While in Feltham Young Offenders' Institution and Brixton Prison, both in London, interviewees said they acquired the human and social capital necessary to be competitive on the open criminal market. One of the strongest critiques of Elijah Anderson's (1999) 'code of the streets' thesis is indeed that, 'The walk, the pose, the language, the argot, the dress, the focus in one's eyes, and the studied indifference all bespeak prison' and not the street (Miller, 2001, p. 157). Prisons (and exclusion schools and special classes, tracks, or programs at regular schools, for that matter; think *The Breakfast Club*) are also selective environments for recruitment because strong markers inherently segregate them:

> [They] already had crime in common. ... The odd thing about a Peckham boy and a New Cross boy is that Peckham and New Cross are not supposed to get on together, yeah? But they sit next to each other all day in a cell, then drive home in the same car when they are out. Doesn't add up, does it?
>
> Member 12

In prison, gang members are confronted by offenders from other regions but can gather both *indirect* (for example, the nature and extent of crimes they are arrested and convicted for or the length and type of sentence they are serving) and *direct* information about them to identify those who are cooperative and endowed with special talents to perpetrate crimes:

> One of the guys, like, literally I could tell him, 'take this chair and go smack it over his head' and he would've done that. He would've gone out and done anything for me, do you know what I mean? So, just being in prison is not enough, it's what you do in prison. One dude I was in there with, one of the white boys, he used to look like a

tramp or whatever, I see him recently, I was doing clothes shopping. 'Oh, bruv, I know you're making money, man, come on, man, bring me in, bring me in, bring me in.' I told him straight, 'you ain't one of my colleagues, you ain't one of the people that I roll with'. You've just got to tell them the truth sometimes. ... He was a dickhead inside, he'd be a liability outside.

Member 12

Alas, a prison record *per se* is 'not enough' because the proximity of prison quickly exposes individual character flaws.

Of course many volunteers have never committed a crime or been to prison. Novice criminals are a concern for gangs because their criminality may turn out to be inefficient or inexpedient, which on the streets increases the likelihood of casualties, collateral damage, prolonged police attention, and reduced profit margins. Ironically, gang members generally do not consider former inmates who got caught as unsuccessful or incapable because prison plays such an important role in their lives. Much like the way in which volunteers without any accumulated violence capital must fight to signal their toughness, therefore, volunteers without extensive criminal credentials must commit a crime in the presence of the gang to signal their criminal potential:

It's basically not what you say but what you do. Like if you back your chat, say you say 'I'm going to shoot this person for doing what he done to me two years ago', you pull out a gun and then you, you bring the older lot down and you shoot him. ... They standing like a witness ... that shows them you're serious, yeah and they'll give you respect. People that were looking, 'see what he done?'

Member 41

Crime conveys information: it is an honest signal because it implies strategic costs (for example, possible arrest, incarceration, or lethal retaliation from another gang). Public displays of criminality amplify these costs, which explains in part the emerging phenomenon of young people photographing or filming brazen and extravagant acts of crime and violence and posting them online (see Chapter 4). As Erving Goffman (1967, p. 262), whose seminal work on 'impression management' comes close to signaling theory, observes, 'serious action itself involves an appreciable price'. In the digital age of perfect remembering, moreover, technology ensures the signal is received and facilitates the exchange of compromising or 'hostage-information' (Gambetta, 2009b, p. 71).

Mutual offending behavior likewise becomes a way of confirming a sense of self as loyal or belonging to the gang. As Gambetta (2009b, p. 61) observes, 'Illicit acts carried out jointly create a bond among participants, not just generically because sharing significant experiences does that, but also because each will have incriminating information on everyone else.' Member 30 gave the following explanation:

> You're going to have to be doing certain things that we do. You're going to have to be in my shoes, you're going to have to be doing what I'm doing. 'Cus from when I see you do what I'm doing, there's no way you can be a snitch because then I know that you've done it. See if you go and talk then you've done it as well.

In other words, collective criminality requires that recruiters and volunteers trust one another not to inform in the sense that 'I've got shit on you, you've got shit on me' (see Hamill, 2011, p. 115). Crime also gives gang members an additional reason to keep their activities secret, which, in turn, reinforces a strong sense of loyalty and cohesion within the gang. Gang members are known to take this one step further, however, and keep used weapons as forensic evidence to blackmail volunteers with should they ever defect.

### Vouching and referrals

Gang 'elders' are the primary receivers of signals and thus most gang recruitment comes through them. While any gang member can *initiate* the recruitment process (indeed this is one of the privileges of being a gang member), only a gang elder or above can *complete* it. Once a potential gang member signals properties to a gang elder and a gang elder screens them, the next step is for a gang elder to select that individual as someone they are willing to vouch for. Vouching within gangs can take subtle forms, but, as Member 10 explained, more often it is represented by the way in which gang elders 'hand down' their 'street names' and known aliases to their 'protégées' with the prefix 'little' or 'younger' attached. Caesar's 'younger', for example, might be named 'Little Caesar'.

Street names are part of a new lexicon of words that help dramatize the persona of individual gang members (Felson, 2006). As one youth mentor explained, initiating 'street characters'—and talking in the third person about them—enables gang members to create distance between *actor* and *action*:

> On the streets, a gang member is never a 'murderer' or 'criminal', he's a 'badman' or 'don'. They don't 'kill' a real person, they just 'burst',

'pop', or 'wet up' another street name. It's fantasy. It dehumanizes, like, if I don't say his real name, his 'government name', then he don't really exist.

Such 'euphemistic language' serves as yet another example of gang members' 'moral disengagement' (Bandura, 2002) or 'neutralization' of harmful acts against others (Sykes and Matza, 1957).

Street names reflect upon status, rank, and personal accomplishments within the gang, but also emphasize the characteristics gang members seek to represent (such as a penchant for violence). Developing and inheriting a 'good name' (in the Biblical sense, see Proverbs 22:1), therefore, is paramount in what John Pitts (2008, p. 101) describes as 'gangland'. According to infamous LA gang member Sanyika 'Monster' Shakur (1993, p. 379),

> The purpose of all gang members is to develop a reputation. You must build the reputation of your name, you must build your name in association with your gang—so when your name is spoken your gang is also spoken of in the same breadth, for it is synonymous.

Back in London, Member 6 explained:

> You might have an older brother who's a nice guy at college, doing his A-Levels, working part-time at Sainsbury's. But if you're in a gang, you don't want to be 'younger' him. You don't want his endorsement. You want to be a badman's younger, the younger of someone with a reputation … for doing stuff.

Gang members without a name, Member 39 said, are anonymous to the streets:

> [S]omeone came up to me and go 'what you doing, do you know who my brother is?' I said 'who the fuck is your brother, brother? I'll kill your brother, bruv.' That's how it is. I ain't heard of you. And if I ain't heard of you, then I ain't heard of him. I don't care. That's how it is.

Hence why the correct response on the street to the fundamental question, 'Are you a gang member?' is simply 'Ask another gang member'—a reference to the strength of one's reputation and the 'common knowledge' of one's peers (Chwe, 2001). As Member 26 explained:

> If you're in, you're in, you don't have to talk about it … if you've got your respect, you don't need to say anything, don't need to show

off, people don't like that. ... The one's who are showing off have something to prove.

Gang membership only exists because several gang members share this information, know that they share it, and know that others know that they share it. Such is broadly analogous to the way in which Mafiosi distinguish connected guys ('friend of mine') from made members ('friend of ours') (Pistone with Woodley, 1989, p. 156).

When derived from the street name of a gang elder, therefore, a volunteer's street name becomes an honest signal of referral to the gang. As Member 19 explained, the cost lies in the inability to mimic such an endorsement: 'It's like a younger sister or brother relationship. You can't just, like, be someone's younger and them not know you.' Gang elders essentially recruit others in their own image and mentor them in the way of the gang. Member 43 noted, 'Slowly [a younger] will start screaming out whatever crew you're repping, he'll get a tag, he'll start wearing the colors you're wearing, he'll wear the same coat, he'll start talking the way you're talking.' Such behavior is reflective of imitation not initiation, however, because a younger is not yet authorized to exploit the shared reputation asset of the gang by the elders who 'own' it. At this stage, Member 43 added, 'They're associated with the gang but not initiated. They're not real gang members.'

Elder referral is an important screening mechanism because gang members are judged by whom they associate with. Gang elders have built the reputation of their name, thus by handing it down they have staked their entire livelihood on the success of that volunteer. If responsibility for a volunteer were defused across a larger number of gang members, the consequences of mistaken selection would be less dire for any given gang member; thus lowering the risk for bringing on new members. Forcing someone to stake his or her reputation on a new recruit ensures the bar remains high, at least for that individual.

### Screening

Reputations and referrals pertain only to evidence of trustworthiness 'acquired indirectly through a third party' (Gambetta, 2009b, p. 15). But to paraphrase H. Ross Perot, talk is cheap because words are plentiful. On the streets, Member 10 observed, deeds are precious:

Talk is cheap bruv, so if you wants to roll with us, if you want in on this thing, you better prove yourself. You gotta do something for us, you gets me? ... You prove yourself ... more or less by actions.

Gangs directly evaluate the commitment and competency of volunteers, as follows:

> I think people shy away from the fact that you have to have walked it before you get into a gang. Or you have to do something bad before you get into a gang. It's no one off thing. It takes time and effort. It's about who's got the heart for it? Who's got the balls for it? And there might be different tests you put different people through, you know?
>
> Member 29

Gangs test volunteers to determine the similarity of their values and abilities to those of other gang members and to see if their personal identities can be merged into that of the group. Such tests are tantamount to the practice of intense and lengthy interviews, written examinations (such as psychometric personality tests to assess the correct cultural fit and case studies to test problem-solving skills), and medical assessments in the legitimate business world. Volunteers subject themselves to such tests and in doing so they signal their fitness for gang membership.

As Member 12 explains below, volunteers are constantly scrutinized, even during the most benign group activities:

> It might be something as simple as, you know, we bring a whole lot of girls, we're sort of having a barbecue. You know, all the guys in the gang are there. ... You see what they're like in that environment and that's how you work people out. ... After a few drinks, can I leave the room and trust this boy with my girl? Can I trust this boy with the money on the table? When it comes to girls and money, that's when you see people's true colors.

During such encounters, gang members may also ask questions of volunteers, which provoke gossip or invite exaggeration, in order to see if certain secretive qualities are revealed or not. Gang members likewise pretend not to know about things which in reality they know full well about in order to measure the validity of any stories told by volunteers. In Member 46's words, 'real gang members will openly disrespect [those who] ... listen in on everything or ... come with every gossip and spread it everywhere. They can't be trusted.'

By spending more and more time in the company of a gang and its members, volunteers enable themselves to be monitored and thus create opportunities to signal their loyalty. Member 43 elucidated: 'All your time has to go into ... the gang, that is your life. Got nothing else to do but be out on the street with your other crewmembers ... it's basically your life.' Indeed, time not spent with the gang must be reasonably accounted for and gang members will ask subtle probing questions to check people's movements and make inferences about their acquaintances and behavior, such as: 'Were you in the shop yesterday, I thought I saw you? Who was that you were with, I've not seen them around here?' (Member 43).

Member 21 asserted that by dutifully and punctually 'showing up' to gang functions and activities, volunteers subject themselves at the very least to 'monitoring'. He explained: 'You've always got to be there. ... If you call man down for a beef, even if he don't make it in time, just the fact man show is important. You know where he be at all times.' But 'If something goes down and you're there', Member 40 clarified, 'you have to back it [because] if you don't back it, you now become the next victim'. He went on, 'If people don't see you there when shit really does go to the fan, they're going to think you're fake and [that] you talk a lot but you don't show your actions.' To specifically test for loyalty (and wean out possible police informants), gang members will even stage or set up low-level criminal tasks involving recruiters and volunteers, such as domestic burglaries and street robberies, and then observe whether or not the police proceed to make arrests of the specific individuals involved. Associate 5 observed, 'They could be sending you out to go and rob somebody or to go and stab up somebody. It depends on what they ask you to do and if you go and do it that's how you can get your status built up a bit more.' These events test both the loyalty and criminal potential of volunteers.

Volunteers are similarly tasked with running general errands for the gang, which can be as innocuous as collecting a food order from the takeaway or as dangerous as handling someone's backpack filled with drugs. Over time the volunteer might assume the role of what Member 21 described to me as 'golf caddy' and be asked to carry, clean, or conceal weapons for the gang. Member 50 explained:

> We call them send-outs. So I've just committed a crime with a gun and I'm going to ask you to clean it, yeah. Now, if you're lucky the gun won't go off in your face and you'll leave your fingerprints on the gun instead of me because you don't know how to clean the gun, do you? No, you're an 11-year-old kid.

Gang elders will later contact them at random asking for a particular weapon to be delivered, which further tests the resolve of the individual (not only must they deliver the weapon, it must be the correct one). There are popular examples of this behavior. During the investigation into the 2010 Hackney murder of Agnes Sina-Inakoju, 16, for example, police seized a cache of weapons that the indicted members of the London Fields Boys had hidden under the bed of a nine-year-old boy. The haul included two sub-machineguns, a semi-automatic self-loading pistol, a single-barrel shotgun, and a converted BBM Olympic revolver (Evans and Fernandez, 2011). As a 13-year-old boy, moreover, Elijah Kerr buried a revolver for gang members in his balcony garden for three months. For his efforts, Elijah became the youngest ever member of the Brixton '28s', a precursor to the PDC gang (Pritchard, 2008). Handling weapons is risky, not least because the items are often previously 'used' and therefore implicated in unsolved crimes. In the end, 'If they need to prove themselves to me, I can put anything on them', Member 10 said.

### Burning bridges

Finally, gang members signal loyalty by 'burning bridges' back to mainstream civilian life (Gambetta, 2009b, p. 37). Such is achieved in ways subtle and not. Gang members will assault or insult old friends, quit their jobs, or fail to attend or even enroll in the school examinations necessary to secure further education, employment, or training. They also get tattoos. A gang tattoo is a reliable signal because it incorporates predation risks with high production and opportunity costs (it even implies economic costs to erase them). Gang tattoos are not necessarily large or ostentatious, but they are often conspicuously placed in difficult-to-conceal areas, such as on the hands or face. About 10 percent of interviewees had conspicuous gang-related tattoos, but they were all senior members with at least four years in the gang. Many had prison records.

The tattoos of British gang members are not nearly as significant as the tattoos of Yakuza or Russian Mafia members, and full-body or facial tattoos are rare in London compared to Los Angeles or Latin America (Goldberg, 2001). Arm and neck tattoos, however, are increasingly common, particularly in south London. Senior members of the Wandsworth-based 'Stick'em Up Kids', for example, invariably wear 'SUK' tattoos. Elijah Kerr has the letters PDC etched prominently on the side of his neck. In one of his rap songs Elijah even boasts, 'I love PDC so much I scarred it on my skin.' His brother Chris likewise has the words 'Prey Days Change' inked on his chest. One interviewee, Member 14, even had his postcode tattooed on his forearm, 'so people know where I'm from and who I'm repping'.

The Latin word for tattoo is 'stigma'; the degree of stigma associated with gang tattoos is of course contingent upon the 'decoding capacity of the audience' (Goffman, 1963, p. 51). As many consider gang tattoos a mark of criminality, such public proclamations of affiliation make it difficult to live outside the world of the gang and work in the client-facing formal labor market (Gambetta, 2009b). Speaking of a friend, Member 2 astutely observed: 'He can't really get a job now, 'cus he's got his gang name tattooed across his fingers.'

But as discussed previously, gang members are adept at transforming the negative views of them in the mainstream into something positive in the underworld, such as the prestige attached to the size and scope of one's prison record. Gang tattoos essentially convert stigma into emblem; they shock and awe (depending on the receiver), becoming signs of individual prestige, worn with pride like military honors (Goldberg, 2001; Phelan and Hunt, 1998). Like engagement rings or athletic letter jackets, moreover, gang tattoos may also serve a more mutable function to signal commitment, thus deterring rivals by demonstrating an established relationship. As a permanent signal of group identity, tattoos hinder the ability of the bearer to create or join new gangs, which is important given the mobility of individuals across gangs and consequent shifting of alliances.

## Concluding remarks

To explain gang recruitment, existing scholarship has attended to the profiles and motivations of gang members, but has failed to take into account that recruitment is essentially an exchange between two actors (recruiters and volunteers) that is based upon mechanisms that are governed by the constraints of secrecy and violence within which gang members live (Hamill, 2010). This chapter has explored such mechanisms through the theoretical lens provided by signaling theory, with emphasis on the strategies used by recruiters and volunteers to address and solve pertinent problems of asymmetrical information. This chapter has demonstrated how gangs can infer trustworthiness from contextual properties such as previous encounters, but also directly through interpersonal cues and by observing behavior *in situ*.

Gangs first identify prospective members by utilizing their proximity and territorial control. Signs of locality and personal identity are examples of 'indices' or 'automatic cues' that are present anyway, meaning that true possessors need do nothing more to display them. The strength of these signs lies in the fact that they are near impossible to mimic. As such, mistakes made by gangs in assessing trustworthiness at this stage are not made at the level of the trustworthiness of the signs, but because the properties of locality, ethnicity, and so on, poorly discriminate between trustworthy and untrustworthy individuals. African heritage, for example, may signal violence proficiency (which is desirable), but also the potential for indiscriminate violence (which is undesirable). Gangs thus use the remainder of the recruitment process to screen for signs of disciplined violence potential, criminal competency, and group loyalty, which constitute trust-warranting proprieties within this context.

This chapter thus used signaling theory to provide a new interpretation of well-studied social problems and processes in a context about which we know all too little. Empirical research on signaling theory among humans is scarce. The novel application of this theoretical framework in the context of London street gangs provides a new way of thinking about and understanding, *inter alia*, the dynamics of acquiring and performing a street reputation (Anderson, 1999; Garot, 2007). Elijah Anderson (1990, p. 176), a key writer on impression management in the inner city, for example, once described how law-abiding black males purposely 'put on a swagger' or adopt a menacing stance to intimidate others and keep social predators at bay. Anderson saw that the right looks and moves ensured safe passage. The problem is that a masculine walk or evil stare are cheap signals that are easily mimicked—they do not even come close to discriminating between *bona fide* models and dishonest mimics. In the game of gang recruitment, only hard-to-fake signals overcome the burden of proof.

That gang members attend to hard-to-fake signals should not be surprising. Lauren Rivera (2010) observes how elite nightclub doormen make hundreds of similar status decisions every night, admitting only the rich and famous based on signs as subtle as the type of wristwatch someone is wearing. In clubland, mistaken selection can tarnish the image of the club or discourage big spending among patrons. In gangland, the stakes are much higher. Individual gang members guard the collective reputation of their gangs. They must regulate what outsiders are able (or disposed) to say about them. This is true both in recruitment and in retirement, the subject of our next chapter.

# 6
# Gang Desistance

Gang membership is often considered a transitory state, partly because of the youthfulness of gang members. Longitudinal research in schools indeed indicates that the majority (approx. 55–69 percent) of gang members remain so for one year or less (for a review, see Pyrooz, Decker, and Webb, 2010). The problem is that serious gang members are typically not represented in school-based surveys because they drop out, are too old to attend school, or are simply excluded from such surveys owing to their embedment in gangs and their engagement in crime and analogous acts (Hughes, 2005). The surveys used also include such essentialist and all-encompassing definitions of gang membership that anyone who has ever attended a school or partaken in a night on the town with their friends might qualify.[1] Suffice it to say, we are only just beginning to understand how youths extricate themselves from gangs.

Thus far we have explored the origins and organization of gang careers. This chapter examines how gang careers end, thus contributing to a growing literature on gang desistance (see Decker and Lauritsen, 2002; Decker and Van Winkle, 1996; Pyrooz and Decker, 2011; Pyrooz, Decker, and Webb, 2010). Eleven interviewees presented themselves to me as either 'ex' or 'former' gang members and associates. I appreciate this is not a statistically representative sample, but as Plato once said, 'You cannot conceive the many without the one.' Interviewees desisted from gangs both 'abruptly' and 'gradually' (Decker and Lauritsen, 2002). Either way, desistance was associated with the interplay of a number of factors, including, in some cases, a pattern of declining involvement as gangs themselves divided or diminished.

## General maturation

'Maturational reform', a term first coined by David Matza (1964, p. 22), is a common process observed in criminology. Individuals essentially 'grow up' and move out of crime associated with the 'storm and stress' of adolescence and into more conventional pursuits associated with the stability of adulthood, such as education, employment, marriage, and families (Laub and Sampson, 2003; Thornberry et al., 2003). They may even 'burn out', not least because, as discussed in Chapter 3, gang life is a 'young man's game'. Member 46 reflected on the process of ageing:

> When you're younger it's all about what you've got now and how fast you can get it. But then when you're older, remember you're more wiser when you're older, you're more mature so you're more, like, worried about what's going to happen to you, your family or what's going to happen to the people that you love. ... You've got more to lose. You can't, like, make a bullet bounce back off you. You can't make a stab wound not go in you.

With maturation came the recognition of the impact of gang membership upon themselves, their victims, and their personal relationships. Interviewees with close friends in rival gangs, for instance, found that personal loyalty could supersede gang loyalty, particularly in the precious minutes before an impending attack:

> I grew up with that boy, went school with him, but 'cus he lives there [in a rival area are] we supposed to have beef? It's not like that. If something's about to go down here, someone's gonna get shanked, he calls me, like 'bruv, you need to go home'. He makes sure I'm out the area and I do the same for him. ... Is it a conflict of interest? Maybe. But then some mans just need to get what's coming to them.
>
> Member 30

Two interviewees desisted following general pressure from a partner or the responsibilities of parenthood, offering support to Thrasher's (1927, p. 170) notion that sex associated with love and marriage is 'the chief disintegrating force in the gang'. I left the field following the birth of my son, in part because my wife and I agreed that it was a bad idea for a parent to be hanging around late at night with drug dealers. Gang members, it seems, acknowledge the same.

Others desisted after a specific traumatic event, such as a serious injury or bereavement, that lay bare the effect that gang membership was having on their lives. One gang member, for example, quit his gang after he was beaten so badly by rivals that he was left blind in one eye. He fell victim to the 'boomerang effect' of gang violence—what goes around comes around—and came to realize that his gang could not protect him at all times as advertised, which in turn exposed the futility of his membership.

There is an upper limit to gang violence and the tolerance that individual gang members have for that violence (see also, Decker and Van Winkle, 1996). The irony is thus that a 'critical incident' (Ferguson, Burgess, and Hollywood, 2008, p. 133), such as the victimization of one's friends, can discourage gang membership just as easily as encourage it. Member 12 mused:

> Trust me, it's not an easy life. ... Sometimes you don't know what the next move is. Sometimes your friend has died, like, and you want to just spew up ... you've been crying the whole night and people don't see that. People don't understand that ... sometimes you've got to make decisions you didn't want to make, and you end up getting yourself involved in something. ... Life looks very different you've been shot at or stabbed several times and your insides are on the outside and the doctors are looking at you, like 'shit, how he not dead'.

Member 3 indeed eventually left gang life because he 'didn't want to be next' after his friend was stabbed to death.

Desistance was, in some cases, also precipitated by contact with the criminal justice system. Prison is integral to gang life, as discussed in Chapters 3 and 5, but to suggest that all gang members who go to prison come out worse than when they went in would be grossly negligent. Time behind bars taught Member 49, for example, some realistic exit strategies that made him resent his gang. He said, 'Whoever told you that, "yeah, prison's alright", they're telling you shit. No one wants to go to prison. ... I can't even stand the cell, yeah. I get claustrophobic. I can't breathe.'

Likewise prison was a 'wake up call' for Member 6:

> When you go to prison, you go to prison alone. I know 'cus I've been there. You've got to remember that in prison you get moved from one prison to another prison. You could get moved overnight.

You could get moved to Scotland where it's like, 'Who are you?' Your gang is nothing to them up there. Your gang can't protect you. ... Enough of these guys will come out and they won't tell these kids about it, about the realities. They like 'oh it was a holiday. I just lifted weights, got muscly, and played PlayStation all day. I ran that place, rah rah rah.' They don't hear the reality. The story's not told because it's catastrophic for our rep, you understand. I mean, what man wants to admit they were scared to go to sleep, or stuck on lockdown 23 hours a day, or raped, or made someone's bitch. Trust me, you don't say nothin'.

Member 6 actually got credit for having served time in prison for his gang, which enabled him to live life separate from gangs when he got out.

## Retirement

The barriers to aging out did not, as might be expected from some myths of gang life, originate in gangs refusing to let members resign. Assuming one has a 'legitimate' reason for leaving—for health reasons, family, or employment—then there is no need for gangs to react violently. Gangs are happy enough to let people leave under certain conditions because a truly 'reluctant gangster', in Pitts's (2008) words, with full access to the secrets of the group, threatens the longevity of the gang and the freedom of its members. A gang is greater than the sum of its parts. It is rarely the case that a gang member below elder rank knows *too* much. Most gang members are totally dispensable and other youths are queuing up to replace them:

When I got taken out of the loop, the system makes this assumption that because I'm out of the loop, it's just all going to stop. The guys just find somebody else. And they probably find him very quickly. They probably set me up in the first place.

Member 50

Continuing members simply need assurances that former members will not divulge their secrets or provide evidence against them to the police. Comparisons exist with the way in which corporations in legitimate markets often require employees to sign legally binding 'nondisclosure' agreements that protect confidential information acquired during the employee's tenure at the corporation, or 'non-compete' agreements, which prohibit work in a related or rival business for a certain period of time, within a certain geographical area.

Enforcement mechanisms of course differ in gangs, because in gangland a signature making a promise is not enforceable. But gang members still announce their 'retirement' in much the same way that disgraced politicians, out-of-favor *aides-de-camp*, and fired CEOs broadcast that they want to 'spend more time with family'. Gangs cannot afford the perception that members defect because they are dissatisfied or that their organization made a hiring mistake. After all, gangs endure in part because they become the lens through which their members view life. Gang members succumb to what is known in the corporate and political world as 'groupthink'—the collective tunnel vision that group members develop as they begin to think alike (Janis, 1982). This pluralistic ignorance—the belief that everyone else in the gang believes something that, in reality, no one else actually believes—is what keeps the gang alive.

Retirement entails desistance from crime and the development of a lifestyle less likely to bring oneself into conflict with police. Desistance from crime, however, is not functionally the same thing as desistance from gangs. Day-to-day involvement diminishes, but connections to gangs and contact with gang members remain, not least because gang life may be all a retiree has. As one outreach worker told me, some gang members are simply unable to 'drift away':

> These kids don't work. They don't go to school. They don't go away on holiday or leave their local estate for that matter. Everyone knows everyone else's business. It's an incestuous lifestyle. Without the excitement and gossip they would have nothing to talk about. They need the gang. They need the rivalry and drama for any sense of identity.

It is much easier for gang associates to drift in and drift out of gang life because of less allegiance or weaker ties to the group or other gang members. If you watch gang members, Member 46 said, you notice that they share a 'close proximity' with each other on road. Gang members walk, stand, and sit with other gang members. In doing so, they reveal to the community at large their status as an active gang member. Gang associates and retirees, by contrast, 'come and go' and generally 'stand off to the side' or walk as adjunct of a group. But by hanging *around* the gang as opposed to hanging *with* the gang, retirees make themselves available for ongoing monitoring.

Retired gang members remain inactive most of the time but can be coaxed out of 'retirement' if the situation merits it, as Member 12 explained: 'You're never out of this game ... an old enemy sees you out on the street, you don't have time to tell them you're reformed now.' Indeed, some retirees continue to live in gang space and associate with gang members out of necessity because they once maintained a reputation such that their family and friends remain vulnerable to reprisals. Member 50 said:

> They'll just come straight to you. You know, you've got enough kids on mopeds, you know, stabbings, shootings, whatever. Those things happen very quick. [It can] be very methodical, 'I'm going to teach you a lesson and I'm going to do it systematically', basically and 'I will hit but I won't ever miss. I'm going to teach you a lesson, and that is I'm going to get your wife, get your child.'

The suspicion and labeling of people within and without gangs certainly complicates gang desistance. For example, 'When an individual has made the decision and taken the steps to leave a gang, but is still in a police database and treated by the police as a gang member, rival members may continue to perceive that individual as an active member and attack him as if he were still a gang member' (Curry and Decker, 1998, p. 7). Gang members on probation, Member 2 argued, are especially vulnerable:

> If you're on probation you're obliged to be there. If you're obliged to be there then I know every single time that you're getting there. So I had people all the time, yeah, 'I'll see this one at probation. I'll see this one at the Y[outh] O[ffending] T[eam]', and I set them up. Bam.

To further complicate matters, some retirees said they felt obliged on occasion to 'front out' or display uncustomary levels of aggression toward police in public to signal that they were 'still down for the street'. Such behavior typically results in a public order arrest, which keeps retirees in the system longer.

## A new life?

The problem remains of how to find alternative forms of occupation and meaning. Some interviewees processed through various points of the criminal justice system found valued and purposeful education, employment, and training, but they were a minority. The gang life leaves stigmata on former members. They often carry criminal records, violent reputations, tattoos, scars, ongoing vulnerability to reprisals and a residual territorial confinement into their uncertain futures. Member 43 observed:

> [There's] places you can't go because you was in that certain gang, because of the stuff you've done. ... If I get seen I'm either going to get robbed, stabbed or whatever. ... there's certain areas now, like where my friend got killed, I can't really go 'cus, it'll be a problem.

The costly signals that secure gang membership, in other words, make gang desistance prohibitively expensive. Member 51, for example, said that without even any GCSEs, which she perceived as the baseline requirement for an alternative career, her only option was to go back to making money through 'shotting and stealing'.

For some 'retired' interviewees, youth work and church membership provided alternative, legitimized pursuits. Organized religion is arguably the only alternative form of collective youth organization to gangs. It offers protection, identity, group belonging, and—in some cases—a sense of solid militancy. Gang members are honorably discharged, therefore, because they essentially swap one gang for another. Much like you should never hit a man in glasses, moreover, gang members generally do not hit a colleague who claims to have found God. Religion is indeed a powerful and persuasive 'get out of gang free' card. To use Richard Dawkins's (1989) apt expression, any rational inquiry is expected to 'respectfully tiptoe away' once religion enters the equation. It is dangerous to question from within, and rude to question from without. Religious organizations are aware of this, and in some cases actively seek to recruit and reform gang members.[2]

But long-term unemployment, recurrent imprisonment, and poverty await many of the people who cannot perform the identities of the retired gangster or the reformed youth worker as they age. Hence why many gang members choose never to leave:

> This is a good life, a fast life. A lot of us are grown men and we've been living this way a long time. We've grown to love to live like this, you feel me? I don't want to be anywhere else. This is my home. Here I feel comfortable.
>
> Member 9

And hence why those that do leave typically find solace in the effervescent gang intervention industry or in selling their story to the press. Once the medium for promoting gang reputations, media appearances have indeed become a means for retired gang members to communicate personal reformation to the widest possible audience:

> Depending on how much people know about you, that's what it really boils down to. Because of how much people know or, or know you're involved with certain things. Some of the guys, when I've done that some of the TV interviews and that, I've had like phone calls and stuff like that with people going, 'no, you're a liar, you're this and that'. You've just got to have other people to verify that, you know, you're not in the game no more. And I say, 'That's good that you're able to show your face on TV and say, 'you know, I'm not involved with these two', you know what I mean?' It's like a public way of saying this is not my game no more.
>
> Member 12

This perhaps explains why many 'veteran' gang members are safe to parade around on television wearing gang colors.

Gang members that were most successful in staying out of trouble after desistance were those that maintained a constant vision of a crime-free life, regarding their past behavior as being something which they had done once but which was now no longer a part of their lives. Member 43, now a qualified youth worker, maintained that gang exit, just like gang entry, is a process grounded in choices:

> I was two-minded. I had two things going on in my head, which was doing the drugs thing, making money from drugs, but also keeping my education and trying to help other young people. Other young people out there are just daft-minded, they just want to do the drugs and get money out of drugs and just leave, which is impossible. My mind was not only on the drugs but on university long term. I left [the gang] because I found something what I was really good at and I wanted to pursue for the future. For people to stop they have to be dedicated to one thing outside the gang. That's it, dedicated.

## Concluding remarks

Once someone joins a gang it is not the case that they can never get out. The myths that gang members must be beaten out of their gangs or kill their parents in order to leave, etcetera, are exactly that—myths. My fieldwork experience suggests that gang members decide to leave gangs all the time. Getting out and staying out, however, requires resolve, not least because gang members must continue to signal some of the trust-warranting properties that guaranteed them entry into gangs in the first place. Retirees must stay loyal to their gangs and, in some cases, live in constant fear of reprisals. The somewhat predicable conclusion is thus that while it is good that gang members choose to desist from gangs, it is much better to have never joined in the first place. Which brings me to my final topic for consideration: gang prevention and intervention.

# 7

# Gang Prevention and Intervention

When I first met Inspector Allen Davis in the summer of 2008 he had not long returned from a trip to the United States, which, in his own words, had 'revolutionized' his thinking about gang intervention. This admission worried me. Allen had visited California, the state people usually visit to learn how *not* to intervene with gangs. In Los Angeles County alone there are an estimated 1000 gangs and over 80,000 gang members. Approximately 10,000 young people have been killed in gang conflicts there over the past two decades (Howell, 2012). But here was Allen telling me that he's found the secret to gang prevention. And predictably for an American gang project, it was an acronym: GREAT.

GREAT stands for Gangs Resistance Education and Training, a gang and delinquency-prevention program delivered by law enforcement officers within a school setting. To Alan's credit, GREAT is one of the only primary gang prevention programs evaluated with both longitudinal quasi-experimental and randomized experimental designs featuring matched comparison groups (Esbensen et al., 2011). Results suggest GREAT 'appears to have short-term effects on the intended goals of reducing gang involvement (but not general delinquency) and improving youth–police relations, as well as on interim risk or skills' (Esbensen et al., 2011, p. 67). Nevertheless, I was skeptical.

Effective intervention rests on effective delivery. Police officers are not educators—if you don't believe me, sit in on one of their monotonous PowerPoint briefings. Police are neither trained to deliver dynamic curricula nor differentiate instruction according to students' readiness, interest, or learning profile. In other words, police officers may be *experienced* in delivering preventative messages (law enforcement personnel have long attended schools to discuss topics such as stranger danger and substance misuse) but they are not necessarily *adept* at doing so.

The 'Just Say No' approach typically employed by police, for example, misfires because 'children have difficulty resisting temptation, and temptation increases as objects are forbidden' (Hardy, 2002, p. 110). Just ask the high school students who posted the deathly hilarious viral video of a police officer accidently shooting himself in the foot (literally and figuratively) while preaching firearm safety to children (YouTube, 2007). A few hours in a classroom is hardly enough time to break the cycle of gangs, moreover, because the pressure to join still exists in their communities.

I gave Allen the benefit of the doubt. Allen was in charge of the Kennington Task Force, a team of 26 officers that was initially set up to deal with street robbery in Lambeth North, the area encompassing North Brixton, Stockwell, Vauxhall, Clapham, and Kennington. The street robbery task force evolved in 2006 to become one of London's first gang units, but unlike most gang units it dared to dream beyond the dead end of gang suppression. Change was necessary because gang members were responsible for the vast majority of street robbery in the area. Street robbery had become an initiation rite for those wanting to join the gangs. The proceeds of crime were funding the gangs. And the fear of crime was fuelling their reputation.

The task force worked out of in a tiny office in a nondescript police station. I visited many police offices during my fieldwork, but this one was truly remarkable. It was data driven. There were hotspot maps and anacapa charts on the wall. Photographs of gang members were linked to known associates and organized according to gang name and color. Gang histories and argot were recorded for posterity. And all these data had been collected in the strangest of ways. The gangs had consciously given it away. This was a plain-clothes unit comprised of ex-military commandos and aspiring detectives; degreed officers with customer service experience, even a part-time law student. The gangs respected them, in part because they treated the gangs with respect. Officers would stop by unannounced not necessarily to search or arrest gang members but simply to talk to them. And by talking to gang members, even counseling them, police gathered tidbits of information that they pieced together to form the concise intelligence picture now posted around the office.

Allen and his team used this intelligence to enact 'Operation Layercake', which involved targeting gangs individually from the top down and the bottom up. It was an innovative approach that deserves attention beyond that which it received in the July 2008 edition of *The Job*, the Met's bi-monthly magazine for officers and staff. From the top down, police executed search warrants and a series of coordinated dawn raids on the gangs' highest-ranking members, which resulted in 13 arrests for class A and C drugs offenses, grievous bodily harm, robbery, theft, violent disorder, even murder. From the bottom up, police sent letters to the parents of minor gang members, then conducted home visits to present them with tangible evidence of their child's involvement in gangs.

Police sat down with 30 gang members aged 14 to 18 and their families to deliver a simple message: if you don't get out you either follow the others and go in or—in the context of escalating teenage homicide at the time—you go under. They found that parents were often surprised and shocked to find out about their child's involvement in gangs, and most were appreciative of the personal and proactive approach taken. Home visits were an opportunity to educate parents about the warning signs of gang membership, encourage them to take responsibility for their child's behavior, and build trust for the future. The home visits indeed led to the formation of a parent contact group—a monthly forum for families to voice opinions and for police to disseminate information and mediate disputes. The home visits also enabled law enforcement to verify home addresses, ascertain levels of parental support and risk at home, and cultivate covert human intelligence sources—the latter being an unintended consequence of gang members' positive encounters with police officers.

Police used the threat of acceptable behavior contracts (ABCs) and antisocial behavioral orders (ASBOs)—more on these later—to back up the home visits and to persuade parents to get their children back into education, employment, or training. Police offered help to those who wanted it. Layercake included a strong diversionary element wherein police officers facilitated individual gang desistance with the help of local partners. One gang member, who had expressed an interest in working with animals during his home visit, won a work placement at a local city farm. Others signed up to the local football academy and army cadets. While only a minority took up diversionary offers, parental disapproval combined with knowledge that they were now on first-name terms with police disrupted gang activity and inflicted gang members with paranoia. And the police followed up, visiting families again on the pretext of giving all of them a Christmas card.

Layercake achieved modest success on the back of officers who understood the local gang context and the importance of mixing tough enforcement with community engagement. Allen wanted those same officers to drive forward gang prevention based upon the GREAT model.

He had partnered with Nick Mason, another member of the California delegation and Chair of the Lambeth Summer Projects Trust, one of the largest police and community partnerships in London, to pilot an abbreviated version of GREAT at Vauxhall City Farm, a local hub for youth enrichment. The pilot was named 'Be a shepherd, not a sheep' in homage to the farm setting and, in further departure from GREAT, it was delivered by task force officers accompanied by youth workers and education officers at the farm. Out of curiosity, I agreed to go watch. That was in the summer of 2008. Allen, Nick, and I have worked together ever since.

## Growing Against Gangs

'Be a shepherd, not a sheep' was well intentioned but misguided. The curriculum was too close to its American counterpart and lacked local flavor. The venue was a distraction. And the audience of primary school-aged children was too young to receive anything more than a cursory look at gang life. Over the next two years, therefore, we revised the curriculum to better reflect the vast local knowledge I received researching gangs and Allen and his team developed policing them. We collaborated with the Association of Surgeons of Great Britain and Ireland on knife crime prevention and with Victim Support Services on gang-related sexual violence prevention. We hired local community filmmakers to develop ancillary materials, including live action dramas and documentary-style interviews with academics, bereaved families, and leading practitioners in the field. And we partnered with local secondary schools, including a teacher-training site, to better incorporate interactive teaching techniques, but also integrate the project into the fabric of the school.

We piloted and re-piloted lessons. We also changed the name of the project to 'Growing Against Gangs and Violence' (GAGV). Under the auspices of helping youths to (a) avoid gang membership, violence, and criminal activity, and (b) develop a positive relationship with law enforcement, we brought the sporadic community engagement of individual officers and police agencies under one roof and became a conduit for specialist law enforcement to access schools to and talk to children about the realities of gang enforcement and the experiences they had of the gang members they dealt with. We simplified the key preventative messages, leaving goal setting to teachers and anger management training to agencies better equipped to deliver it. Instead, we exposed and dissected the pyramid scheme gangs operate at the expense of their younger members. We found that a frank discussion about the true social and economic realities of gang life resonated far more with young people than the typical 'moral' debate in which adults pass judgment on gangs as either 'good' or 'bad', or indeed the gory images and horror stories youths are accustomed to receiving from police officers, not least because youths at risk of joining gangs already live in violent circumstances.

GAGV is today the only early intervention education and prevention program in London that is universally delivered in schools and provides for the joint youth engagement of the Metropolitan Police Service's Safer Neighbourhood Teams, Safer Schools Partnerships, Central Operations, Specialist Operations, and Specialist Crime Directorates. As of December 2012, GAGV had been delivered in 10 London boroughs to more than 20,000 young people in over 150 schools. Initial independent process evaluations suggest that GAGV is administered with fidelity and school personnel view it favorably (Horvath, 2011). Preliminary results from an outcome evaluation are equally promising (Project Oracle, 2011).

GAGV is really all that remains of Allen's gang taskforce, which was disbanded in 2009 and its officers moved on to other assignments following a shift in administration and operational priorities—to the detriment of local gang expertise and overall police corporate memory. GAGV was a foreign import but outgrew the capacity of the indigenous task force because it adapted quickly to its local surroundings. The implication is that gang prevention and intervention cannot be transplanted from abroad without some degree of compromise. But with each new arrival from out of the country there is a risk this point gets lost in translation. The remainder of this chapter thus explores some of the other ideas and initiatives exported from abroad to Britain and the opportunities and challenges they bring with them.

## Police gang units

As criminological ideas have flowed across the Atlantic, so too have cultural and political messages about what the gang is and appropriate responses to its existence. In the UK, the most recent official pronouncements focusing on gangs as the source of large proportions of violent crime call for tough crackdowns on gang members in ways that echo US efforts—of dubious effectiveness (Densley, 2011; Hallsworth and Brotherton, 2011)—at the suppression of gangs. The report that presents this strategy (HM Government, 2011) reproduces the language of 'risk factors' and effectiveness that dominates contemporary discussions of crime prevention (for example, see Sherman et al., 2006).

But, in common with this paradigm, it presents a vision of the etiology of gang offending that occludes analysis of the social contexts within which risk factors—that only by regression analysis promote gang membership—develop. Indeed, our knowledge of risk factors as either causal or contingent is quite unrefined and our assessment of specific traits as 'maladaptive' is of itself contextually dependent: unqualified pathologizing may conflate context with internal cause. The only concession to wider social influences, however, is to acknowledge the role of 'local attitudes to the illegal economy or high crime rates' (HM Government, 2011, p. 16). The strategy document does not mention evidence that violent crime is closely associated with, for example, income inequality at both the national and neighborhood level (Nadanovsky and Cunha-Cruz, 2009; Whitworth, 2012; Wilkinson and Pickett, 2008). Social factors thus are reduced to faulty attitudes toward illegality and the tautological cause of victimization—high crime rates.

Who better to consult on dealing with high crime rates than former Los Angeles and New York police commissioner Bill Bratton? In the days following the 2011 UK riots, Bratton was indeed invited by Prime Minister David Cameron to help enact tough new anti-gang measures. Bratton is an unashamed proponent of 'broken windows' theory (Wilson and Kelling, 1982), and many analysts credit his related 'quality of life' and 'zero tolerance' rubrics with making New York safer under Mayor Rudolph Giuliani (see Gladwell, 2000; Zimring, 2011). But not all are convinced Bratton (1998) can take credit for the 'turnaround' and great crime drop in New York, with economic shifts, demographic changes, gentrification, diminished demand for crack cocaine, mass incarceration, the deterrent and incapacitation effect of technology, reduced atmospheric lead density (Reyes, 2007), legalized abortion (Donohue and Levitt, 2001), even mean reversion (Harcourt and Ludwig, 2006), touted as equally plausible explanations.

Bratton has a wealth of experience. His visiting Downing Street thus was not without merit. But there was something odd about someone who famously helped levy a new tax to pay for the recruitment of 5000 extra police officers advising a coalition government cutting police budgets by 20 percent over three years and shedding thousands of front line jobs. There was also something sad about said government ignoring their homegrown expertise on gangs (I'm still waiting for my invite). Lest we forget the history and problem profile of Los Angeles are very different from London, not least with regard to access to firearms.

Bratton's emphasis on confrontation is real cause for concern. Based in part upon his recommendations, for example, the MPS launched the new Trident Gang Crime Command in February 2012. This expanded the remit of Trident from its previous focus on shootings in the black community to proactively tackling wider gang crime. It remains to be seen whether or not prioritizing generic quality-of-life crime detracts from the specific problem of gun crime or damages the community-oriented reputation of Trident's previous incarnation. It is also unclear whether or not this shift in priority was dictated by politics or operational necessity. According to Vincent Webb and Charles Katz (2003), police gang units are created as a result of rational considerations (that is, to address real growth in gangs and gang-related crime), moral panic (that is, to validate that the 'gang problem' actually exists), institutional considerations (that is, to communicate to local stakeholders that law enforcement is responding to the problem), or financial considerations (that is, to secure grant money from central government). All of the above seem to apply in the case of Trident Gang Crime Command.

The opening of Trident Gang Crime Command is the strongest evidence yet that Britain is at least beyond its state of denial about gangs. This is a good thing. Inaction comes at a price—Edmund Burke (1770) describes best what happens when 'good men do nothing'. But as the American experience makes clear, overreaction is equally dangerous. The original war on gangs, with its special sentencing provisions for gang-related crimes, only initiated more gangs and assimilated them into prison gangs (see Bjerregaard, 2003; Fleisher, Decker, and Curry, 2001; Klein, 1995; Spergel, 1995; Wacquant, 2001).

The creation of Trident Gang Crime Command actually marks Britain's progression to stage five of the six-stage response to gangs that is commonplace across the Atlantic (see Curry and Decker, 1998). Here are the stages. Stage one: reports surface on early warning signs of gang formation, such as the appearance of graffiti tagging or episodes of 'random' or 'senseless' youth violence. Stage two: police and municipal leaders inevitably downplay the evidence of an emerging gang problem, attributing the violence either to 'outsiders' or otherwise 'gang like' groups. Stage three: 'denial' turns to frank admission in the face of public anxiety and mounting irrefutable evidence of a gang problem. Stage four: public and media overreaction ensues, which results in a call for immediate action. Stage five: special police squads and specific 'anti-gang units' are formed to suppress the gangs.

Britain only has stage six—that is, the multiplication of gangs and gang members in spite of (or because of) heightened intelligence about gangs and increased arrests of gang members—to go. Based on largely unhelpful quarterly comparisons, the Metropolitan Police Service (2012c) claim that serious violence among young people in London has fallen 34 percent since their crackdown on gangs began, from which the media has inferred that the Trident Gang Crime Command is a success, which is of course purely speculation. What we do know is that Trident 2.0 was launched publicly with a mass photocall in Trafalgar Square and a series of coordinated police raids in less picturesque locales that resulted in 515 'gang-related' arrests and the recovery of 14 guns, 37 knives, half a kilo of crack/cocaine in Southwark and 67 grams of heroin in Lewisham. Of the 515 people arrested, however, only 254 were charged, which implies there was no evidence against 233 of them (Metropolitan Police Service, 2012a).

As presented in Chapter 1, interviewees are already wary of police, in part because of concerns about racial profiling and the possibility of being wrongfully accused. American-style 'zero tolerance' of gangs can only exacerbate their suspicions. A gang is neither a precise nor legal term. But gangs are synonymous with communities of color and routinely classified by law enforcement agencies according to the phenotypic distinctiveness of their members (Alexander, 2008). As such, 'zero tolerance' could quickly become divisive along racial lines.

In England and Wales, black people are still six times more likely than white people to be stopped and searched by police under section 1 of the 1984 Police and Criminal Evidence Act (House of Commons Home Affairs Committee, 2007). This rises to 30 times more likely when police use powers granted by section 60 of the 1994 Public Order Act, which allows people to be stopped and search without reasonable suspicion (EHRC, 2012). The younger-age structure of the black population and over-representation of young black males in the street retail sector of the drug market and as victims and perpetrators of youth violence explain only some of this variation (House of Commons Home Affairs Committee, 2007).

By residing in more heavily patrolled urban neighborhoods, the activities of black youths are also more public than their white suburban counterparts. Adolescents are generally more autonomous than ever before (Margo et al., 2006), but they increasingly occupy spaces devoid of the protective authority of adults. Adults are stuck at work or have retreated into their homes, abandoning the streets to the young and to the impersonal authority of the state. Bus conductors, park keepers, truancy officers, and other public authority figures are relics of a bygone age. The police are now the first and only line of defense.

And this enables a broad swath of antisocial behavior and historically recurring forms of street crime to be consciously and subconsciously reconstituted as 'black specific' transgressions, 'somehow expressive of the ethnicity of those who carry them out' (Gilroy, 1987, p. 117).

Only 2.3 percent of section 60 stops and searches in England and Wales resulted in an arrest in 2010–11, and fewer than one in five of these arrests were for offensive weapons (EHRC, 2012). Such a low 'hit' rate is not necessarily a bad thing. One purpose of stop and search is to deter gang members from carrying weapons, because when guns and knives are around pushing and shoving escalate into shanking and shooting. Perhaps that deterrence has taken place. To avoid a weapons possession arrest if they were stopped, interviewees kept caches of weapons in communal locations rather than on their person. They gave the guns to their 'youngers' or girlfriends to carry, or simply kept them at home. Member 50 said:

> What's happened is, they're making the sentencing harsher for carrying a gun. So rather than me take the risk, I'm the middleman ... I've got a 'young gun'. That's the term for the kids around here. I'll get them to hold on to that gun for me. ... If he gets stopped by the police, that's five years for him. I don't care. Bye, bye. I'll just get another young gun.

The Met stopped 33 per 1000 black people in 2012–11 (EHRC, 2012). In heavily policed neighborhoods, where the average young man is stopped and searched multiple times a year, Associate 4 told me, 'Only an idiot walks around with a gun in his pocket.' The implication is perhaps that real gang members are too organized and savvy to be caught by a stop and search. If police are setting up knife arches on the street and outside transportation hubs, crime simply moves out of sight and out of mind into the stairwells and back alleys—the boundaries of the policed area. After all, if those who carry weapons do so to protect themselves in areas they perceive to be unsafe, then disarming gang members does little to address what exactly causes such fear and anxiety in the first place.

There is no clear prevention alternative to stop and search (Zimring, 2011), but my time interviewing police tells me that unlike in the movies, cops rarely prevent and solve crimes or apprehend criminals by rolling up on bad guys. Police follow leads based on reliable information from ordinary citizens who are eager to help. And if ordinary citizens think of the police as the rough men who humiliate their children by throwing them against a wall when their only crime is walking home from school, ordinary citizens will refuse to help. But if zero tolerance and its focus on minor infractions is a civil liberties concern, then the government's new civil gang injunctions, which fully complement the theory of broken windows, take things to a whole new level.

## Civil gang injunctions

Recent changes brought about by section 34 of the Policing and Crime Act 2009 permit civil courts to make injunctions aimed specifically at preventing 'gang-related violence'. Dubbed 'gangbos', many believe these injunctions to be an extension of the discredited Anti-Social Behavior Order (ASBO), which Labour introduced under the 1998 Crime and Disorder Act—coincidently the same piece of legislation that reduced the age of criminal responsibility in England and Wales from 14 to 10 and thus redefined the notion of *doli incapax*, enshrined in law since the fourteenth century—and the Conservatives axed in 2012 after it was revealed that of the 20,231 ASBOs issued between June 1, 2000 and the end of 2010, more than half—11,432—were breached at least once. In total there were 51,976 separate breaches of ASBOs—an average of 4.5 for each offender (Slack, 2012). More than half of those proved to have breached their order received an immediate custodial sentence, swelling already overcrowded prisons. ASBOs were also criticized for punishing vulnerable people and criminalizing everyday incivility—section 1 of the 1998 Crime and Disorder Act encompassed behavior 'likely to cause harassment, alarm and distress' but was otherwise lawful. The Youth Justice Board (2006) reported that ASBOs were actively sought as a 'badge of honor'—a hard-to-fake signal of antisocial tendencies.

Given the controversy surrounding ASBOs and the government's supposed commitment to restoring civil liberties, the survival alone of gangbos is noteworthy. Gangbos are civil orders that can be granted if the court thinks that on the balance of probabilities someone aged 18 years or over has engaged in, or has encouraged or assisted, 'gang-related violence' and the injunction is necessary either to prevent repetitive gang-related violence or to protect the individual from future gang-related violence. Notably, the application can be made using hearsay testimony and police intelligence without the need for any direct evidence. Proponents of the orders argue such is necessary to circumvent an identified barrier to tackling gang-related violence using the criminal justice system; namely, that witnesses are often too afraid to cooperate with police or give evidence (Whitehead, 2011). Nevertheless, this is a surprisingly low threshold, especially given the fact that the 2009 Policing and Crime Act fails to define what constitutes a gang—referring only to groups 'associated with a particular area' that have an 'identity' and consist of three or more people—and 'violence' includes the threat of violence, minor property damage, and graffiti.

The conditions that can be imposed also far outstrip even ASBO punishments. The new order enables the courts to impose a range of indefinite restrictions or requirements on 'gang members', from not entering areas compromised by gangs to not associating with named members of a gang, and from not using the Internet to encourage or facilitate gang activity to not wearing particular items of clothing, such as balaclavas or gang colors. Unlike ASBOs, there is no facility to make applications for gang injunctions upon conviction of a criminal offense. Breach of injunction restrictions is also not a criminal offense, but rather a civil contempt of court, which carries a maximum punishment of two years in custody and/or an unlimited fine. This means that gangbos are less likely than ASBOs to become another 'badge of honor', which is a good thing. Yet when one considers that the restrictions listed above can be imposed without the need for police arrest, prosecution or conviction and that the government plans to extend the legislation out to 14 to 17-year-olds with little further testing (Home Office, 2009), the consequences look increasingly cruel and unusual.

The order is not without any safeguards. The respondent is able to make an application to vary or discharge the order once in place; there is a right of appeal; and any breach must be demonstrated to the criminal standard of proof (Whitehead, 2011). Positive conditions can also be attached to the order, such as mentoring and job training. And gangbos may hypothetically provide young people with the 'excuse' they need to disengage with gangs. Whereas ASBOs were only prohibitive in nature, gangbos indeed offer the incentive of compulsory support to change, a concept that may soon become commonplace following government plans to introduce crime prevention orders—an order with the same blueprint as a gangbo but targeting antisocial behavior.

So, will gangbos work in reducing gang-related violence as intended? Results from the pilot in Birmingham were overwhelmingly positive (Home Office, 2009), but evidence from American cities shows that similar measures in place since the 1980s have displaced, rather than reduced, gang activity (Myers, 2009) and discriminated against children of color unfortunate enough to live in areas identified as gang 'hotspots' (Barajas, 2007; Rosenthal, 2001). Any positive reductions in gang-related violence were also short-lived (Grogger, 2002; Maxson, Hennigan, and

Sloane, 2005) meaning that gang injunctions did little to reduce police enforcement efforts. Indeed, many gang members defiantly continued to commit crimes post-injunction, stopping only when incarcerated (O'Deane, 2011).

Gang injunctions do not apply to entire gangs. The government thinks that targeting specific individuals will have a knock-on effect on other gang members. As Member 50 warned in Chapter 6, however, removing a gang member is like beheading a Hydra: more will grow back in its place. Don't just take his word for it: an assessment of Operation Headache in Chicago, for example, concluded that, in the short term, federal prosecution and imprisonment of Gangster Disciples leaders simply allowed other gangs to expand their operations (see Papachristos, 2001). In large corporate gangs, new leaders are quickly appointed. In smaller gangs with less organization and less territory, however, the removal of gang leadership may prompt the remaining gang members to retreat indoors. Reduced physical presence and visual control, in turn, may encourage other gangs to encroach upon their territory, resulting in more violence as outsiders fight to take control (Sobel and Osoba, 2009). The Centre for Social Justice (2012), an independent think-tank set up in 2004 by Iain Duncan Smith MP, indeed claims that arrests of nearly 200 gang leaders since the 2011 riots have led to 'chaos, violence and anarchy' in London as gang youngers seek to fill a power vacuum. Not one to let evidence get in the way of a good press release, however, their assessment is based entirely on consultation with an undisclosed, but presumably small, given the report is only 15 pages long including the preamble and executive summary, number of 'community leaders' whose livelihoods depend upon said 'chaos, violence, and anarchy'.

The government also optimistically claims that gang injunctions are a tool to tackle the problem of gang violence *before* criminalizing young gang members. But as the evidence in Chapters 3 and 5 demonstrates, a gang member's offending history often has its genesis in serious violence. Moreover, if social media is the *lingua franca* of gang members, as is argued in Chapter 4, a condition such as not to appear on YouTube inciting violence will be difficult if not impossible to enforce with Internet access freely available and so many websites to police.

Civil injunction is no substitute for the full force of the criminal law in dealing with serious gang violence. They 'allow for guilt by association and a short cut into custody' (Sankey, 2011). But where there is evidence of violence, or a threat of violence but insufficient evidence to prosecute, gangbos do provide an alternative (or additional) action. Furthermore, 'without notice' applications could enable immediate action to try to pre-empt violence from occurring, particularly at 'periods of high tension, where lethal reprisal is most likely' (Home Office, 2009), or for example, where intelligence from social networking sites indicates imminent large-scale violence organized by a few individuals. There is currently no other formal means of targeting individuals in this way. 'Gang injunctions also serve as a risk management tool for the police and can be used in relation to more established criminals, for example, gang members who are due to be released from prison and are at risk from rival gangs' (Whitehead, 2011).

At the end of the day, the success or failure of gangbos rests on the capacity of local councils and police to identify credible threats and distinguish gangs from benign peer groups. In this respect, Britain may also want to adopt one more idea from America: gang audits (see Papachristos, 2012). Gang audits are a survey or census of a neighborhood's gang landscape—the nature and extent of the groups, where they congregate, and, most importantly, who is actively involved in violent disputes and with whom. Gang audits emerge from regular working sessions with law enforcement, community stakeholders, outreach workers, researchers, and so on, who pool and piece together as much information as they can in a systematic way to produce (a) consensus data on gangs and their activities and (b) social network maps of gang violence, with the objective of directing intervention and police efforts accordingly. Targeted interventions and data-driven policing strategies such as this yield dramatic results in reducing gang-related violence (Braga and Weisburd, 2012). All we have to do is work together, which history tells us is easier said than done.

## Problems with partnership

The British government recognizes that 'you can't arrest your way out of the problem' of gangs (HM Government, 2011, p. 4). Trident now has 1000 officers and additional resources, including Operation Connect, which is the closest the MPS has come to adopting ideas from the much-hailed Operation Ceasefire (see below), to develop a coordinated police response to gang crime, while working with partners to prevent gang recruitment and divert young people away from gangs. Support for 'partnership' fits well with the broader drive for small government, local accountability, and an increased role for citizens—popularly, albeit vaguely, characterized as 'the big society' by Prime Minister David Cameron. But this does feel a bit like *déjà-vu*, which begs the question, what we can learn from previous examples of partnership working around gangs?

During my fieldwork I gained access to Operation Connect's predecessor, the 'Network Alliance', which was similarly intended to promote the sharing of good practice among the Metropolitan Police Service, the councils of the represented boroughs (Croydon, Greenwich, Lambeth, Lewisham, Southwark, and Waltham Forest), the Home Office, the Probation Service, local Crime and Disorder Reduction Partnerships and Victim Support Services. The Network Alliance, in turn, built on earlier work delivered through the original 'Five Borough Alliance' (formerly the 'Five Borough Gangs Project'), a 'multi-agency programme set up in 2006 to develop long-term, effective solutions to serious violence, including gang-related issues' (Jacobson and Burrell, 2007, p. ii).

A range of initiatives were piloted and coordinated across the Network Alliance, although most of them appeared to be exercises in promoting the very existence of the Network Alliance among parents and families, not in tackling gangs *per se*. A telephone and text-messaging information service sponsored by the Network Alliance, for instance, failed to engage at all with *any* young people. The Network Alliance was also relatively unsuccessful in comprehensively mapping youth provision across the boroughs, one of its stated aims. One practitioner described its efforts thus: 'So many small but obvious projects were missing that it was like giving someone a road map for Christmas; a road map that's two years out of date and with only the motorways highlighted.'

The theoretical advantages of partnerships are well rehearsed and stem from the lateral thinking, 'It takes a village to raise a child'. Stakeholders thus tended to take for granted the benefits of partnership working without properly examining its perils and pitfalls. Network Alliance was often held up externally as an example of good practice, its partners praised for taking a leading role in the fight against gangs. But the reality behind the scenes was very different from the image portrayed. Practitioners complained that Network Alliance played almost no leadership role at all and at three years old it was already showing signs of advanced senescence. The central problem was the view of local authorities as relatively ineffective at making decisions or taking action due in part to overall institutional inertia. The partnership itself was also characterized as 'ridden with conflict', symptomatic of a power imbalance inherent in the way in which gang intervention is typically funded by the Home Office but administered by the police on their premises.

As a consequence, communication was closed between boroughs, representation from some boroughs and agencies was sporadic at best, and far too much time was devoted to, in one representative's words, 'playing politics' and personal 'empire building'. More time was spent reconciling differences in organizational structures, professional values, and accountability and reporting mechanisms, than in actually implementing solutions. But every minute spent in a meeting (and there were a lot of meetings) meant a loss of direct service and potentially a loss of income. One representative, for example, questioned the value of having 27 different people, each representing agencies as diverse as housing, probation, and police, spend two hours deliberating the merits of a sports recreation program with a target group of only eight teenagers. And yet, the one intervention that excited practitioners most during my research was predicated on lengthy meetings, multiagency working, and targeted intervention. Its name is Operation Ceasefire.

## Operation Ceasefire

Perhaps no gang intervention has received more plaudits than the Boston Gun Project, also known as Operation Ceasefire (Braga, Kennedy, and Tita, 2001; Braga et al., 2001; Kennedy, 1997). Pioneered by David Kennedy and colleagues at Harvard University's John F. Kennedy School of Government, Operation Ceasefire sees gang members, by invitation, collectively attend a series of formal staged face-to-face forums or 'call-ins' with police officers, criminal justice practitioners, and community representatives to help them understand the consequences of their actions. What differentiates Operation Ceasefire from other gang interventions is its focus not on gang membership *per se*, but rather the violence perpetrated by a small number of chronic offenders associated with gangs.

Operation Ceasefire evokes a classic deterrence strategy—that is, violence can be prevented when the perpetrator perceives the costs to outweigh the benefits of committing it. Ceasefire's so-called 'pulling levers' approach holds all gang members accountable for violence committed by any one of them (Kennedy, 1997). Gangs are warned that if violence occurs then the consequences will be swift, certain, and severe, with federal prosecution for possession—not use—of illegal firearms. There are never enough resources to tackle every gang, so police focus instead on one gang at a time, informing its members that unless they put their guns down, law enforcement will concentrate entirely on investigating every crime and exploiting every legal vulnerability the gang has. The implication is that when the police focus like that, in a manner reminiscent of the aftermath of an officer shooting, they will win and the gang will lose.

When Operation Ceasefire began in 1996, the message, 'Don't be the next group in Boston that kills somebody', clearly resonated with the gangs: 'The shooting just stopped', David Kennedy told me when we met at a 2011 Minnesota Public Radio reception. The city's homicide rate indeed plummeted from a record 152 in 1990 to 31 in 1999, but it is difficult to specify cause and effect because Operation Ceasefire encompassed a number of different strategies and no real control group was used (evaluation was based on a basic one-group time series design, see Braga, Kennedy, and Tita, 2001; Braga et al., 2001). However, the 'pulling levers' philosophy has since been replicated with similar success in cities throughout the United States (Braga and Weisburd, 2012) and, more recently, in Strathclyde, Scotland (Henley, 2011).

The tactic was first used in England and Wales in January 2012. Enfield police staged a call-in at Wood Green Crown Court, a setting intended to reinforce the gravitas of gang crime. Media coverage of the event suggests that the Enfield call-in in many ways stayed true to its heritage, but some changes are needed if it is to recreate the benefits of its Boston counterpart. First, only one third of gang members (10 people) invited to the Enfield call-in actually turned up, compared to 40 on average in Strathclyde. The result was that the gang members were embarrassingly 'outnumbered by journalists' (Davey, 2012).

One possible explanation for such low response is the venue. Operation Ceasefire is about bringing all interested parties to the table as equal voices, but the court setting implies an inherent status divide. 'It tells people that this is a lecture not a conversation', said Paul Iovino, Commander of the gang unit in my new home of St Paul, Minnesota (personal communication, July 23, 2012). Hence why when Iovino implemented his interpretation of Operation Ceasefire in St Paul, he staged the call in at a place of civic importance—the Neighborhood House, a vibrant community hub that since 1897 has provided a safe space for immigrants, refugees, and low-income populations. Police posted flyers around the neighborhood to raise awareness and provided food and free childcare during the event to encourage families to attend. Most importantly, they recruited gang members by serving warrants without making an arrest. Such appeared to foster a degree of trust because while attendance was not mandatory, Iovino and his team achieved nearly full participation from the gang and the surrounding community.

I suspect what happened in Enfield is that police underestimated antipathy toward them among black residents and thus failed to truly cultivate the moral voice of the community. Operation Ceasefire works only when police and the people who care most about the gang members—mothers, grandmothers, the clergy, and so on—are singing from the same hymn sheet. Only then will community elders monitor the social networks for signs of impending action and help reinforce or 'retail' the message that violence will incur consequences (Kennedy, Piehl, and Braga, 1996). In this context, 'People begin seeing ghosts', Iovino told me. 'They think every black SUV parked outside is a police undercover vehicle waiting for them to slip.' But to get to this point requires buy-in from formal and informal leaders—and that means elected officials need to show up for more than just a publicity picture. If a community has a long history of silence on violence, senior police officers must publicly acknowledge that silence is not a form of consent for gangs, but rather a manifestation of anger against them.

Silence is born out of concerns about racial profiling and the possibility of being wrongfully accused, as outlined above and in Chapter 1. Anger, in turn, festers, because at the same time, the community thinks, at best, the police are not going to help and, at worst, the police are part of a deliberate plan to do them damage. As discussed in Chapter 1, signs reading 'no blacks, no dogs', the 'sus laws' and resulting 1981 Brixton disorders (Scarman, 1982), the Stephen Lawrence inquiry (Macpherson, 1999), continued black deaths in police custody (approximately 120 since 1997, see Independent Police Complaints Commission, 2011) and so on, are living memory in London's black communities. Law enforcement must embrace this difficult past to move forward in the present. At the same time, the community must concede the times in which it shut the police out and perpetuated conspiracy theories about them. The police and the community need to engage with each other to unlock the failed narrative that gang crime is cultural, the entire black community is 'in on it', and no one wants to help. The conversation starts with a simple apology.

The above speaks to my second piece of advice for Enfield: dial down the rhetoric. In the transcript from the Enfield call-in, the local Chief Inspector boasts, 'You may think you belong to a big gang, you may be 50 people, even 100, but we have 32,000 in our gang. It's called the Metropolitan Police' (Davey, 2012). Mr Kibblewhite's tough talk implies a war of attrition on the streets of London that subverts the very nature of policing by consent. Moreover, it reinforces the view of police as the 'biggest gang', which emerged frequently during my fieldwork (and later research into the 2011 UK riots, see Prasad, 2011) as a means to condemn basic police incivility and the oppressive paramilitary policing of poor black communities. The last thing the public wants to hear is law enforcement celebrating its likeness to groups that operate outside the law.

Third, don't let the gang call your bluff. Chief Inspector Kibblewhite also told the Get Money Gang, 'We know where you live, who your families are, where you go to school. ... If your parents are on benefits we might be coming to see if they are lawful' (Davey, 2012). The problem is, police have been saying such things for years, but nothing ever happens—the next day is business a usual for the gang. Gang members recognize idle threats when they receive them, not least because they spend most of their lives being threatened. The reality is that the gang gets away with almost everything and the police know it. When they say, 'We know everything you're doing', police effectively submit, 'And we're letting you do it'. We have known since Cesare Beccaria wrote *On Crimes and Punishments* in 1764 that deterrence is predicted on the certainty and celerity of punishment. Broken promises undermine the entire call-in process. This is why St Paul police reinforced their Operation Ceasefire-inspired intervention with 30-, 60-, and 90-day follow-up visits.

Fourth, the stick without the carrot does not work. What was surprising about the Enfield 'call-in' was the absence of a community or social service message. Instead, the participants endured a long lecture about the realities of gang crime and the prospect of jail time, and were told simply to 'Go away and think about it' (Davey, 2012). The idea of being apprehended, convicted, and serving a long sentence assumes that gang members do not want a stable future jeopardized by being wrapped up in the criminal justice system. But as discussed in Chapter 1, a stable future is not something that gang members typically look forward to.

One of the unintended consequences of reaching in and stopping gang violence, moreover, is disciplining the gangs and the drug markets. The violence may stop, but the gangs and their economic activities continue (Kennedy, 2011a). Operation Ceasefire thus evolved over time to engage in an agreement with the gang members about a possible way out of gang life. Gang members were offered 'carrots' of counseling, education, employment, training, and treatment, enforced by a 'stick', such as the threat of deportation or 10 years without parole in a federal penitentiary. Gang members knew such services existed before, just not where and how to access them. Failure of the London project to recruit local service providers and evolve along similar lines will result only in its extinction.

Fifth, if the 'call-in' is the direction of travel then the Government must put its money where its mouth is and pay for it long term. According to media reports, a further two call-ins are planned in Enfield, using a £10,000 Home Office grant (Davey, 2012). This begs the question, what happens once the £10,000 grant is spent? Three call-ins alone will not solve Enfield's gang problem, but at the same time, three call-ins are little to show for £10,000 of taxpayer money. Should the Government stick or twist? They should stick. Operation Ceasefire has at least produced some tangible results (albeit in different contexts), which is more than can be said for a battery of other pilot gang interventions the Government has bankrolled in recent years—'more pilots than Heathrow airport', as one practitioner had it. The problem is that academia is painfully slow—detailed analysis, peer review, and replication of results takes years. Politicians, who travel from one media-driven micro-controversy to the next, thus grow impatient waiting for results and turn to quick fixes to satisfy their constituents, spending money to address gang problems on a reactionary level.

The original 'Boston Miracle' (McDevitt et al., 2003) did not last because the City let it fall apart. Success in gang intervention depends on certain people who are in certain positions, and when they move on (as they inevitably do in public life) the attention fades and the political will evaporates. The irony of solving a problem is that a problem no longer needs solving. And a problem that no longer needs solving no longer needs funding. In theory, only the best evidence-based practice should get funded. In reality, plenty of weak practice gets funded because it is in the right place at the right time and sounds intuitive to someone with the ear of those in power. Sacred cows make the best hamburgers and as one practitioner argued, decision-makers are 'all too easily seduced by those proficient in producing beautiful glossy documents and speaking with authority in public'.

Far too many initiatives are tried in the court of public opinion without any hard data. I recall one project that received £5000 of public money for gang members to deliver 'inspirational' lectures to school children on the back of an business plan that was at best two pages of typeface. In the absence of information, untested assumptions and hunches will continue to drive critical policy decisions. Which brings me to …

## Gang, interrupted

Operation Ceasefire must never be confused with CeaseFire Chicago,[1] an initiative of the Chicago Project for Violence Prevention at the University of Illinois at Chicago, which received international recognition courtesy of an article in the *New York Times Magazine* (Kotlowitz, 2008) and a critically acclaimed promotional movie, *The Interrupters* (2011). CeaseFire utilizes a 'public health' approach to violence prevention (see Hemenway, 2006), whereby outreach workers—many of whom are ex-offenders and former gang members—mediate conflicts between gangs to prevent retaliatory shootings and interrupt potentially violent situations. CeaseFire's founder, epidemiologist and physician, Gary Slutkin, is extremely vocal about the merits of treating violence as an infectious disease, to the extent that when he and I were guests on BBC Radio 5 Live (2012), I barely got a word in. In nearly 20 years, however, Slutkin has not published anything about CeaseFire in a peer-reviewed journal, which suggests it may lack real substance beyond the media hype.

CeaseFire was anointed a success well before external evaluation. Indeed, it was the benefactor of so much political and economic capital—perhaps at the expense of smaller and equally successful programs—that when CeaseFire was finally evaluated nearly a decade after its founding, no one even cared about the negative or null results. By then its street work efforts were so deeply integrated into larger community-level activism that CeaseFire transcended violence intervention to become a 'social movement' that was simply 'too big to fail' (see Papachristos, 2011).

But what do the data tell us? An independent evaluation of the project funded by the National Institute of Justice highlights statistically significant declines in gang-related shootings and reciprocal homicides in neighborhoods where CeaseFire is active (Skogan et al., 2009). But close inspection of the report's technical appendices, specifically the analyses of Richard Block and Andrew Papachristos, respectively, reveals, 'except for one of seven Chicago neighborhoods, there is no demonstrable effect of CeaseFire's programming *by their own data*' (Hagedorn, 2011, original emphasis). An audit detailing CeaseFire's misappropriation of public funds likewise found the project could not isolate the effects of its efforts in reducing shootings, adding that although shootings had decreased in some CeaseFire zones, other non-CeaseFire zones experienced greater decreases (Office of the Auditor General, 2007).

Even if declines in violence are real, CeaseFire may not be the cause. I remain unconvinced that violence is a disease or that violence is always 'retaliation' that is amenable to 'interruption'. Civil or international wars, for instance, are incongruous with the public health rationale. Violence is a choice. Hence why in absence of priority rights, ownership in the criminal economy is guaranteed by violence (Gambetta, 1993). Violence, to paraphrase the novelist Raymond Chandler (1954), is also a 'symptom' with deep structural roots untouched by CeaseFire. Violence was already declining when CeaseFire began, and changes in police strategy, housing policy, and neighborhood demographics—to name but a few variables—are not measured. CeaseFire is (rightly) active in areas with higher than expected numbers of homicides and potentially dramatic year-to-year variations in homicide rate. As such, 'regression toward the mean' (that is, the tendency for high scores, homicides in this case, to decline over time toward the average) might better explain the declines.

The above has not deterred Jason Featherstone at Surviving Our Streets (2010), a London-based CeaseFire replication project, from making bold claims that the interrupter 'model has been independently *proven* to reduce violence' (my emphasis) and that—with proper funding, of course—his team of Mixed Martial Artists could have prevented the 2011 UK riots (see Gryniewicz, 2012). Aside from the fact that no program of cause and effect can ever be 'proven' to work (it can only be disproven, see *Daubert v. Merrell Dow Pharmaceuticals, 509 US 579* (1993)), Featherstone conveniently ignores the fact that other CeaseFire replication projects in Baltimore (Webster, Vernick, and Mendel, 2009), Newark (Boyle et al., 2010), and Pittsburgh (Wilson and Chermak, 2011) provide little evidence of a convincing CeaseFire effect and on balance the results are overwhelmingly negative.

Featherstone is not alone in his denial of science. The vast majority of community-based gang interventions 'have not been independently evaluated, and most have not been evaluated at all' (Silvestri et al., 2009, p. 44). In some cases this is ascribable to simple budgetary restrictions and/or the recent genesis of initiatives. In many more instances it is owing to a belief endemic among service providers that evaluation distracts from provision and that 'box ticking' is the work of bureaucrats—real work at the margins is 'unquantifiable' thus cannot be measured. But because providers describe their practices so informally, it is difficult to capture precisely what it is many of them actually do.

The Greater London Authority is admirably attempting to tackle the perception that evaluation equals a customer satisfaction survey handed out and completed at the end of an event, through Project Oracle (2012). Opened in 2010 but relaunched in 2012, Project Oracle aims to increase replication of projects that work and reduce wasteful duplication of projects that don't by holding them accountable to robust and widely adopted standards of evaluation and evidence. Above-average projects, according to Project Oracle's 'Evaluation Standards Framework', must evince a deterrent effect or positive effect, external replication, and a consistent pattern of statistically significant effects, and effects that are sustained beyond treatment for at least one year with no known negative or harmful ramifications. Good intentions are no longer enough, says the Greater London Authority. In order to prove effective in reducing gangs and gang-related activity, programs and projects must be constantly evaluated and amenable to change in response to results.

Any academic worth his or her salt will applaud Project Oracle's efforts. But herein lies the paradox. Oracle status is encouraged but not enforced, and projects generally lack the talent to evaluate internally and the money to pay others to do it externally. Austerity cuts and general declines in philanthropic activity mean fewer resources to dedicate to expensive evaluations. Even projects flush with HM Government's (2011) 'Ending Gang and Youth Violence' money must spend it all by March 31, 2013 (Centre for Social Justice, 2012). Projects already bemoan government short-termism and the fact they spend increasing amounts of time fundraising rather than in actual delivery—a scenario broadly analogous to the way in which a member of the US House of Representatives must actively campaign for re-election throughout the duration of his or her two-year term. Evaluation is just one more bill to pay. Practitioners thus see Oracle as aspirational but largely irrelevant. At the time of writing, only my own GAGV project is validated beyond the minimum standards of evidence, which practitioners are interpreting as reason not to improve their evidence base over time, as Oracle intends.

As more and more agencies jump on the gang bandwagon, however, the innovative practice of small volunteer and community-based organizations is in danger of being crowded out by the substandard practice of vast corporate entities led by career officials who appear to care more about their position in the hierarchy than about the mission of the project. As one outreach worker observed, 'there are a number of poverty pimps out there exploiting people's fears and making a quick profit. For them it's not about changing lives, it's about business. But you cannot compete against them when you're already operating over capacity.' You can observe them, in Arthur Miller's (1949) words, 'riding on a smile and a shoeshine', at any one of the hundreds of gang and serious youth violence conferences housed in London each year—£250 per head structured venting sessions, which practitioners attend not to learn from the experiences of others but to hear the sound of their own voice on the microphone during the rhetorical question and answer session. Token 'reformed' gang members typically accompany them on stage as living proof that one's brand of intervention works. And even when their views are not really valued by the audience, former gang members are assured of rapturous applause simply for being young and having an opinion.

Which brings me back to CeaseFire, which continues to thrive politically and economically despite its flawed intervention model. CeaseFire is based on an old approach commonly referred to as 'street work' wherein outreach workers work directly with gangs and gang members to provide services (for a review, see Tita and Papachristos, 2010). But as Mac Klein's (1971) influential action research in Los Angeles discovered, conventional street work with gang members can unintentionally contribute to a gang's attractiveness, which in turn can increase solidarity and delinquency among its members. In Klein's (1995, p. 45) words, the street workers' 'active group programming, their anti-police attitudes, and their total commitment to their groups had become even stronger glue than the [gang] members' original need to come together for identity, status, and belonging'. Klein's study confirmed, in part, Lewis Yablonsky's (1959) fear that group structure could be projected on to gangs through usual notions and expectations of gangs as 'groups'.

Through the spectacle of street work, moreover, many *former* gang members who are hired to intervene in gangs obtain the notoriety and status they once sought to gain or possessed through gang membership (Klein, 2011). I italicize the word 'former' above because many of the *former* gang members working in the gang intervention industry are also nothing of the sort. Between 2007 and 2012, for example, at least six CeaseFire employees were charged with drugs and firearms offenses while on the organization's payroll (Main, 2012). Closer to home, I met gang members strategically qualifying as youth workers via private accreditation and diploma mills in order to exploit London's bourgeoning gangs industry, demonstrate a legitimate source of income, and better account for time spent in the company of criminals. Member 12, who retired from gang life some years ago, told me, 'I can still make a phone call and get people to, you know, do things.'

Gang members of course can change for the good, but building an intervention solely around their status as gang members creates the perverse incentive for them to exaggerate their previous role in the gang and in violence. Such is why the designation 'former gang member' appears now to extend to every young black male in Britain who has passed through Brixton and is willing to talk to the press.

CeaseFire and its ilk assume that juvenile delinquents respect the older former gang members, but what if the old guard is completely out of touch with the younger generation? As the great *New York Times* columnist Red Smith once said, you do not need to have experienced something in order to do it: 'If that were true, then only dead men could write obituaries.' In my experience, street workers are unfamiliar with current research and unprepared to manage the trauma associated with gang violence. CeaseFire offers only 'sporadic' training for its case managers and no 'regularly scheduled training sessions' for its violence interrupters, in part because ex-offenders presume they learned all they need to learn from the streets (Skogan et al., 2009, pp. 63–6).

Such considerations explain why CeaseFire also does not work with law enforcement by design or as a matter of principle—the 'code of the street' says police should not be trusted (Anderson, 1999). What results are memorial marches and prayer vigils that (a) thrust victims' families into the spotlight, thereby denying them any emotional due process, and (b) enable gang members' stylized and scripted grief (for example, T-shirts and websites dedicated to 'fallen soldiers'); but do little to change community norms. To the contrary, they actually feed the community's profound distrust of and alienation from the police by tacitly sending the message, 'We don't trust them either' (Kennedy, 2011b). Suffice it to say, I very much admire the young men and women who work hard and risk their lives to interrupt violence on behalf on CeaseFire. But as it encroaches upon British soil, it is incumbent upon us all to be skeptical of CeaseFire as an institution and not be seduced by its propaganda machine.

## Entrepreneurial zeal

In a June 2012 speech, Shadow Business Secretary Chuka Umunna argued one possible solution to London's gang problem was to appeal to gang members' 'entrepreneurial zeal' and channel the considerable energy gangs devote into building up their brands into building legitimate businesses (Watt, 2012). The Minister's comments recall my meeting with Member 3, a gang member who talked about how much he hated school and how his worst subject was mathematics. And then he took me through the calculations he did every day: how much product passed through his hands, how it was divided, prices at wholesale and retail, the profit margins. For example:

> Say I buy one ounce of skunk from a dealer for £120. There is 28 grams in one ounce. An eighth is three and a half grams. Now, an eighth is £20 and, well I sell eight of them, that's £160. That's £40 profit. So, I flip this three times, I have £120 profit meaning I now buy two ounces. Now every deal I'm making at least £80 profit. Some of this has to go back in, like on scales [to weigh the drugs], and bags to sell, but you know what I mean. Do this five, six, seven times … and you have enough to move up a level. Now, the dealer is getting to know you better and you're buying bigger bits so he'll

probably give you a deal. So, you buy a half box, that's nearly £200 profit on every £450 invested. You see, it soon adds up. But where before you were just selling to your friends or people at school, now you might be setting up a line and having others sell for you. The next level is a quarter K. Nine ounces. That's ... 250 grams ... 72 eighths, at £20 each, that's £1400, so over £600 profit. Do that a couple times and you move up again, this time to a half K. From that point on, you're nearly doubling your money each time. Then it gets serious.

Member 11, another gang member, once said: 'Certain man learn maths through drugs ... in school they don't learn maths but on the road they learn maths. We got 14 year olds like accountants.' Member 3 was living proof.

Few research studies have found exceptional organizational and leadership abilities among gang members (Spergel, 1995). Many of the attributes needed in gang business, such as aggressiveness, however, could actually be considered as positive, even required, factors for succeeding in legitimate business. Herb Kelleher, co-founder and CEO of Southwest Airlines, the single best-performing stock from 1972 to 1992, for instance, '*bullies* competitors' and '*battles* with politicians', and for his efforts, *Fortune Magazine* crowned him 'America's best CEO' (Labich, 1994, my emphasis). Mr Umunna's proposition thus begs the question, would making legitimate business a more feasible avenue for young people reduce the appeal of gangs and provide gang members with a 'ladder up'? Could gangs be redirected to become providers of *legal* goods and services?

In theory, job-training programs should reduce crime, improve earnings, and reduce long-term costs, but if in practice job training leads to dead-end jobs then illegal opportunities may become even more attractive to youths. As Member 50 warned:

Why do you think that young people [aren't] tolerant about getting [legal] employment? They find the ideas difficult to grasp because in the business they're involved in they get a credit line, a company phone, company car, bodyguards, you know, and these are all metaphorical statements.

Street skills do not necessarily translate into marketable skills in the actual business world. Gang tattoos and prison records make gang members virtually unemployable, while low levels of formal education make it difficult for them to negotiate increasingly complex official and legal documents and requirements pertaining to licensing and regulation in the private sector.

However, there is precedent for this type of thinking. In the late 1960s, for example, Chicago's largest and most sophisticated gang structure, the Vice Lords, changed its name to the Conservative Vice Lords (CVL), became incorporated, and gained entrée to the political establishment (see Dawley, 1992). Essentially, gang members were paid with public funds to transform the gang into a force for good. The CVL opened small businesses, established prominent social and cultural centers, and launched campaigns to beautify the Lawndale neighborhood under the slogans 'grass, not glass' and 'making the West Side the best side' (Conservative Vice Lords Inc., 1969). A zero-tolerance crusade against gangs by Chicago Mayor Richard J. Daley brought this promising social experiment to an untimely end and shortly after its funding was cut, the Vice Lords once again became a negative presence. Nevertheless, the Conservative Vice Lords' story offers a blueprint for innovative gang intervention.

Admittedly, the contemporary context is different from 1960s Chicago. The CVL were very much steeped in the traditions of the Civil Rights Movement, for example; and emerged at a time before young blacks became actively involved in the street retail sector of the drugs market. The choices were more limited for generations past. Either you found a way to participate in the mainstream economy or you starved. Youths today know that a tolerable-to-good life is achievable outside the hostile mainstream economy, where, interviewees argued, potential so often goes unnoticed. Far from reducing crime, drugs prohibition has indeed fostered gangsterism on an unprecedented scale. So long as there is a market for illegal drugs there will be a supplier. In order to redirect gang members' 'entrepreneurial zeal', therefore, we first need a sensible debate about the decriminalization, medicalization, and prescription of drugs through licensed outlets (Stevens, 2011).

Gangs flourish in the drugs market because contracts are not legally enforceable. When one cannot sue to obtain drugs or money owed, violence is needed. Since there is safety in numbers, gangs are needed. The irony of course is that gangs are not the most economically efficient organizations—they have long, complex, opaque, and at times unreliable supply chains that feature price mark-ups and product dilution at every step. Gangs also routinely lose inventory to rival action and police enforcement, which is directed at street-level drug sales. The government could instead tax and regulate the drugs trade and use the funds raised (and saved on policing drug-related crime) to educate the public and to treat addiction properly. No longer would drug dealing be a viable alternative to work in legitimate markets.

Let me be clear, I'm not advocating the government write gang members a blank check. Budget with no oversight is a big problem. When the Almighty Black P Stone Nation, another Chicago gang, received federal community block grant money from the US Office of Economic Opportunity in the 1970s, for example, its leader Jeff Fort went to prison for defrauding the government of nearly $1,000,000 (Moore and Williams, 2011). Still, the government could hire gang members to do all kinds of work, from cleaning communities to raising and renovating new homes as part of a community self-build scheme. Gang members could help escort youths to school in the morning or operate supervised after-school activities in the evening. This would move people from welfare to work and in the process create much-needed hope, solving the 'burning bridges' predicament discussed in Chapter 5.

At time of writing, another interesting experiment is under way—the Almighty Latin King and Queen Nation, an internationally franchised Chicago 'supergang', has been formally accepted as a 'cultural association' in the Spanish community of Catalonia, including its provincial capital, Barcelona. Such an initiative is unique even among Spanish municipal administrations. Madrid, for example, still defines the Latin Kings as an organized crime group (Tremlett, 2006). It remains to be seen whether or not Barcelona will be rewarded for putting their faith in gangs and social integration. During the 1990s, the Latin Kings in New York recruited members on much the same anti-drug, anti-crime, anti-violence, pro-health, and pro-education platform that exists in modern-day Barcelona (Brotherton and Barrios, 2003). Following two decades of violence perpetrated by callous corporate drug dealers and a state waging a war of attrition at street level, the gang's revival among the city's disenfranchised Latino community 'represented an indigenous attempt to impose order and structure on what had become an unmanageable situation' (Curtis, 2003, p. 51). As the styles and sensibilities of the gang came to dominate youth discourse, however, the message diluted. In the end, the drug business underwrote much of the economic activity of the gang.

History tells us that major changes in behavior occur with the emergence of mass social movements that challenge the status quo. Change is often messy, as the Arab spring now illustrates. But as John Goldthorpe (1980, pp. 158–60) writes, the 'achievement of a genuinely open society ... is ... only likely to be brought about through collective action on the part of those in inferior positions'. Gangs could be a catalyst for positive social change, but only with some direction and a little faith on behalf of those in positions of power.

## Concluding remarks

The great theoretical physicist Albert Einstein once defined insanity as 'doing the same thing over and over again and expecting different results'. If Britain is to learn anything from the United States, therefore, it needs to learn from its mistakes; but also from the truly innovative practice that goes against the grain and challenges conventional wisdom. What Britain needs is a 'comprehensive model' of prevention and intervention that recognizes the gang phenomenon for what it really is: a complex interaction of individual and situational variables (Spergel, 1995).

Gang prevention and intervention must be rational and based on the best possible evidence. We know that current public perception overestimates the number of young people involved in gangs and gang-related activity; that fear of crime and personal safety is of equal concern to young people as it is to adults; and that personal encounters between young people and individual officers play a crucial role in how the police service is perceived overall (Pitts, 2008). These considerations should be at forefront of government thinking about gang prevention and intervention, even though some of the evidence presented above suggests otherwise. In the end, the failure of politicians, police, and practitioners to come together and thoughtfully adapt American ideas to specific local conditions, as the gangs themselves are doing (see Chapter 4), will result only in the repetition of history and a parallel and equally unwinnable war on gangs.

# Conclusion

'Gradually, then suddenly' is how the author Ernest Hemingway (1926) describes the process of going bankrupt in his classic, *The Sun Also Rises*. Gradually, then suddenly is also how Britain's gang problem unfolded. It started with a few people perhaps knowingly doing something a bit wrong, but then it became the norm. To blame gangs on poverty of aspiration or poverty of opportunity denies of the complexity of the problem. The problem runs much deeper. Street gangs are a product of the political and economic arrangements of British society. They are the bastard children of complex social processes that promote upward mobility and material wealth but more often result in 'sociocultural and racial exclusion' (Pitts, 2008, p. 39) or, in Jock Young's (1999) words, cultural 'bulimia'. Thrasher (1927, p. 20) once said, 'the gang develops as one manifestation of the economic, moral, and cultural frontier'. Thus I agree with John Hagedorn (2007), gangs are 'responding to the conditions of globalization, just as they responded to the conditions of industrialization'.

Gang life expresses values not in direct opposition to any privileged cultural mainstream, but rather thoroughly intertwined with it. Following Matza and Sykes (1961), it is safe to say that 'subterranean' values are not merely oppositional but are just under the skin of life in late modernity. The 'code of the street', as Anderson (1999) puts it, shares many tropes and assumptions with the code of the suites. The commitment to short-term profit at the expense of longer-term value and the need to demonstrate willingness to experience and dole out personal harm in order to progress is, according to Karen Ho's (2009) ethnography of Wall Street, not confined to London gangs. Indeed, gang members might recognize some of the questionnaire items that Eric Stewart and Ronald Simons (2010) use to operationalize Anderson's code of the street (such as 'sometimes you have to use physical force or violence to defend your rights', or 'sometimes you need to threaten people in order to get them to treat you fairly') in the reactions of the British government to perceived threats from Afghanistan, Iraq and Iran.

Interviewees described their association with gangs as a career that was available to them when other avenues of vocational engagement were not. This is not a novel finding, but it does provide useful replication of results of some US studies (Levitt and Venkatesh, 2000; Sánchez-Jankowski, 1991). Britain's 'emerging' gang situation stands in stark contrast to America's 'chronic' gang problem (Spergel, 1995, p. 180). But street gangs represent a persuasive aspiration on both sides of the Atlantic. Economic exclusion from the fruits of consumerism in combination with the contemporary and generationally transmitted experience of racism, both real and perceived, give credence and legitimacy to the development of an, at times self-righteous, subterranean culture based in part on the superficial adulation of what George Orwell (1946) called the 'false values of American film'. The rejection of the recruitment of black young men to menial, low-status occupations through slavery, immigration and social exclusion as discussed in Chapter 1 is ironically now being performed, at least in part, by the self-relegation of black young men to violent, low-status and usually low-paid work on the street.

There once was an American brand of gangs. This is now an Anglo-American brand born out of an Anglo-American style of neoliberalism, rooted in free market regulation that—in contrast with the Germanic or Scandinavian system of managed capitalism—promotes high levels of inequality (Wilkinson and Pickett, 2008). Britain and America are 'two countries separated by a common language', says George Bernard Shaw. By reading media, gangs learned to interpret. Satellite television, launched in 1989, and the Internet, ubiquitous by 1996, contributed to the cultural diffusion of the gang lifestyle (Hagedorn, 2008). But in copying the same, at times mythical, templates, gangs began to converge and reproduce in their own image. Gangs in Britain indeed almost compete with each other to see which best conforms to the American 'gang' prototype. It remains to be seen whether or not British gangs have achieved optimal levels of organization or if optimal levels even exist. The question for practitioners and policymakers is how best to intervene without further reinforcing gang structure.

Not all gangs fully evolve. Gangs that fail to acquire the necessary resources of violence, territory, secrecy and intelligence may regress or become extinct. The takeaway points are that gangs exist on a spectrum from the simple to the complex, and the search for one unanimous and universal statement on gangs across contexts may be a fruitless endeavor. But fully evolved gangs are really no different from legitimate enterprises that address agency problems through careful and competitive selection procedures, training and credentialing, and the establishment of ethics codes that curb individual self-interest and opportunism.

## Implications

This case study also adds to the evidence from other contexts that groups constrained by asymmetric information and at risk of infiltration rely upon hard-to-fake signals to efficiently and effectively recruit (Hamill, 2010; Pizzini-Gambetta and Hamill, 2011); including organized criminals (Gambetta, 2009b), rebel insurgents (Humphreys and Weinstein, 2008; Viterna, 2006; Weinstein, 2005, 2007), and radical and extremist groups (Gambetta and Hertog, 2007; Hamill, 2011; Hegghammer, 2010; Krueger, 2007; Krueger and Malecková, 2002). The processes described in Chapter 5 specifically are also broadly analogous to the processes of initiation, indoctrination and membership control employed by cults and communes (Knox, 1999) and the lengthy, phased recruitment of Outlaw Motorcycle Clubs, whereby prospective members transition from 'Hang-around' (that is, they are invited to some club events or to meet club members at known gathering places) to 'Prospect' or 'Probate' (that is, they participate in some club activities and run errands for the gang while being evaluated for suitability as a full member) and eventually to 'Full Member' status (that is, they are granted voting rights and permission to wear the top and bottom 'rockers' of the gang) (Barker, 2007).

The understanding gained from this research, therefore, provides an input in the applications of gang research to understanding other subterranean groups (Decker and Pyrooz, 2011b). Street gangs, organized criminals, rebel insurgents, and radical and extremist groups, differ in many respects, but are wedded in their need to find trustworthy members in a context in which information does not flow freely and alternative mechanisms need to be implemented for the recruitment process to take place. Given the neighborhood and friendship base for most gangs and the youthfulness of most gang members, a question for future research is whether or not recruitment into gangs is a less formal process than recruitment into other extra-legal organizations. The implication, however, is that signaling theory might offer the most compelling narrative for understanding recruitment into all such groups. As statisticians George Box and Norman Draper (1987, p. 424) famously observed, 'All models are wrong, but some models are useful.' In this context, signaling theory is very useful.

Consistent with signaling theory, this book also has also demonstrated how actions that are in usual circumstances costly to those that carry them out (for example, fighting, going to prison, participating in criminal acts), may actually facilitate entrée into gangs. As Goffman (1967, p. 217) fortuitously observed, only those who engage in 'fateful' activities can truly test their characters, and certain skills and attributes can only be claimed in social situations 'where the action is' and something of consequence is risked. Displays of crime and violence are utilitarian—they are hard-to-fake signals and hard-to-fake signals deter opportunists and free riders. A question for future research, therefore, is do gangs face greater free-rider problems as they grow in size? If the answer is yes, a second question materializes: must prospective members exhibit even costlier signals and/or does the screening become more rigorous under increased selective pressures? Either way, the policy implications in the context of the Prime Minister's 'war on gangs' are clear: lengthy prison sentences and gang injunctions risk becoming yet another means for gang members to signal their criminal credentials. Member 13 explained, 'There's always someone out there who's willing to go the next step just to prove himself ... to do what it takes to show that, "do you know what, I'm the real deal, I can roll with you".'

My talking with gang members leads me to conclude, in line with other critical commentators in this area (Alexander, 2008; Hallsworth and Brotherton, 2011; Hallsworth and Young, 2008), it would be dangerous to reduce the problem of street violence in London to the phenomenon of the gang. Policy analyses that make this mistake by isolating gangs and their members from the social contexts in which they act are destined to repeat the failures of previous, US attempts at gang suppression outlined in Chapter 7. That being said, it is possible that my own focus on gangs encouraged interviewees to over-emphasize their attachment to gangs and the role of gangs in their offending and other activities, thus inadvertently contributing to the suppression agenda. I fully acknowledge that gang members engage in *both* legal and illegal activity with each other, but my emphasis has been on the latter because crime is integral to the *raison d'être* of the group (see Klein and Maxson, 2006). The solution to such uncertainties would not be to create research with a harder veneer by replicating this problem over a larger sample using standardized rather than semi-structured interviews. Rather, it would be to develop a deeper ethnographic engagement with similar young people, ideally in ways that followed their biographies longitudinally and that enabled them to produce and interpret data about their own lives (see, for example, Venkatesh, 1997).

Are my findings merely a product of the city studied or the methodology used? Gang evolution, organization, recruitment, desistance, and so on, are processes that unfold over time. A further limitation of my own data, therefore, is that it is cross-sectional and based in part upon retrospective accounts. Although I observed gangs at the stages outlined in Chapter 2, for instance, I would need longitudinal data from inception to truly test whether or not gangs progress through stages in sequence. Likewise, I would ideally need to observe a series of volunteers gain entrée into gangs from first contact (which may be in early childhood) all the way through to initiation in order to test the presence of the recruitment screening processes described in Chapter 5. Such is an important avenue for future research, but implies predictive skills beyond the capacity of the 'risk factor' crowd.

Regardless of whether gangs recruit different people at different times depending on their needs, I am confident gangs' need for trustworthy people remains constant. Gangs have the capacity to use coercion in recruitment, but rarely do because: (a) they have a willing pool of volunteers; and (b) there is too much at stake for them to neglect the trust-warranting properties. The risks of allowing people who are merely 'players' into the gang are evident in this quote from Member 12:

> One thing you say in the game is you can't be half hearted. ... Because someone who's half-hearted is the same person that's going to feed you to the Feds ... [or] your information to someone else.

Suffice it to say, Pitts's (2008) 'reluctant gangster' is probably not gangster at all.

Yet given the challenges facing all young people living in gang-affected communities, the extent to which gang membership is ever truly 'voluntary' is of course questionable. Like lawyers who chase ambulances, gangs certainly do exploit naïve and vulnerable young people. Here's Member 12 again:

> You see, when that child reaches 11 they start going into secondary school, if they haven't got a sense of identity, someone else will give it to them. If they haven't got a sense of belonging, someone else will give it to them. If they haven't got a sense of being loved, someone

else will give it to them. You know who those people are. You know, you find them, or they will find you. And they become part of what we are. Some are extrovert and some aren't, you know. The ones that aren't they're, they are very, very, very, very, very, very useful to someone. No one suspects them.

While gangs are selective organizations that deliberately narrow the recruitment pool, the caveat is thus that they select from an already narrow pool of individuals. Such individuals are often the easiest to entice and entrap because the less an individual has in the first place, the less bridges they must burn in the end. The present research, therefore, lends support to the 'enhancement' model of understanding the gangs–delinquency nexus (Battin et al., 1998; Esbensen and Huizinga, 1993; Esbensen, Huizinga, and Weiher, 1993; Gatti et al., 2005; Gordon et al., 2004; Lacourse et al., 2003; Thornberry et al., 1993, Thornberry 1998; Zhang, Welte, and Wieczorek, 1999). In other words, youths who join gangs may already display a higher level of delinquency than their non-gang peers, but the complex processes of joining a gang exacerbate this delinquency. Additional research is needed to further untangle this complex relationship.

Many of the ideas in this book are amenable to further empirical testing. For example, it may be possible to test the claim that high levels of violence related to gangs will be more common in the presence of causal configurations that combine the presence of high inequality (along class and ethnic lines), high social validation of consumerism, high social visibility of violence, high youth unemployment, high concentration of poverty, high levels of violent maltreatment of children, high levels of confrontational policing of young people and low social mobility. These terms will all require careful operationalization, but would be especially amenable to the kind of qualitative comparative analysis performed by Federico Varese (2011) and Charles Ragin (2008) on different topics.

## The last word

Young people have long been associated with heightened rates of delinquent behavior. In *The Winter's Tale*, William Shakespeare (1623) ruefully describes the activities of what we would now call adolescent males as 'getting wenches with child, wronging the ancientry, stealing, fighting' (Act III, Scene iii). Delinquent youths gathered in groups on street corners have likewise long given the public pause, as in previous 'moral panics' around Garrotters, Hooligans, Mods and Muggers. What, then, is different about this latest incarnation of the 'folk devil' (Cohen, 2002), beyond its penchant for hooded sweatshirts?

When I embarked on this project nearly six years ago such was the first question I sought to answer. Upon moving back to Britain to study gangs in this context, however, my compatriots greeted me with disdain. Violent activity of a territorial nature conducted by 'gangs' with recognizable leadership and specific roles for participants was the exception, not the rule (Patrick, 1973). Gangs were home in America, they told me. I was encouraged to go join them and, preferably, get lost in the ocean en route. Much to some people's disappointment, I found the gangs Britain denied existed. Not because I was 'looking' for them in the myopic sense bemoaned by British criminologists, but because gangs were all present and correct. And in the end, the differences are everything and nothing.

# Appendix 1: Sample Demographics

Demographic information for sample of gang members and associates (N=69)

| # | Name | Rank | Age | Sex | Ethnicity | Years in gang | Retired | Jail |
|---|------|------|-----|-----|-----------|---------------|---------|------|
| ALFA GANG, CROYDON | | | | | | | | |
| 1 | *Associate 1* | – | 15 | F | Mixed | 1–3 | | |
| 2 | *Member 1* | Younger | 15 | M | Black British | 1–3 | | |
| 3 | **Member 2** | Younger | 15 | M | Black British | 1–3 | | |
| 4 | Member 3 | Inner Circle | 18 | M | Black British | 4–6 | | |
| 5 | *Associate 2* | – | 15 | F | Black British | 1–3 | | |
| 6 | Member 4 | Elder | 17 | M | Black British | 1–3 | | |
| 7 | Member 5 | Elder | 17 | M | Black British | 1–3 | | X |
| BETA GANG, CROYDON | | | | | | | | |
| 8 | *Member 6* | Inner Circle | 30 | M | Black British | 7–9 | | X |
| 9 | *Member 7* | Elder | 20 | F | Black British | 4–6 | X | |
| 10 | Associate 3 | – | 19 | F | Black Caribbean | 1–3 | X | |
| 11 | **Member 8** | Inner Circle | 22 | M | Black Caribbean | 4–6 | | X |
| 12 | Member 9 | Inner Circle | 24 | M | Black British | 4–6 | | X |
| 13 | Member 10 | Elder | 24 | M | Black British | 4–6 | | |
| 14 | Member 11 | Elder | 19 | M | Black British | 4–6 | | |

(continued)

Continued

| # | Name | Rank | Age | Sex | Ethnicity | Years in gang | Retired | Jail |
|---|------|------|-----|-----|-----------|---------------|---------|------|
| CHARLIE GANG, HACKNEY | | | | | | | | |
| 15 | *Member 12* | Inner Circle | 26 | M | Black African | >10 | X | X |
| 16 | Member 13 | Elder | 19 | M | Black British | 4–6 | X | |
| 17 | *Associate 4* | – | 25 | M | Black Caribbean | 1–3 | | |
| 18 | Associate 5 | – | 24 | M | Asian British | 1–3 | | |
| 19 | Member 14 | Elder | 20 | M | Black British | 4–6 | | |
| 20 | *Associate 6* | – | 32 | F | Black British | 7–9 | X | X |
| 21 | Associate 7 | – | 26 | F | Black African | 4–6 | X | |
| DELTA GANG, HACKNEY | | | | | | | | |
| 22 | Member 15 | Elder | 16 | F | Black British | 1–3 | | |
| 23 | Member 16 | Younger | 16 | F | Black British | 1–3 | | |
| 24 | Member 17 | Elder | 19 | F | Black British | 1–3 | | X |
| 25 | Member 18 | Younger | 15 | F | Black British | 1–3 | | |
| 26 | Member 19 | Elder | 17 | F | Black British | 1–3 | | |
| ECHO GANG, HARINGEY | | | | | | | | |
| 27 | Member 20 | Elder | 17 | M | Black Caribbean | 1–3 | | |
| 28 | *Member 21* | Younger | 15 | M | Black Caribbean | 1–3 | | |
| 29 | *Member 22* | Younger | 16 | M | Black British | 1–3 | | X |
| 30 | Associate 8 | – | 15 | M | Black Caribbean | 1–3 | | |
| 31 | Associate 9 | – | 15 | M | Black British | 1–3 | | |
| 32 | Member 23 | Younger | 14 | M | Black British | 1–3 | | |
| FOXTROT GANG, HARINGEY | | | | | | | | |
| 33 | *Member 24* | Elder | 17 | M | Black British | 1–3 | | |
| 34 | Associate 10 | – | 20 | F | Mixed | 4–6 | | |

## GOLF GANG, LAMBETH

| | | | | | | | |
|---|---|---|---|---|---|---|---|
| 35 | *Member 25* | Younger | 17 | M | Black British | 1–3 | |
| 36 | Associate 11 | – | 15 | M | Black British | <1 | |
| 37 | Associate 12 | – | 18 | M | Black British | 1–3 | |
| 38 | Member 26 | Elder | 18 | M | Black Caribbean | 1–3 | X |
| 39 | Member 27 | Younger | 18 | M | Black Caribbean | 1–3 | |

## HOTEL GANG, LAMBETH

| | | | | | | | |
|---|---|---|---|---|---|---|---|
| 40 | **Member 28** | Inner Circle | 24 | M | Black Caribbean | 4–6 | |
| 41 | Member 29 | Inner Circle | 20 | M | Black Caribbean | 4–6 | X |
| 42 | *Member 30* | Inner Circle | 21 | M | Black Caribbean | 4–6 | |
| 43 | Member 31 | Elder | 19 | M | Black African | 1–3 | |
| 44 | Member 32 | Elder | 19 | M | Black African | 1–3 | X |
| 45 | Member 33 | Elder | 20 | M | Black African | 1–3 | |
| 46 | Member 34 | Younger | 17 | M | Black British | 1–3 | |
| 47 | Member 35 | Younger | 17 | M | Black British | 1–3 | |
| 48 | Member 36 | Elder | 19 | M | Black African | 1–3 | X |

## INDIA GANG, LAMBETH

| | | | | | | | |
|---|---|---|---|---|---|---|---|
| 49 | **Member 37** | Elder | 19 | M | Black African | 4–6 | X |
| 50 | Member 38 | Elder | 20 | M | Black British | 4–6 | |
| 51 | *Associate 13* | – | 19 | F | Mixed | 1–3 | |
| 52 | Associate 14 | – | 18 | F | Black British | 1–3 | |
| 53 | Member 39 | Elder | 19 | M | Black African | 1–3 | X |
| 54 | Member 40 | Elder | 18 | M | Black British | 1–3 | |
| 55 | Member 41 | Younger | 17 | M | Black British | 1–3 | |
| 56 | Member 42 | Elder | 19 | M | Black British | 1–3 | |
| 57 | **Associate 15** | – | 16 | F | Black British | <1 | |

*(continued)*

Continued

| # | Name | Rank | Age | Sex | Ethnicity | Years in gang | Retired | Jail |
|---|------|------|-----|-----|-----------|---------------|---------|------|
| **JULIET GANG, LAMBETH** | | | | | | | | |
| 58 | *Member 43* | Elder | 19 | M | Black African | 1–3 | X | |
| 59 | *Member 44* | Inner Circle | 25 | M | Black Caribbean | >10 | | X |
| 60 | *Member 45* | Inner Circle | 26 | M | Black British | >10 | | X |
| **KILO GANG, LEWISHAM** | | | | | | | | |
| 61 | *Member 46* | Elder | 25 | M | Black African | 4–6 | X | |
| 62 | Member 47 | Inner Circle | 28 | M | Black African | 7–9 | | X |
| 63 | Member 48 | Elder | 24 | M | Black British | 7–9 | | |
| 64 | Member 49 | Elder | 19 | M | Black British | 4–6 | | X |
| **LIMA GANG, SOUTHWARK** | | | | | | | | |
| 65 | *Member 50* | Elder | 33 | M | Black Caribbean | 4–6 | X | X |
| 66 | Member 51 | Elder | 34 | F | Black Caribbean | >10 | X | X |
| 67 | *Member 52* | Younger | 15 | M | Mixed | 1–3 | | |
| 68 | *Associate 16* | – | 16 | M | Black Caribbean | 1–3 | | |
| 69 | Associate 17 | – | 13 | M | Black Caribbean | <1 | | |

*Note:* Names in **bold** denote when interview was recorded and transcribed verbatim. Names in *italics* denote interviewees who were interviewed on more than one occasion. Names in ***bold italics*** denote interviewees both recorded and revisited.
*Source:* Author's compilation. Names listed in order interviewed/referred per gang.

180

# Appendix 2: Glossary of Terms

*Street culture has produced a distinctive language and so, in the interest of reference and clarity, I have compiled the following glossary of terms from the interview transcripts.*

| | |
|---|---|
| 5–O: | Police (origin: 'Hawaii 5–0') |
| Amp: | Amplified, as in being too much |
| Badman: | Notorious, someone with 'bare ratings' |
| Bait: | Obvious |
| Balled/to ball: | To engage in threatening eye contact (origin: 'eyeball') |
| Ballin': | Living the good life |
| Bang: | Punch |
| Banging: | Very good |
| Bare: | A large or sufficient amount or quantity |
| Bars: | A measure of music, as in 'spit some bars' (to sing something) |
| Battle: | Rap competitions that are sometimes drawn out over time |
| Beat: | Sex |
| Beef: | Argument/fight/confrontation/conflict/vendetta |
| Bell(ed): | A telephone call |
| Ben: | A £10 bag of drugs |
| Big up: | To compliment |
| Blap Blap: | The sound of a gun discharging |
| Blaze: | To smoke cannabis |
| Block: | A council estate (origin: the area bounded by four streets) |
| Blowing: | Running or depart quickly |
| Blud: | A close companion who can be family or friend |
| Bly: | Chance |
| Booky: | Suspicious |
| Bore: | To stab someone (origin: transitive verb to 'hollow out') |
| Bounce: | to exit a location/situation |
| Boyed: | Insulted |
| Brainer: | Oral sex |
| Brap: | A sign of approval (often used repeatedly and loudly) |
| Breed: | Wanting to impregnate a girl |
| Brethren: | A close companion who can be family or friend |
| Bruv: | A close companion who can be family or friend (origin: 'brother') |
| Buff: | Physically attractive |
| Burner: | A firearm |
| Burst: | To stab or shoot someone |
| Bust a nut: | To ejaculate |
| Butters: | Ugly (origin: 'butt ugly') |
| Calm-stige: | Content (a portmanteau word from 'calm' and 'prestige') |
| Certified: | Serious girlfriend |
| Chief: | Unintelligent |

| | |
|---|---|
| Chirps(ing): | Sweet talking/flirting |
| Chug: | Physically attractive |
| Chung: | Extremely attractive |
| Country: | Places outside of London where youngers are sent to deal drugs |
| Crack: | Hard crystalline form of cocaine broken into small pieces and smoked |
| Criss: | New (origin: 'crisp') |
| Crow: | Cannabis |
| Dash: | To throw something away |
| Deal: | To sell illegal drugs |
| Dis: | To disrespect someone or something (origin: disrespect) |
| DJ: | A disc jockey, someone who uses samples of recorded music to make new music |
| Drapse: | To be roughed up or held up |
| Dutty: | Dirty |
| Elder: | Older or more senior gang member |
| Emcee/MC: | Master of Ceremonies |
| Ends/Endz: | A neighborhood, esp. one's own neighborhood/gang territory |
| Fam: | A close companion who can be family or friend (origin: 'family') |
| Feds: | The police (origin: abbreviation of 'federal agent') |
| Flip/Flipping: | Turning the proceeds of a 'hustle' or robbery into profit (origin: to 'flip' a property, that is, buy and sell quickly and profitably using a fraudulent evaluation of its worth) |
| Floss: | Flaunt |
| Food: | Illegal drugs |
| Front: | Behavior assumed to conceal one's genuine feelings |
| Frontline: | The area in gang territory where the 'action' happens |
| G: | Gangster/gang member |
| Gallis: | Womanizer |
| Gassed: | Talking nonsense/excited (origin: to fill a tank with gasoline) |
| Gem: | Fool |
| Ghost: | To be frequently absent |
| Green: | Cannabis |
| Greezy: | Bad |
| Grime: | A style of urban music that evolved primarily out of UK garage, Caribbean dancehall and American hip-hop |
| Grimy: | Something not good |
| Grips/to Grips up: | To be roughed up or held up |
| Gwap: | Money |
| Gyal-dem: | Girls |
| Hench: | Muscular (origin: 'Henchmen') |
| Hip-hop: | A style of popular music of US black and Hispanic origin, featuring rap with an electronic backing |
| Hood: | Gang territory (origin: abbreviation of 'neighborhood') |
| Hustle: | Obtain by illicit action/swindle/cheat |

| | |
|---|---|
| Hype: | To promote or publicize without real foundation |
| Innit: | 'Isn't it', often put at the end of a sentence for effect |
| Jack(ed): | To illegally seize something (origin: abbreviation of 'hijack') |
| Jam(ming): | Relax |
| Jezzie: | A promiscuous girl (origin: 'Jezebel') |
| Junge: | A promiscuous girl |
| Klep: | Steal (origin: abbreviation of 'kleptomania') |
| Kodee: | A close companion who can be family or friend |
| Liccie: | Small |
| Lick: | Attack/attack someone |
| Link: | Casual sexual partner |
| Long: | Something arduous, complex or time-consuming |
| Madness: | A chaotic event involving a number of young people |
| Man Dem: | Group of men/gang |
| Mans: | Oneself or another individual |
| Marvin: | hungry (rhymes with 'starving') |
| Merk: | To insult or to injure |
| Mission: | *See* 'long' |
| Moist: | No ratings/weak/effeminate |
| Moved/to move: | Violence or the visible threat of violence |
| Nang: | Good |
| Neek: | A portmanteau word from 'nerd' and 'geek' |
| O.G.: | Original Gangster, older gang member |
| On it: | Willing to participate |
| Ones: | By oneself |
| Owned: | To be humiliated or manipulated by others |
| P's/Paper: | Money |
| Peel: | To rob someone |
| Peng: | Attractive girl |
| Pop: | To stab or shoot someone |
| Posting the strip: | Hanging out in front of an estate |
| Props: | Peer respect |
| Pure: | Complete/total |
| Put in work: | Contributing to gang business |
| Rambo: | Large knife |
| Rap: | A type of popular music of US black origin in which words are recited rapidly and rhythmically over a pre-recorded, typically electronic instrumental backing |
| Ratings: | Level of peer respect |
| Rep: | To represent an area or gang/or reputation |
| Respect: | Esteem for or a sense of the worth or excellence of a person |
| Rinsed: | Consuming something |
| Rock: | Attack someone |
| Rolling: | Hanging out |
| Rude boy: | *See* 'badman' |
| Rush: | To approach and threaten or use violence in/or to rob |
| Screw(ing): | Look at someone more than twice/a 'dirty look' |
| Shank(ed): | A knife/to stab or be stabbed |
| Shook: | Frightened or nervous (origin: to 'shake' with fear) |

| | |
|---|---|
| Shot(ting): | To sell things illegally on the street, mainly drugs |
| Slip(ping): | To go through an area that you are not from; especially on your own and/or through an area that rival where you live and/or without any form of protection |
| Snake: | A traitor/act of treachery |
| Snitch: | A traitor/informer |
| Spit: | Perform rap music |
| Spud: | Fist bump |
| Stack: | To form a large quantity/build up money |
| Stick up: | An armed robbery in which a gun is used to threaten people |
| Strap(ped): | A firearm/carry a firearm |
| Stripes: | Level of peer respect |
| Tax: | *See* 'jack' |
| Tekkers: | Technique |
| Tiny: | Young gang member |
| Touch skin: | Unprotected sex |
| Vexed: | Irritated |
| Wavey: | High or drunk |
| Weed: | Cannabis |
| Wet(ted up): | Stab/to be stabbed |
| Wha'gwan: | 'What's going on?', often used as a greeting |
| Wifey: | Serious girlfriend, literally 'wife' material |
| Yard: | House or place where one lives |
| Younger: | Younger or subordinate gang member |
| Yout: | Youth or young person |

# Notes

## Introduction

1. According to the Metropolitan Police Service (2012b), 'a decision on gang membership is made based on the strength of the intelligence and the strength of the association. For example, a nominal linked to a gang through one historic piece of intelligence would be considered low strength intelligence and a nominal linked to a gang through, for example, his cousin would be a low strength of association. When compiling gang related data those nominals that are low for both strength of intelligence and association are not included'.

2. Gang members generally feel the media portrays their lives inaccurately, thus I had distinguish my work from any previous, primarily journalistic, research in which some of them had taken part. Among gang members, journalists are know for dropping in en masse following a teenage homicide and immediately pulling out once a sufficient sound bite is obtained, even staging conflict and encouraging the wearing of gang costumes and brandishing of weapons for the cameras. To prove I had no imminent deadline and I was not working a particular angle, I spent weeks hanging out in some communities before ever really asking a question. I also did not pay interviewees for their participation.

3. I also registered my research with the Metropolitan Police Service, in part to obtain some top cover for time spent in the company of criminals, but also because I needed to pass a criminal background check to access police, prisons, schools, and so on.

4. Aldridge, Medina, and Ralphs (2008) report experiencing a similar problem with the perception of 'gang' research in 'Research City'.

5. Young black men primarily fear being attacked by someone of the same ethnicity. In the period from 2002 to 2005, in 74.2 percent of homicide cases with a suspect where the victim was black, the perpetrator was also black (House of Commons Home Affairs Committee, 2007, pp. 16–17).

6. Signaling theory developed independently in economics (Grafen, 1990a, 1990b; Ross, 1977; Spence, 1974) and in biology (Johnstone, 1997; Zahavi, 1975, 1977; Zahavi and Zahavi, 1997), but its applications are found in anthropology (Cronk, 1994; Irons, 2001; Sosis, 2003; Sosis and Bressler, 2003), political science (Fearon, 1997; Morrow, 1999; Weinstein, 2005), management (Connelly et al., 2011), and analytical sociology (Gambetta, 2009b; Gambetta and Hamill, 2005; Hamill, 2011).

## 1  Gangs and Society

1. The price of the average home in London is now £295,000. The average salary is £38,600. Mortgage companies are generally willing to offer around four times one's salary, which means the average London worker can buy half an average home (Economist, 2012b).

2. Ironically this statement was made not long before Chris Brown was convicted of domestic violence.
3. For more on how persistent contact with authority can reinforce gang identities see Klein (1971), McAra and McVie (2005), and Short and Strodtbeck (1965).
4. 'No blacks, no dogs' is a reference to the infamous signs that were placed in the windows of some pubs and rented accommodation during the post-war immigration of workers from the West Indies to the UK.
5. General Certificate of Secondary Education. An academic qualification roughly equivalent to an American high school diploma.
6. Youth unemployment figures are always considerably higher than the general population, in part owing to the difficulty of tracking students through this data. Most students are excluded from official figures because they are classed as 'economically inactive', that is, people who are not currently in work or looking for work, but any student actively looking for full-time or part-time work but unable to find it would be classed as unemployed. It should be noted, however, that black people are less likely to enter higher education than most other ethnic groups.

## 2   Gang Evolution

1. Despite accounting for 11 percent of Londoners, black people of all ages accounted for 67 percent of those accused of supplying crack cocaine and almost 40 percent of those found in possession of the drug during 2003–4. Arrest referral statistics for the same period indicate also that almost half of arrestees who reported using crack cocaine but no other drug were black (House of Commons Home Affairs Committee, 2007).
2. Amway is a private American direct-selling company and manufacturer that uses network marketing to sell health, beauty, and home care products. Avon Products, Inc. is a public American multi-level marketing company, which traditionally uses both door-to-door sales people ('Avon ladies') and brochures to advertise its line of cosmetics. In addition to selling, both companies offer representatives the ability to be involved in network marketing or 'leadership' programs, whereby representatives recruit, mentor, and train others.
3. In some more articulated and established gangs, youngers have their own youngers known as 'tinies', but because my assessment of gang youngers essentially and equally applies to gang tinies (in other words, youngers look like elders from the point of view of tinies), they are not the subject of this book.
4. Illegal firearms possession carries a five-year minimum sentence.

## 3   Gang Organization

1. Lewisham's gangs are collectively known as 'blue borough' after the color of their local authority logo, street signs and wheelie bins.
2. Hence why I was unable to obtain anything close to equivalent the extraordinary financial records Levitt and Venkatesh (2000) use in their economic analysis of a drug-selling gang.

# 4   Gangs, Media, and Technology

1. 'The Movie and the Dime Novel' was curiously edited out of Thrasher's second edition because, according to James Short's (1963, p. ii) introduction, film had seemingly less impact on modern boys and the 'novelty' of media had largely expired. Short acknowledged, however, that 'little is known concerning the influence of any of these media on the behaviour of gang boys, or of children generally'.

# 5   Gang Recruitment

1. The Regulation of Investigatory Powers Act 2000 provides a statutory basis for the authorization and use by UK public authorities of covert surveillance and 'covert human intelligence sources'. Under section 26(8) a person is a 'source' if: (a) he establishes or maintains a personal or other relationship with a person for the covert purpose of facilitating the doing of anything falling within paragraph (b) or (c); (b) he covertly uses such a relationship to obtain information or to provide access to any information to another person; or (c) he covertly discloses information obtained by the use of such a relationship or as a consequence of the existence of such a relationship. In some instances, the tasking given to a source will not require them to establish a personal or other relationship for a covert purpose, but rather to present purely factual information, for example, about the layout of commercial premises.

# 6   Gang Desistance

1. According to Gatti et al. (2005, p. 1180), for example, anyone in the past 12 months who has been 'part of a group or gang that did reprehensible acts' qualifies as a gang member. For Bendixen et al. (2003, p. 94), 'a member of a group or gang that has bullied or pestered other people' or 'a member of a group or gang that has drunk alcohol and then been noisy and rowdy' is equally culpable.
2. During the fieldwork, police even expressed concern that radical Mosques were giving vulnerable youths an escape route from gangs in exchange for a commitment to Jihad, but I found no concrete evidence of such practices.

# 7   Gang Prevention and Intervention

1. Perhaps to reduce name confusion (or hide from bad press), CeaseFire Chicago changed its name to 'Cure Violence' in 2012.

# Bibliography

Aldridge, J. and Medina, J. (2008) *Youth Gangs in an English City: Social Exclusion, Drugs and Violence*, ESRC End of Award Report, RES-000-23-0615 (Swindon: Economic and Social Research Council).

Aldridge, J., Medina, J., and Ralphs, R. (2008) 'Dangers and Problems of Doing "Gang" Research in the UK', in F. van Gemert, D. Peterson, and L. Inger-Lise (eds) *Street Gangs, Migration, and Ethnicity* (Devon, UK: Willan).

Alexander, C. (2000) *The Asian Gang: Ethnicity, Identity, Masculinity* (Oxford: Berg).

Alexander, C. (2008) *Rethinking Gangs* (London: Runnymede Trust).

Anderson, E. (1990) *Streetwise: Race and Class in an Urban Community* (Chicago, IL: University of Chicago Press).

Anderson, E. (1999) *Code of the Street: Decency, Violence, and the Moral Life of the Inner City* (New York, NY: W. W. Norton).

Avon (n.d.) *You Make the Rules. You Enjoy the Profits!* http://www.youravon.com/repsuite/static/bar/earnings_avon.html [accessed September 20, 2012].

Ayling, J. (2011) 'Gang Change and Evolutionary Theory', *Crime, Law and Social Change*, 56, 1–26.

Bacharach, M. and Gambetta, D. (2001) 'Trust in Signs', in K. Cook (ed.) *Trust in Society* (New York, NY: Russell Sage Foundation).

Ball, J., Milmo, D., and Ferguson, B. (2012) 'Half of UK's Young Black Males are Unemployed', *The Guardian*, March 9, http://www.guardian.co.uk/society/2012/mar/09/half-uk-young-black-men-unemployed [accessed September 20, 2012].

Bandura, A. (1977) *Social Learning Theory* (New York, NY: General Learning Press).

Bandura, A. (2002) 'Selective moral disengagement in the exercise of moral agency', *Journal of Moral Education*, 31, 101–119.

Bannister, J., Pickering, J., Batchelor, S., Burman, M., Kintrea, K., and Mcvie, S. (2010) *Troublesome Youth Groups, Gangs and Knife Carrying in Scotland* (Edinburgh: Scottish Government).

Barajas, F. (2007) 'An Invading Army: A Civil Gang Injunction in Southern California Chicana/o Community', *Latino Studies*, 5, 393–417.

Barker, T. (2007) *Biker Gangs and Organized Crime* (Newark, NJ: Anderson).

Batchelor, S. (2009) 'Girls, Gangs, and Violence: Assessing the Evidence', *The Journal of Community and Criminal Justice*, 56, 399–414.

Batey, A, (2010) 'So Solid Crew: "What We're Doing is Bigger than Music"', *The Guardian*, January 14, http://www.guardian.co.uk/music/2010/jan/14/so-solid-crew-interview [accessed September 20, 2012].

Battin, S., Hill, K., Abbott, R., Catalano, R., and Hawkins, J. (1998) 'The Contribution of Gang Membership to Delinquency Beyond Delinquent Friends', *Criminology*, 36, 93–115.

BBC News (2008a) 'Gun Smuggling "Common" in UK Army', 25 April 25, http://news.bbc.co.uk/2/hi/uk_news/7366279.stm [accessed September 20, 2012].

BBC News (2008b) 'Teenage Rapper Jailed for Killing', December 1, http://news.bbc.co.uk/2/hi/uk_news/england/london/7758574.stm [accessed September 20, 2012].

BBC News (2009) 'Police Informant Payouts Top £6m', July 29, http://news.bbc. co.uk/2/hi/uk_news/8173638.stm [accessed September 20, 2012].

BBC News (2012) 'Leroy James Murder: Youth Detained for Boy's Enfield Killing', September 21, http://www.bbc.co.uk/news/uk-england-london-19671918 [accessed September 21, 2012].

BBC Radio 5 Live (2012) 'Double Take', February 5, http://www.bbc.co.uk/iplayer/ episode/b01bmmlm/double_take_05_02_2012/ [accessed September 20, 2012].

Beccaria, C. ([1764] 1963) *On Crimes and Punishments* (Indianapolis, IL: Bobbs-Merrill).

Bendixen, M., Endresen, I., and Olweus, D. (2003) 'Variety and Frequency Scales of Antisocial Involvement: Which One is Better?', *Legal and Criminological Psychology*, 8, 135–50.

Bennett, T. and Holloway, K. (2004) 'Gang Membership, Drugs and Crime in the UK', *British Journal of Criminology*, 44, 305–323.

Best, J. and Hutchinson, M. (1996) 'The Gang Initiation Rite as a Motif in Contemporary Crime Discourse', *Justice Quarterly*, 13, 383–404.

Biernacki, P. and Waldorf, D. (1981) 'Snowball Sampling: Problems and Techniques of Chain Referral Sampling', *Sociological Methodology*, 10, 141–163.

Bjerregaard, B. (2003) 'Anti-Gang Legislation and its Potential Impact: The Promises and the Pitfalls', *Criminal Justice Policy Review*, 14, 171–192.

Bjerregaard, B. (2010) 'Gang Membership and Drug Involvement: Untangling the Complex Relationship', *Crime and Delinquency*, 56, 3–34.

Blair, T. (1993) 'Why Crime is a Socialist Issue', *New Statesman*, January 29, 27–28.

Blaxter, L., Hughes, C., and Tight, M. (1996) *How to Research* (Buckingham, UK: Open University Press).

Bliege Bird, R. and Smith, E. (2005) 'Signaling Theory, Strategic Interaction, and Symbolic Capital', *Current Anthropology*, 46, 221–248.

Bourgois, P. (1995) *In Search of Respect: Selling Crack in El Barrio* (Cambridge: Cambridge University Press).

Box, G. and Draper, N. (1987) *Empirical Model Building and Response Surfaces* (New York, NY: John Wiley and Sons).

Boyle, D., Lanterman, J., Pascarella, J., and Cheng, C. (2010) *Impact of Newark's Operation Ceasefire* (Newark: Violence Institute of New Jersey, University of Medicine and Dentistry, New Jersey).

Bradshaw, P. (2005) 'Terrors and Young Teams: Youth Gangs and Delinquency in Edinburgh', in S. Decker and F. Weerman (eds) *European Street Gangs and Troublesome Youth Groups: Findings from the Eurogang Research Program* (Walnut Creek, CA: AltaMira Press).

Braga, A. and Weisburd, D. (2012) *The Effects of 'Pulling Levers': Focused Deterrence Strategies on Crime* (Oslo, Norway: Campbell Collaboration).

Braga, A., Kennedy, D., and Tita, G. (2001) 'New Approaches to the Strategic Prevention of Gangs and Group-Involved Violence', in C. R. Huff (ed.) *Gangs in America*, 3rd edn (Newbury Park, CA: Sage).

Braga, A., Kennedy, D., Waring, E., and Piehl, A. (2001) 'Problem-Oriented Policing, Deterrence, and Youth Violence: An Evaluation of Boston's Operation Ceasefire', *Journal of Research in Crime and Delinquency*, 38, 195–225.

Bratton, W. (1998) *Turnaround: How America's Top Cop Reversed the Crime Epidemic* (New York, NY: Random House).

Brotherton, D. and Barrios, L. (2003) *Between Black and Gold: The Street Politics of the Almighty Latin King and Queen Nation* (New York, NY: Columbia University Press).

Bugliosi, V. and Gentry, C. (1974) *Helter Skelter: The True Story of the Manson Murders* (New York, NY: W. W. Norton).

Burke, E. (1770) *Thoughts on the Cause of the Present Discontents* (New York, NY: New York Public Library).

Campbell, A. and Muncer, S. (1989) 'Them and Us: A Comparison of the Cultural Context of American Gangs and British Subcultures', *Deviant Behavior*, 10, 271–88.

Campbell, D. (1994) 'Breaking the *Shame Shield:* Thoughts on the Assessment of Adolescent Child Sexual Abusers', *Journal of Child Psychotherapy*, 20, 309–326.

Cameron, D. (2011) 'Speech on the Fight-Back after the Riots', *New Statesman*, August 15, http://www.newstatesman.com/politics/2011/08/society-fight-work-rights [accessed September 20, 2012].

Chandler, R. (1954) *The Long Goodbye* (Boston, MA: Houghton Mifflin).

Chang, J. (2007) 'It's a Hip-Hop World', *Foreign Policy*, 163, 58–65.

Centre for Social Justice (2009) *Dying to Belong: An In-Depth Review of Street Gangs in Britain* (London: CSJ).

Centre for Social Justice (2012) *Time to Wake Up: Tackling Gangs One Year after the Riots* (London: CSJ).

Chin, K. (1996) *Chinatown Gangs: Extortion, Enterprise and Ethnicity* (New York, NY: Oxford University Press).

Cho, I. and Kreps, D. (1987) 'Signaling Games and Stable Equilibria', *Quarterly Journal of Economics*, 102, 179–221.

Chu, Y. (2000) *The Triads as Business* (London: Routledge).

Chwe, M. (2001) *Rational Ritual: Culture, Co-Ordination and Common Knowledge* (Princeton, NJ: Princeton University Press).

Citizens Report (2012) *Mapping the Location and Victim Profile of Teenage Murders in London from 2005 to 2012*, http://www.citizensreportuk.org/reports/teenage-murder-london.html [accessed September 20, 2012].

Citizen's UK (2012) *Citizens' Inquiry into the Tottenham Riots: The Report*, http://www.citizensuk.org/about/reports/ [accessed September 20, 2012].

Clarke, R. and Cornish, D. (1986) *The Reasoning Criminal: Rational Choice Perspectives on Offending* (New York, NY: Springer-Verlag).

Cobain, I. and Siddique, H. (2009) 'Former Soldier Set Up Secret Gun Factories to Supply Street Gangs', *The Guardian*, 21, http://www.guardian.co.uk/uk/2009/sep/21/former-soldier-gun-factories [accessed September 20, 2012].

Cohen, S. (2002) *Folk Devils and Moral Panics*, 3rd edn (London: Routledge).

Cohen, L. and Felson, M. (1979) 'Social Change and Crime Rate Trends: A Routine Activity Approach', *American Sociological Review*, 44, 488–608.

Collins, R. (2008) *Violence: A Micro-Sociological Theory* (Princeton, NJ: Princeton University Press).

Collins, R. (2009) 'Micro and Macro Causes of Violence', *International Journal of Conflict and Violence*, 3, 9–22.

Connelly, B., Certo, T., Ireland, R., and Reutzel, C. (2011) 'Signaling Theory: A Review and Assessment', *Journal of Management*, 37, 39–67

Conservative Vice Lords Inc. (1969) *A Report to the Public, 1968–69*, http://www.gangresearch.net/chicagogangs/vicelords/vltitle.html [accessed September 20, 2012].

Cronk, L. (1994) 'Evolutionary Theories of Morality and the Manipulative Use of Signals', *Zygon: Journal of Religion and Science*, 29, 81–101.

Cronk, L. (2005) 'The Application of Animal Signaling Theory to Human Phenomena: Some Thoughts and Clarifications', *Social Science Information/Information Sur Les Sciences Sociales*, 44, 603–620.

Curry, G. and Decker, S. (1998) *Confronting Gangs: Crime and Community* (Los Angeles, CA: Roxbury).

Curtis, R. (2003) 'The Negligible Role of Gangs in Drug Distribution in New York City in the 1990s', in L. Kontos, D. Brotherton, and L. Barrios (eds) *Gangs and Society: Alternative Perspectives* (New York, NY: Columbia University Press).

Daily Mail (2007) 'Straw Blames Absent Dads for Gang Violence', August 27, http://www.dailymail.co.uk/news/article-476837/straw-blames-absent-dads-gang-violence.html [accessed September 20, 2012].

Daily Mail (2010) '"Terror Zone" Teen Gang Behind £1m Crime Spree Jailed for 40 Years', May 22, http://www.dailymail.co.uk/news/article-1186402/terror-zone-teen-gang-1m-crime-spree-jailed-40-years.html [accessed September 20, 2012].

Dasgupta, P. (1988) 'Trust as a Commodity', in D. Gambetta (ed.) *Trust: Making and Breaking Cooperative Relations* (Oxford: Basil Blackwell).

Davenport, J. (2007) 'Named: The 257 London Gangs', *Evening Standard*, August 24.

Davey, E. (2011) 'Peckham Murder "Snitch" Leaflet: What Has Changed?', *BBC News*, January 19, http://www.bbc.co.uk/news/uk-england-london-12217949 [accessed September 20, 2012].

Davey, E. (2012) 'Gang Members Face Stark Choice at Gruesome Day in Court', *BBC News*, January 31, http://www.bbc.co.uk/news/uk-england-london-16825265 [accessed September 20, 2012].

Davies, A. (1998) 'Youth Gangs, Masculinity and Violence in Late Victorian Manchester and Salford', *Journal of Social History*, 32, 349–369.

Dawkins, R. (1989) 'The Irrationality of Faith', *New Statesman*, March 31.

Dawley, D. (1992) *A Nation of Lords: The Autobiography of the Vice Lords*, 2nd edn (Prospect Heights, IL: Waveland Press).

Debarbieux, E. and Baya, C. (2008) 'An Interactive Construction of Gangs and Ethnicity: The Role of School Segregation in France', in F. van Gemert, D. Peterson, and I. Inger-Lise (eds) *Street Gangs, Migration and Ethnicity* (Devon, UK: Willan).

Decker, S. and Curry, G. (2002) 'Gangs, Gang Homicides, and Gang Loyalty: Organized Crimes or Disorganized Criminals', *Journal of Criminal Justice*, 30, 343–352.

Decker, S. and Lauritsen, J. (2002) 'Breaking the Bonds of Membership: Leaving the Gang', in C. R. Huff (ed.) *Gangs in America III* (Thousand Oaks, CA: Sage).

Decker, S. and Pyrooz, D. (2011a) 'Gangs, Terrorism, and Radicalization', *Journal of Strategic Security*, 4, 151–166.

Decker, S. and Pyrooz, D. (2011b) *Leaving the Gang: Logging off and Moving on*, http://www.cfr.org/counterradicalization/save-supporting-document-leaving-gang/p26590 [accessed September 20, 2012].

Decker, S. and Van Winkle, B. (1996) *Life in the Gang: Family, Friends, and Violence* (New York, NY: Cambridge University Press).

Decker, S. and Weerman, F. (2005) *European Street Gangs and Troublesome Youth Groups: Findings from the Eurogang Research Program* (Walnut Creek, CA: AltaMira Press).

Decker, S., Bynum, T., and Weisel, D. (1998) 'Gangs as Organized Crime Groups: A Tale of Two Cities', *Justice Quarterly*, 15, 395–425.

Decker, S., Katz, C., and Webb, V. (2008) 'Understanding the Black Box of Gang Organization: Implications for Involvement in Violent Crime, Drug Sales, and Violent Victimization', *Crime and Delinquency*, 54, 153–72.

Decker, S., Van Gemert, F., and Pyrooz, D. (2009) 'Gangs, Migration, and Crime: The Changing Landscape in Europe and the United States', *Journal of International Migration and Integration*, 10, 393–408.

Densley, J. (2011) 'Ganging up on Gangs: Why the Gangs Intervention Industry Needs an Intervention', *British Journal of Forensic Practice*, 13, 12–24.

Densley, J., Davis, A., and Mason, N. (2013) 'Girls and Gangs: Preventing Multiple Perpetrator Rape', in M. Horvath and J. Woodhams (eds) *Handbook on the Study of Multiple Perpetrator Rape: A Multidisciplinary Response to an International Problem* (London: Routledge).

Densley, J. and Mason, N. (2011) 'The London Riots: A Gang Problem?', *Policing Today*, 17, 14–15.

Department for Communities and Local Government. (2007) *The English Indices of Deprivation 2007*, NRAD 05137 (London: DCLG).

Department for Work and Pensions (2012) *Social Justice: Transforming Lives*, http://www.dwp.gov.uk/docs/social-justice-transforming-lives.pdf [accessed September 20, 2012].

Deuchar, R. (2009) *Gangs: Marginalised Youth and Social Capital* (Stoke on Trent: Trentham).

Donohue, J. and Levitt, S. (2001) 'The Impact of Legalized Abortion on Crime', *Quarterly Journal of Economics*, 116, 379–420.

Downes, D. (1966) *The Delinquent Solution* (New York, NY: Free Press).

Dr Seuss (1961) *The Sneetches and Other Stories* (New York, NY: Random House).

Drugscope (2012) *Cocaine and Crack*, http://www.drugscope.org.uk/resources/drugsearch/drugsearchpages/cocaineandcrack [accessed September 20, 2012].

Economist (2012a) 'Assimilating Plutocrats', June 2, http://www.economist.com/node/21556251 [accessed September 20, 2012].

Economist (2012b) 'Home is where the Money is', June 30, http://www.economist.com/node/21557531 [accessed September 20, 2012].

EHRC (2012) *Race Disproportionality in Stops and Searches under Section 60 of the Criminal Justice and Public Order Act 1994* (Manchester: Equality and Human Rights Commission).

Elevation Networks Trust (2012) *Race to the Top: the Experiences of Black Students in Higher Education* (London: The Bow Group), http://www.bowgroup.org/news/half-black-students-feel-government-discriminatory-employer.

Elster, J. (1979) *Ulysses and the Sirens: Studies in Rationality and Irrationality* (Cambridge: Cambridge University Press).

Elster, J. (2000) *Ulysses Unbound: Studies in Rationality, Precommitment, and Constraints* (Cambridge: Cambridge University Press).

Erikson, E. (1977) *Toys and Reasons: Stages in the Ritualization of Experience* (New York: W. W. Norton).

Emler, N., and Reicher, S. (1995) *Adolescence and Delinquency: The Collective Management of Reputation* (Oxford: Blackwell).

Esbensen, F. and Huizinga, D. (1993) 'Gangs, Drugs, and Delinquency in a Survey of Urban Youth', *Criminology*, 31, 565–589.

Esbensen, F., Huizinga, D., and Weiher, A. (1993) 'Gang and Nongang Youth: Differences in Explanatory Variables', *Journal of Contemporary Criminal Justice*, 9, 94–116.

Esbensen, F., Peterson, D., Taylor, T., Freng, A., Osgood, D., Carson, D., and Matsuda, K. (2011) 'Evaluation and Evolution of the Gang Resistance Education and Training (G.R.E.A.T.) Program', *Journal of School Violence*, 10, 53–70.

Evans, R. and Fernandez, C. (2011) 'Found Under a Nine-Year-Old's Bed: The Weapons Arsenal of Gang who Killed Schoolgirl, 16', *Daily Mail*, April 12, http://www.dailymail.co.uk/news/article-1376085/Schoolgirl-dreamed-going-Oxford-gunned-gang-queued-takeaway.html#ixzz26wwQ6Y71 [accessed September 20, 2012].

Fagan, J. and Wilkinson, D. (1998) 'Gun, Youth Violence and Social Identity in Inner Cities', *Youth Violence*, 24, 105–188.

Fearon, J. (1997) 'Signaling Foreign Policy Interests', *Journal of Conflict Resolution*, 41, 68–90.

Felson, M. (2006) 'The Street Gang Strategy', in M. Felson (ed.) *Crime and Nature* (Thousand Oaks, CA: Sage).

Ferguson, N., Burgess, M., and Hollywood, I. (2008) 'Crossing the Rubicon: Deciding to Become a Paramilitary in Northern Ireland', *International Journal of Conflict and Violence*, 2, 130–137.

Fleisher, M. (2005) 'Fieldwork Research and Social Network Analysis: Different Methods Creating Complementary Perspectives', *Journal of Contemporary Criminal Justice*, 21, 120–134.

Fleisher, M., Decker, S., and Curry, G. (2001) 'An Overview of the Challenge of Prison Gangs', *Corrections Management Quarterly*, 5, 1–9.

Forbes, W. (2008) *The Investigation of Crime* (New York, NY: Kaplan).

Frank, R. (1988) *Passions within Reason: The Strategic Role of Emotions* (New York, NY: W. W. Norton).

Freeland, C. (2012) *Plutocrats: The Rise of the New Global Super-Rich and the Fall of Everyone Else* (New York, NY: Penguin).

Frere-Jones, S. (2005) 'True Grime', *The New Yorker*, March 21, http://www.newyorker.com/archive/2005/03/21/050321crmu_music [accessed September 20, 2012].

Frum, D. (2009) 'Bristol's Myth', Frum Forum, March 12, http://www.frumforum.com/bristols-myth/ [accessed September 20, 2012].

Gambetta, D. (1993) *The Sicilian Mafia* (Cambridge, MA: Harvard University Press).

Gambetta, D. (2009a) 'Signalling', in P. Hedstrom and P. Bearman (eds) *The Oxford Handbook of Analytical Sociology* (Oxford: Oxford University Press).

Gambetta, D. (2009b) *Codes of the Underworld: How Criminals Communicate* (Princeton, NJ: Princeton University Press).

Gambetta, D. and Hamill, H. (2005) *Streetwise: How Taxi Drivers Establish Their Customers' Trustworthiness* (New York, NY: Russell Sage Foundation).

Gambetta, D. and Hertog, S. (2007) 'Engineers of Jihad', *Sociology Working Papers 2007/10*, Oxford.

Garot, R. (2007) '"Where You From!" Gang Identity as Performance', *Journal of Contemporary Ethnography*, 361, 50–84.

Gatti, U., Tremblay, R., Vitaro, F., and McDuff, P. (2005) 'Youth Gangs, Delinquency and Drug Use: A Test of Selection, Facilitation, and Enhancement Hypotheses', *Journal of Child Psychology and Psychiatry*, 46, 1178–1190.

Gibbs, N. (2012). 'Your Life is Fully Mobile', *Time*, August 16, http://techland.time.com/2012/08/16/your-life-is-fully-mobile/ [accessed September 20, 2012].

Gilligan, J. (1997) *Violence: Reflections on a National Epidemic* (New York: Vintage Books).

Gilroy, P. (1987) *There Ain't No Black in the Union Jack* (London: Unwin Hyman).

Gintis, H., Smith, E., and Bowles, S. (2001) 'Costly Signaling and Cooperation', *Journal of Theoretical Biology*, 213, 103–119.

Gladwell, M. (2000) *The Tipping Point: How Little Things can make a Big Difference* (New York, NY: Little Brown).

Goffman, E. (1963) *Stigma: Notes on the Management of Spoiled Identity* (London: Penguin)

Goffman, E. (1967) *Interaction Ritual: Essays on Face-to-Face Behavior* (New York: Anchor Books).

Goldberg, L. (2001) *Gang Tattoos: Signs of Belonging and the Transience of Signs*, http://www.linagoldberg.com/gangtattoos/ [accessed September 20, 2012].

Goldson, B. (2011) *Youth in Crisis? 'Gangs', Territoriality and Violence* (Abingdon, UK: Routledge).

Goldthorpe, J. (1980) *Social Mobility and Class Structure in Modern Britain* (Oxford: Clarendon Press).

Good, D. (1988) 'Individuals, Interpersonal Relations, and Trust', in D. Gambetta (ed.) *Trust: Making and Breaking Cooperative Relations* (Oxford: Basil Blackwell).

Gordon, R., Lahey, B., Kawai, E., Loeber, R., Stouthamer-Loeber, M., and Farrington, D. (2004) 'Antisocial Behavior and Youth Gang Membership: Selection and Socialization', *Criminology*, 42, 55–88.

Gossett, J. and Byrne, S. (2002) '"CLICK HERE": A Content Analysis of Internet Rape Sites', *Gender & Society*, 16, 689–709.

Gottfredson, M. and Hirschi, T. (1990) *A General Theory of Crime* (Stanford, CA: Stanford University Press).

Gould, R. (1995) *Insurgent Identities: Class, Community and Protest in Paris from 1848 to the Commune* (Chicago, IL: Chicago University Press).

Grafen, A. (1990a) 'Biological signals as handicaps', *Journal of Theoretical Biology*, 144, 517–46.

Grafen, A. (1990b) 'Sexual Selection Unhandicapped by the Fisher Process', *Journal of Theoretical Biology*, 144, 473–516.

Grogger, J. (2002) 'The Effects of Civil Gang Injunctions on Reported Violent Crime: Evidence from Los Angeles County', *Journal of Law and Economics*, 45, 69–90.

Gryniewicz, J. (2012) *Surviving Our Streets: London*, http://www.insightonconflict.org/2012/06/sos-london/ [accessed September 20, 2012].

Guilford, T. and Stamp Dawkins, M. (1991) 'Receiver Psychology and the Evolution of Animal Signals', *Animal Behaviour*, 42, 1–14.

Gunter, A. (2008) 'Growing Up Bad: Black Youth, "Road" Culture and Badness in an East London Neighbourhood', *Crime Media Culture*, 4, 349–366.

Hagedorn, J. (1988) *People and Folks: Gangs, Crime, and the Underclass in a Rustbelt City* (Chicago, IL: Lake View Press).

Hagedorn, J. (2007) 'Gangs, Institutions, Race and Space: The Chicago School Revisited', in J. Hagedorn (ed.) *Gangs in the Global City: Alternatives to Traditional Criminology* (Urbana, IL: University of Illinois Press).

Hagedorn, J. (2008) *A World of Gangs: Armed Young Men and Gangsta Culture* (Minneapolis, MN: University of Minnesota Press).

Hagedorn, J. (2011) *The Interruptors: Why I Don't Like This Movie*, http://gangsandthemedia.blogspot.com/2011/10/interruptors-why-i-dont-like-this-movie.html [accessed September 20, 2012].

Hall, G. S. (1904) *Adolescence: Its Psychology and its Relation to Physiology, Anthropology, Sociology, Sex, Crime, Religion, and Education* (Englewood Cliffs, NJ: Prentice Hall).

Hall, S., Criticher, C., Jefferson, T., Clarke, J., and Robert, B. (1978) *Policing the Crisis: Mugging, the State, and Law and Order* (London: Macmillan).

Hall, S. and Winlow, S. (2008) *Criminal Identities and Consumer Culture: Crime, Exclusion and the New Culture of Narcissism* (Devon, UK: Willan).

Halliday, J. (2011) 'David Cameron Considers Banning Suspected Rioters from Social Media', *The Guardian*, August 11, http://www.guardian.co.uk/media/2011/aug/11/david-cameron-rioters-social-media [accessed September 20, 2012].

Hallsworth, S. (2011) 'Gangland Britain: Realities, Fantasies and Industry', in B. Goldson (ed.) *Youth in Crisis? 'Gangs', Territoriality and Violence* (Abingdon, UK: Routledge).

Hallsworth, S. and Brotherton, D. (2011) *Urban Disorder and Gangs: A Critique and a Warning* (London: Runnymede Trust).

Hallsworth, S. and Silverstone, D. (2009) '"That's Life Innit": A British Perspective on Guns, Crime and Social Order', *Criminology and Criminal Justice*, 9, 359–377.

Hallsworth, S. and Young, T. (2004) 'Getting Real About Gangs', *Criminal Justice Matters*, 55, 12–13.

Hallsworth, S. and Young, T. (2008) 'Gang Talk and Gang Talkers: A Critique', *Crime Media Culture*, 4, 175–195.

Hamill, H. (2010) *Recruitment into Insurgency and Extra-Legal Organizations*, ESRC End of Award Report, RES-061-23-0131 (Swindon: Economic and Social Research Council).

Hamill, H. (2011) *The Hoods: Crime and Punishment in West Belfast* (Princeton, NJ: Princeton University Press).

Hancox, D. (2009) 'The Triumph of Grime', *The Guardian*, February 13, http://www.guardian.co.uk/commentisfree/2009/feb/14/music-grime-dan-hancox [accessed September 20, 2012].

Hancox, D. (2011) 'Rap responds to the riots: "They have to take us seriously"', *The Guardian*, 12 August, http://www.guardian.co.uk/music/2011/aug/12/rap-riots-professor-green-lethal-bizzle-wiley [accessed September 20, 2012].

Harcourt, B. and Ludwig, J. (2006) 'Broken Windows: Evidence from New York City and a Five-City Social Experiment', *University of Chicago Law Review*, 73, 271–320.

Hardy, M. (2002) 'Behavior-Oriented Approaches to Reducing Youth Gun Violence', *Children, Youth, and Gun Violence*, 12, 101–117.

Heckathorn, D. (1997) 'Respondent-Driven Sampling: A New Approach to the Study of Hidden Populations', *Social Problems*, 44, 174–199.

Heckathorn, D. (2002) 'Respondent-Driven Sampling II: Deriving Valid Population Estimates from Chain-Referral Samples of Hidden Populations', *Social Problems*, 49, 11–34.

Hegghammer, T. (2010) *Jihad in Saudi Arabia: Violence and Pan-Islamism since 1979* (Cambridge: Cambridge University Press).

Hemenway, D. (2006) *Private Guns, Public Health* (Ann Arbor, MI: University of Michigan Press).

Hemingway, E. (1926) *The Sun Also Rises* (New York, NY: Simon and Schuster).

Henley, J. (2011) 'Karyn McCluskey: The Woman who Took on Glasgow's Gangs', *The Guardian*, December 19, http://www.guardian.co.uk/society/2011/dec/19/karyn-mccluskey-glasgow-gangs [accessed September 20, 2012].

Hickey, E. (2012) *Serial Murder and Their Victims*, 6th edn (Belmont, CA: Wadsworth).

Hill, A. (2007) 'Ja-Ja Should Know How Street Gangs Operate: He Runs One', *The Observer*, February 24, http://www.guardian.co.uk/uk/2007/feb/25/ukguns.news [accessed September 20, 2012].

Hill, P. (2003) *The Japanese Mafia: Yakuza, Law, and the State* (Oxford: Oxford University Press).

Hirshleifer, J. (1987) 'On the Emotions as Guarantors of Threats and Promises', in J. Dupré (ed.) *The Last on the Best: Essays on Evolution and Optimality* (Cambridge, MA: MIT Press).

HM Government (2011) *Ending Gang and Youth Violence: A Cross-Government Report Presented to Parliament by the Secretary of State for the Home Department by Command of Her Majesty* (London: HM Government).

Ho, K. (2009) *Liquidated: An Ethnography of Wall Street* (Durham, NC: Duke University Press).

Hobbes, T. (1651) *Leviathan* (Cambridge: Cambridge University Press).

Holstein, J. and Gubrium, J. (1995) *The Active Interview* (Thousand Oaks, CA: Sage).

Home Office (2009) *Impact Assessment of Amending Gang Injunctions to Enable their Use for 14–17 year olds—a Pilot Scheme* (London: Home Office).

Home Office (2011) *An Overview of Recorded Crimes and Arrests Resulting from Disorder Events in August 2011*, http://www.homeoffice.gov.uk/publications/science-research-statistics/research-statistics/crime-research/overview-disorder-aug2011/ [accessed September 20, 2012].

Horvath, M. (2011) *Growing Against Gangs Lesson Four: Gangs, Girls and Consequences, Evaluation Report* (Middlesex, UK: Middlesex University).

Hosking, G. and Walsh, I. (2005) *The WAVE Report 2005: Violence and What To Do About It* (London: WAVE Trust).

House of Commons Home Affairs Committee (2007) *Young Black People and the Criminal Justice System: Second Report of Session 2006–07* (London: HM Stationery Office).

Howell, J. (2007) 'Menacing or Mimicking? Realities of Youth Gangs', *Juvenile and Family Court Journal*, 58, 39–50.

Howell, J. (2012) *Gangs in America's Communities* (Thousand Oaks, CA: Sage).

Hughes, L. (2005) 'Studying Youth Gangs: Alternative Methods and Conclusions', *Journal of Contemporary Criminal Justice*, 21, 98–119.

Humphreys, M. and Weinstein, J. (2008) 'Who Fights? The Determinants of Participation in Civil War', *American Journal of Political Science*, 52, 436–455.

Independent Police Complaints Commission (2011) *Deaths in Custody Study*, http://www.ipcc.gov.uk/en/Pages/deathscustodystudy.aspx [accessed September 20, 2012].

Irons, W. (2001) 'Religion as a Hard-to-Fake Sign of Commitment', in R. Nesse (ed.) *Evolution and the Capacity for Commitment* (New York, NY: Russell Sage Foundation).

Jacobson, J. and Burrell, A. (2007) *Five Boroughs' Alliance: Guidance for the Communications Strategy* (London: University College London).

Janis, I. (1982) *Groupthink: Psychological Studies of Policy Decisions and Fiascos* (Boston, MA: Houghton Mifflin).

Jenkins, R. (2009) 'Notorious Gooch Gang Smashed as Leaders Jailed', *The Times*, April 9, http://www.timesonline.co.uk/tol/news/uk/crime/article6046400.ece [accessed September 20, 2012].

Johnstone, R. (1997) 'The Evolution of Animal Signals', in J. Krebs and N. Davis (eds) *Behavioural Ecology: An Evolutionary Approach* (Oxford: Blackwell).

Julien, I. (1994) *The Darker Side of Black* (Normal Films/BBC Television).

Katz, J. (1988) *Seductions of Crime: Moral and Sensual Attractions in Doing Evil* (New York, NY: Basic Books).

Katz, J. and Jackson-Jacobs, C. (2004) 'The Criminologists Gang', in C. Sumner (ed.) *The Blackwell Companion to Criminology* (Oxford: Blackwell).

Kelly, T. (2009) 'Marked Men', *Daily Mail*, June 11, http://www.dailymail.co.uk/news/article-1192286/Notorious-criminal-family-price-heads-Ben-Kinsellas-murderers.html [accessed September 20, 2012].

Kennedy, D. (1997) 'Pulling Levers: Chronic Offenders, High Crime Settings, and a Theory of Prevention', *Valparaiso Law Review*, 31, 449–484.

Kennedy, D. (2011a) *Don't Shoot: One Man, a Street Fellowship, and the End of Violence in Inner-City America* (New York, NY: Bloomsbury).

Kennedy, D. (2011b) 'Whither Streetwork? The Place of Outreach Workers in Community Violence Prevention', *Criminology and Public Policy*, 10, 1045–1051.

Kennedy, D., Piehl, A., and Braga, A. (1996) 'Youth Violence in Boston: Gun Markets, Serious Youth Offenders, and a Use-Reduction Strategy', *Law and Contemporary Problems*, 59, 147–196.

Kirby, T. and Foster, J. (1993) 'Video Link to Bulger Murder Disputed', *The Independent*, November 26, http://www.independent.co.uk/news/video-link-to-bulger-murder-disputed-1506766.html [accessed September 20, 2012].

Klein, M. (1971) *Street Gangs and Street Workers* (Englewood Cliffs, NJ: Prentice Hall).

Klein, M. (1995) *The American Street Gang: Its Nature, Prevalence, and Control* (New York, NY: Oxford University Press).

Klein, M. (2001) 'Resolving the Eurogang Paradox', in M. Klein, H. Kerner, C. Maxson, and E. Weitekamp (eds) *The Eurogang Paradox: Street Gangs and Youth Groups in the U.S. and Europe* (Dordrecht: Kluwer Academic Publishers).

Klein, M. (2004) *Gang Cop: The Words and Ways of Officer Paco Domingo* (Walnut Creek, CA: AltaMira Press).

Klein, M. (2011) 'Comprehensive Gang and Violence Reduction Programs: Reinventing the Square Wheel', *Criminology and Public Policy*, 10, 1037–1044.

Klein, M. and Maxson, C. (2006) *Street Gang Patterns and Policies* (Oxford: Oxford University Press).

Klein, M., Kerner, H., Maxson, C., and Weitekamp, E. (2001) *The Eurogang Paradox: Street Gangs and Youth Groups in the U.S. and Europe* (Dordrecht: Kluwer Academic Publishers).

Knight, G. (2012) 'We Can't Hide Away from Our History of Gritty Youth Culture', *The Guardian*, August 27, http://www.guardian.co.uk/commentisfree/2012/aug/27/gritty-youth-culture-giggs-gang-acquittal [accessed September 20, 2012].

Knox, G. (1999) 'Comparison of Cults and Gangs: Dimensions of Coercive Power and Malevolent Authority', *Journal of Gang Research*, 6, 1–39.

Kotlowitz, A. (2008) 'Blocking the Transmission of Violence', *New York Times Magazine*, May 4, http://www.nytimes.com/2008/05/04/magazine/04health-t.html?pagewanted=alland_moc.semityn.www [accessed September 20, 2012].

Krueger, A. (2007) *What Makes a Terrorist: Economics and the Roots of Terrorism* (Princeton, NJ: Princeton University Press).

Krueger, A. and Malecková, J. (2003) 'Education, Poverty and Terrorism: Is there a Causal Connection?', *Journal of Economic Perspectives*, 17, 119–144.

Kubrin, C. (2005) 'Gangstas, Thugs, and Hustlas: Identity and the Code of the Street in Rap Music', *Social Problems*, 52, 360–78.

Labich, K. (1994) 'Is Herb Kelleher America's Best CEO?', *Fortune*, May 2, 44–52.

Lacourse, E., Nagin, D., Tremblay, R., Vitaro, F., and Claes, M. (2003) 'Developmental Trajectories of Boys' Delinquent Group Membership and Facilitation of Violent Behaviors during Adolescence', *Development and Psychopathology*, 15: 183–197.

Langman, P. (2009) *Why Kids Kill: Inside the Minds of School Shooters* (New York, NY: Palgrave Macmillan).

Laub, J. and Sampson, R. (2003) *Shared Beginnings, Divergent Lives: Delinquent Boys to Age 70* (Cambridge, MA: Harvard University Press).

Laville, S. (2011) 'London Teenagers Found Guilty Over Victoria Station Killing', *The Guardian*, May 16, http://www.guardian.co.uk/uk/2011/may/16/london-teenagers-jail-victoria-station-murder [accessed September 20, 2012].

Laville, S. and Taylor, M. (2012) 'Three Gang Members Guilty of Shooting that Left Girl Paralysed', *The Guardian*, March 26, http://www.guardian.co.uk/uk/2012/mar/26/three-guilty-shooting-girl-paralysed?intcmp=239 [accessed September 20, 2012].

Lawson, G. (2008) 'The Inside Man', *Gentleman's Quarterly*, 78, 84–143.

Lee, H. (1960) *To Kill a Mockingbird* (New York, NY: HarperCollins).

Levitas, R. (2012) 'There May Be Trouble Ahead: What We Know About Those 120,000 Troubled Families', www.poverty.ac.uk/sites/default/files/trouble_ahead.pdf [accessed September 20, 2012].

Levitt, S. and Dubner, S. (2005) *Freakonomics: A Rogue Economist Explores the Hidden Side of Everything* (New York, NY: William Morrow).

Levitt, S. and Venkatesh, S. (2000) 'An Economic Analysis of a Drug-Selling Gang's Finances', *The Quarterly Journal of Economics*, 115, 755–789.

Lewis, P., Newburn, T., Taylor, M., and Ball, J. (2011) *Reading the Riots: Investigating England's Summer of Disorder*, http://www.guardian.co.uk/uk/series/reading-the-riots [accessed September 20, 2012].

Lombardo, R. (1994) 'Recruitment into Organized Crime: A Study of Social Structural Support of Deviance', Unpublished Ph.D. Thesis (University of Illinois, Chicago).

London's Poverty Profile (2011) *Income Inequalities by Wards Within London Boroughs*, http://www.londonspovertyprofile.org.uk/indicators/topics/inequality/income-inequalities-within-london-boroughs/ [accessed September 20, 2012].

London's Poverty Profile (2012) *Unemployment by Borough*, http://www.londonspovertyprofile.org.uk/indicators/topics/work-and-worklessness/unemployment-by-borough/ [accessed September 20, 2012].

Luhmann, N. (1988) 'Familiarity, Confidence, Trust: Problems and Alternatives', in D. Gambetta (ed.) *Trust: Making and Breaking Cooperative Relations* (Oxford: Basil Blackwell).

Macpherson, W. (1999) *The Stephen Lawrence Inquiry: Report of an Inquiry by Sir William Macpherson of Cluny* (London: HM Stationery Office).

Main, F. (2012) 'Six Ceasefire Workers Charged with Crimes in the Past Five Years', *Chicago Sun-Times*, May 31, http://www.suntimes.com/news/metro/12894675-418/six-ceasefire-workers-charged-with-crimes-in-the-past-five-years.html [accessed September 20, 2012].

Malamuth, N., Addison, T., and Koss, M. (2000) 'Pornography and Sexual Aggression: Are There Reliable Effects and Can We Understand Them?', *Annual Review of Sex Research*, 11, 26–91.

Mares, D. (2001) 'Gangstas or Lager Louts? Working Class Street Gangs in Manchester' in M. Klein, H. Kerner, C. Maxson, and E. Weitekamp (eds) *The Eurogang Paradox: Street Gangs and Youth Groups in the U.S. and Europe* (Dordrecht: Kluwer Academic Publishers).

Margo, J., Dixon, M., Pearce, N., and Reed, H. (2006) *Freedom's Orphans: Raising Youth in a Changing World* (London: Institute for Public Policy Research).

Marshall, B., Webb, B., and Tilley, N. (2005) *Rationalisation of Current Research on Guns, Gangs and Other Weapons: Phase 1* (London: University College London).

Matrix Knowledge Group (2007) *The Illicit Drug Trade in the United Kingdom*, Home Office Report 20/07 (London: Home Office).

Matza, D. (1964) *Delinquency and Drift* (New York, NY: John Wiley and Sons).

Matza, D. and Sykes, G. (1961) 'Juvenile Delinquency and Subterranean Values', *American Sociological Review*, 26, 712–719.

Maxson, C., Hennigan, K., and Sloane, D. (2005) '"It's Getting Crazy Out There": Can A Civil Gang Injunction Change a Community?', *Criminology and Public Policy*, 4, 577–605.

Mayer, C. (2008) 'Britain's Mean Streets', *Time*, March 26, http://www.time.com/time/magazine/article/0,9171,1725547,00.html#ixzz2748aCxvb [accessed September 20, 2012].

Mayer, S. (1997) *What Money Can't Buy: Family Income and Children's Life Chances* (Cambridge, MA: Harvard University Press).

Maynard Smith, J. and Harper, D. (2003) *Animal Signals* (Oxford: Oxford University Press).

McAra, L. and McVie, S. (2005) 'The usual suspects? street-life, young people and the police', *Criminal Justice*, 5, 5–36.

McDevitt, J., Braga, A., Nurge, D., and Buerger, M. (2003) 'Boston's Youth Violence Prevention Program: A Comprehensive Community-Wide Approach', in S. Decker (ed.) *Policing Gangs and Youth Violence* (Belmont, CA: Wadsworth).

McGloin, J. and Decker, S. (2010) 'Theories of Gang Behavior and Public Policy', in H. Barlow and S. Decker (eds) *Criminology and Public Policy: Putting Theory to Work* (Philadelphia, PA: Temple University Press).

McVie, S. (2010) *Gang Membership and Knife Carrying: Findings from the Edinburgh Study of Youth Transitions and Crime* (Edinburgh: Scottish Government Social Research).

Merton, R. (1938) 'Social Structure and Anomie', *American Sociological Review*, 3, 672–682.

Metropolitan Police Service (2012a) *Press Release: Met Launches Major Crackdown on Gang Crime* (London: Metropolitan Police).

Metropolitan Police Service (2012b) *Freedom of Information Request Reference No: 2012020002176* (London: Metropolitan Police Service).

Metropolitan Police Service (2012c) *Press Release: Drop in Stabbings and Shootings Among Young People* (London: Metropolitan Police Service).

Michaels, S. (2012) 'Insane Clown Posse to Sue FBI for Including Fans on Gang List', *The Guardian*, August 14, http://www.guardian.co.uk/music/2012/aug/14/insane-clown-posse-fbi-juggalos?newsfeed=true [accessed September 20, 2012].

Mieczkowski, T. (1986) 'Geeking Up and Throwing Down: Heroin Street Life in Detroit', *Criminology*, 24, 645–666.

Miller, A. (1949) *Death of a Salesman* (New York, NY: Penguin).

Miller, J. (2001) 'Bringing the Individual Back in: A Commentary on Wacquant and Anderson', *Punishment and Society*, 3, 153–60.

Ministry of Justice (2012) *Statistical Bulletin on the Public Disorder of 6th–9th August 2011. Full Report*, http://www.justice.gov.uk/statistics/criminal-justice/public-disorder-august-11 [accessed September 20, 2012].

Misztal, B. (1996) *Trust in Modern Societies: The Search for the Bases of Social Order* (Cambridge: Polity Press).

Mollenkopf, J. and Castells, M. (1991) *Dual City: Restructuring New York* (New York, NY: Russell Sage Foundation).

Moore, N. and Williams, L. (2011) *The Almighty Black P Stone Nation: The Rise, Fall, and Resurgence of an American Gang* (Chicago, IL: Chicago Review Press).

Morrow, J. (1999) 'The Strategic Setting of Choices: Signaling, Commitments, and Negotiation in International Politics', in D. Lake and R. Powell (eds) *Strategic Choice and International Relations* (Princeton, NJ: Princeton University Press).

Morselli, C. (2009) *Inside Criminal Networks* (New York: Springer).

Murphy. J. (2009) 'ACPO Comment on Serious and Organised Crime Review', *Police Oracle*, July 13, http://www.policeoracle.com/news/acpo-comment-on-serious-organised-crime-review_19690.html [accessed September 20, 2012].

Murray, J. (2008) 'Media Violence: The Effects are both Real and Strong', *American Behavioral Scientist*, 51, 1212–1230.

Myers, T. (2009) 'The Unconstitutionality, Ineffectiveness, and Alternatives of Gang Injunctions', *Michigan Journal of Race and Law*, 14, 285–306.

Nadanovsky, P. and Cunha-Cruz, J. (2009) 'The Relative Contribution of Income Inequality and Imprisonment to the Variation in Homicide Rates among Developed OECD, South and Central American Countries', *Social Science and Medicine*, 699, 1343–1350.

Nesse, R. (2001) 'The Evolution of Subjective Commitment', in R. Nesse (ed.) *Evolution and the Capacity for Commitment* (New York, NY: Russell Sage Foundation).

O'Deane, M. (2011) *Gang Injunctions and Abatement: Using Civil Remedies to Curb Gang Related Crimes* (Boca Raton, FL: CRC Press).

Office of the Auditor General (2007) *Program Audit of Funding Provided by or through the State of Illinois to the Chicago Project for Violence Prevention for the Ceasefire Program*, www.auditor.illinois.gov/audit...audits/07-ceasefire-pgm-digest.pdf [accessed September 20, 2012].

Olson, M. (1965) *The Logic of Collective Action: Public Goods and the Theory of Groups* (Cambridge, MA: Harvard University Press).

Organization for Economic Cooperation and Development (2011) *Divided We Stand: Why Inequality Keeps Rising*, http://www.oecd.org/document/51/0,3746,en_2649_33933_49147827_1_1_1_1,00.html [accessed September 20, 2012].

Orwell, G. (1946) 'Decline of the English Murder', *Tribune*, February 15.

Ouellette, J. and Wood, W. (1998) 'Habit and Intention in Everyday Life: The Multiple Processes by which Past Behavior Predicts Future Behavior', *Psychological Bulletin*, 124, 54–74.

Padilla, F. (1992) *The Gang as an American Enterprise* (New Brunswick, NJ: Rutgers University Press).

Palfrey, J. and Gasser, U. (2008) *Born Digital: Understanding the First Generation of Digital Natives* (New York, NY: Basic Books).

Papachristos, A. (2001) *A.D., After the Disciples: The Neighborhood Impact of Federal Gang Prosecution* (Peotone, IL: New Chicago Schools Press).

Papachristos, A. (2011) 'Too Big to Fail: The Science and Politics of Violence Prevention', *Criminology and Public Policy*, 10, 1053–61.

Papachristos, A. (2012) 'What is a "Gang Audit"?' *Huffington Post*, July 5, http://www.huffingtonpost.com/andrew-papachristos/what-is-a-gang-audit_b_1651386.html [accessed September 20, 2012].

Pappzd (2012) 'Sneakbo's Gang Affiliation Exposed on BBC Show', http://pappzd.com/2012/04/sneakbo-gas-gang-bbc3-our-crime/ [accessed September 20, 2012].

Patillo, M. (1998) 'Sweet mothers and gang-bangers: Managing crime in a black middle-class neighborhood', *Social Forces*, 76, 747–774.

Patrick, J. (1973) *A Glasgow Gang Observed* (London: Methuen).

Peach, C. (1996) 'Does Britain have Ghettos?', *Transactions of the Institute of British Geographers*, 22, 216–235.

Pearson, G. (1983) *Hooligan: A History of Respectable Fears* (London: Macmillan).

Petersen, R. and Valdez, A. (2005) 'Using Snowball-Based Methods in Hidden Populations to Generate a Randomized Community Sample of Gang-Affiliated Adolescents', *Youth Violence and Juvenile Justice*, 3, 151–167.

Peterson, D., Taylor, T., and Esbensen, F. (2004) 'Gang Membership and Violent Victimization', *Justice Quarterly*, 21, 793–815.

Phelan, M. and Hunt, S. (1998) 'Prison gang members' tattoos as identity work: The visual communication of moral careers', *Symbolic Interaction*, 21, 277–298.

Pistone, J. with Woodley, R. (1989) *Donnie Brasco* (New York, NY: Signet).

Pitts, J. (2007) 'Americanization, the Third Way, and the Racialization of Youth Crime and Disorder', in J. Hagedorn (ed.) *Gangs in the Global City: Alternatives to Traditional Criminology* (Urbana, IL: University of Illinois Press).

Pitts, J. (2008) *Reluctant Gangsters: The Changing Face of Youth Crime* (Devon, UK: Willan).

Pitts, J. (2011) 'Mercenary Territory: Are Youth Gangs Really a Problem?', in B. Goldson (ed.) *Youth in Crisis? 'Gangs', Territoriality and Violence* (Abingdon, UK: Routledge).

Pizzini-Gambetta, V. and Hamill, H. (2011) 'Shady Advertising: Recruitment among Rebels and Mobsters', www.esrc.ac.uk/my-esrc/grants/RES-061-23-0131/outputs/read/5668c3c3-e076-4468-9e88-6ede5117199f [accessed September 20, 2012].

Power, N. (2012) 'Absurd Student Debt has Ended Mass Inclusion—Our Future is at Risk', *The Guardian*, July 3, http://www.guardian.co.uk/commentisfree/2012/jul/03/absurd-student-debt-has-ended-inclusion [accessed September 20, 2012].

Prasad, R. (2011) 'English Riots were "A Sort of Revenge" against the Police', *The Guardian*, December 4, http://www.guardian.co.uk/uk/2011/dec/05/riots-revenge-against-police [accessed September 20, 2012].

Prensky, M. (2001) 'Digital Natives, Digital Immigrants', *On the Horizon*, 9, 1–6.

Press Association (2011) 'Five Teenagers Found Guilty of Killing 15-Year-Old Rival Gang Member', *The Guardian*, November 14, http://www.guardian.co.uk/uk/2011/nov/14/youths-conviction-olumegbon-murder [accessed September 20, 2012].

Pritchard, T. (2008) *Street Boys: 7 Kids. 1 Estate. No Way Out. The True Story of a Lost Childhood* (London: Harper Element).

Project Oracle (2011) *Growing Against Gangs and Violence*, http://www.london.gov.uk/priorities/crime-community-safety/time-action/project-oracle/view-project?pid=39 [accessed September 20, 2012].

Project Oracle (2012) *Project Oracle: Youth Evidence Hub*, http://www.project-oracle.com/ [accessed September 20, 2012].

Pryce, K. (1979) *Endless Pressure: A Study of West Indian Life-Styles in Bristol* (London: Penguin).

Pyrooz, D. and Decker, S. (2011) 'Motives and Methods for Leaving the Gang: Understanding the Process of Gang Desistance', *Journal of Criminal Justice*, 39, 417–425.

Pyrooz, D., Decker, S., and Webb, V. (2010) 'The Ties that Bind: Desistance from Gangs', *Crime and Delinquency*, September 8, 1–26.

Ragin, C. (2008) *Redesigning Social Inquiry: Fuzzy Sets and Beyond* (Chicago, IL: University of Chicago Press).

Reuter, P. (1983) *Disorganized Crime: The Economics of the Visible Hand* (Cambridge, MA: MIT Press).

Reyes, J. W. (2007) 'Environmental policy as social policy? The impact of childhood lead exposure on crime', B.E. *Journal of Economic Analysis and Policy*, 7, 1796.

Rivera, L. (2010) 'Status Distinctions in Interaction: Social Selection and Exclusion at an Elite Nightclub', *Qualitative Sociology*, 33, 229–255.

Robins, L. (1978) 'Sturdy Childhood Predictors of Adult Antisocial Behavior: Replications from Longitudinal Studies', *Psychological Medicine*, 8, 611–622.

Rosenthal, L. (2001) 'Gang Loitering and Race', *The Journal of Criminal Law and Criminology*, 91, 99–160.

Ross, S. (1977) 'The determination of financial structure: The incentive signaling structure', *Bell Journal of Economics*, 8, 23–40.

Ruggiero, V. (2000) *Crime and Markets: Essays in Anti-Criminology* (Oxford: Oxford University Press).

Ruggiero, V. and South, N. (1995) *Eurodrugs: Drug Use, Markets and Trafficking in Europe* (London: University College London Press).

Sagan, C. (1980) 'Encyclopedia Galactica', *PBS: Cosmos*, December 14.

Sageman, M (2008) *The Leaderless Jihad* (Philadelphia, PA: University of Pennsylvania Press).

Sampson, R. (2006) 'How Does Community Context Matter? Social Mechanisms and the Explanation of Crime', in P. Wikström and R. Sampson (eds) *The Explanation of Crime: Context, Mechanisms, and Development* (Cambridge: Cambridge University Press).

Sanchez, R., Hughes, M., and Allen, N. (2012) 'Batman Cinema Shooting: James Holmes "Told Police he was The Joker"', *The Telegraph*, July 20, http://www.telegraph.co.uk/news/worldnews/northamerica/usa/9416529/Batman-cinema-shooting-James-Holmes-told-police-he-was-The-Joker.html [accessed September 20, 2012].

Sánchez-Jankowski, M. (1991) *Islands in the Street: Gangs and American Urban Society* (Berkeley, CA: University of California Press).

Sánchez-Jankowski, M. (2003) 'Gangs and Social Change', *Theoretical Criminology*, 7, 192–216.

Sandberg, S. (2008) 'Street Capital: Ethnicity and Violence on the Streets of Oslo', *Theoretical Criminology*, 12, 153–171.

Sandberg, S. (2010) 'What can "Lies" Tell us about Life? Notes towards a Framework of Narrative Criminology', *Journal of Criminal Justice Education*, 21, 447–465.

Sankey, I. (2011) '"Gangbos" will only Further Infringe Civil Liberties', *The Guardian*, February 3, http://www.guardian.co.uk/commentisfree/libertycentral/2011/feb/03/gangbo-infringe-civil-liberties [accessed September 20, 2012].

Sassen, S. (2007) 'The global city: One setting for new types of gang work and political culture', in J. Hagedorn (ed.), *Gangs in the Global City. Alternatives to Traditional Criminology* (Urbana, IL: University of Illinois Press).

Scarman, L. (1982) *The Scarman Report: The Brixton Disorders 10–12 April 1981* (Harmondsworth: Penguin).

Schelling, T. (1960) *The Strategy of Conflict* (Cambridge, MA: Harvard University Press).

Schelling, T. (1971) 'What is the Business of Organized Crime?', *The Journal of Public Law*, 20, 71–84.

Schneider, J. and Tilley, N. (2004) *Gangs: The International Library of Criminology, Criminal Justice and Penology* (Aldershot: Ashgate).

Shakespeare, W. (1623) *The Winter's Tale* (Oxford: Clarendon Press).

Shakur, S. (1993) *Monster: The Autobiography of an L.A. Gang Member* (New York, NY: Grove Press).

Shapiro, S. (2005) 'Agency Theory', *Annual Review of Sociology*, 31, 263–84.

Sharp, C., Aldridge, J., and Medina, J. (2006) *Delinquent Youth Groups and Offending Behaviour: Findings from the 2004 Offending, Crime and Justice Survey*, Home Office 14/06 (London: Home Office).

Sheldon, R., Tracy, S., and Brown, W. (2004) *Youth Gangs in American Society* (Belmont, CA: Wadsworth).

Sherman, L., Farrington, D., Walsh, W., and MacKenzie, D. (2006) *Evidence-Based Crime Prevention*, revised edn (London: Routledge).

Short, J. (1963) 'Introduction to the abridged edition', in F. Thrasher (ed.), *The Gang: A Study of 1,313 Gangs in Chicago*, 2nd edn (Chicago, IL: University of Chicago Press).

Short, J. and Strodtbeck, F. (1965) *Group Processes and Gang Delinquency* (Chicago, IL: University of Chicago Press).

Silvestri, A., Oldfield, M., Squires, P., and Grimshaw, R. (2009) *Young People, Knives and Guns: A Comprehensive Review, Analysis and Critique of Gun and Knife Crime Strategies* (London: Centre for Crime and Justice Studies).

Simmel, G. (1950) *The Sociology of Georg Simmel* (New York: Free Press).

Skogan, W., Hartnett, S., Bump, N., and Dubois, J. (2009) *Evaluation of Ceasefire-Chicago* (Washington, DC: US Department of Justice).

Skolnick J., Correl T., Navarro, E., and Rabb, R. (1988) *The Social Structure of Street Drug Dealing: Report to the Office of the Attorney General of the State of California* (Berkeley, CA: University of California Press).

Slack, J. (2012) 'May axes the "badge of honour" Asbo in shake-up of laws following 52,000 breaches in ten years', *Daily Mail*, 22 May, http://www.dailymail.co.uk/news/article-2148413/Goodbye-Asbo-badge-honour-prized-young-louts.html [accessed September 20, 2012].

Smith, E. and Bliege Bird, R. (2005) 'Costly Signaling and Cooperative Behavior', in H. Gintis, S. Bowles, R. Boyd, and E. Fehr (eds) *Moral Sentiments and Material Interests: On the Foundations of Cooperation in Economic Life* (Cambridge, MA: MIT Press).

Smith, G. (2009) 'DJ Gang "Used Stolen Credit Cards to Buy their Own Music on iTunes then Pocketed £200,000 in Royalties"', *Daily Mail*, June 11, http://www.dailymail.co.uk/news/article-1192270/dj-gang-downloaded-music-stolen-credit-cards-pocket-200-000-royalties.html [accessed September 20, 2012].

Smithers, R. (2005) 'We Must Tackle Failure of Black Boys—Phillips', *The Guardian*, May 31, http://www.guardian.co.uk/uk/2005/may/31/race.schools [accessed September 20, 2012].

Sobel, R. and Osoba, B. (2009) 'Youth Gangs as Pseudo-Governments: Implications for Violent Crime', *Southern Economic Journal*, 75, 996–1018.

Sosis, R. (2003) 'Why Aren't We All Hutterites? Costly Signaling Theory of Religion', *Human Nature*, 14, 91–127.

Sosis, R. and Bressler, E. (2003) 'Cooperation and Commune Longevity: A Test of the Costly Signaling Theory of Religion', *Cross-Cultural Research*, 37, 211–239.

Spence, M. (1974) *Market Signaling* (Cambridge, MA: Harvard University Press).

Spergel, I. (1995) *The Youth Gang Problem: A Community Approach* (New York, NY: Oxford University Press).

Standing, G. (2011) *The Precariat: The New Dangerous Class* (London: Bloomsbury).

Starbuck, D., Howell, J., and Lindquist, D. (2001) *Hybrid and Other Modern Gangs* (Washington, DC: US Department of Justice).

Stevens, A. (2011) *Drugs, Crime and Public Health: The Political Economy of Drug Policy* (Abingdon, UK: Routledge).

Stevens, A., Radcliffe, P., Pizani Williams, L., Gladstone, B., and Agar, I. (2009) *Offender Management Community Scoping of London Gang Demographics* (Canterbury: University of Kent).

Stewart, E. and Simons, R. (2010) 'Race, Code of the Street, and Violent Delinquency: A Multilevel Investigation of Neighborhood Street Culture and Individual Norms of Violence', *Criminology*, 48, 569–605.

Stouffer, S., Suchman, E., Devinney, L., Star, S., and Williams, R. (1949) *The American Solider: Adjustment During Army Life, Vol. 1* (Princeton, NJ: Princeton University Press).

Sudman, S. and Bradburn, N. (1973) 'Effects of Time and Memory Factors on Response in Surveys', *Journal of the American Statistical Association*, 68, 805–815.

Sullivan, M. (1994) 'Review of "Island in the Street", by Sanchez-Jankowski', *American Journal of Sociology*, 99, 1640–1642.

Sullivan, M. (2005) 'Maybe We Shouldn't Study "Gangs": Does Reification Obscure Youth Violence?', *Journal of Contemporary Criminal Justice*, 21, 170–190.

Summers, C. (2007) 'Is it Wrong to Blame Hip Hop?', *BBC News*, November 13, http://news.bbc.co.uk/2/hi/uk_news/6938411.stm [accessed September 20, 2012].

Surviving Our Streets (2010) *About Us*, http://www.survivingourstreets.com/website/about-us/ [accessed September 20, 2012].

Suttles, G. (1972) *The Social Construction of Communities* (Chicago, IL: University of Chicago Press).

Sykes, G. and Matza, D. (1957) 'Techniques of Neutralization: A Theory of Delinquency', *American Sociological Review*, 22, 664–670.

Tajfel, H. and Turner, J. (1986) 'The Social Identity Theory of Inter-Group Behavior', in S. Worchel and L. Austin (eds) *Psychology of Intergroup Relations* (Chicago, IL: Nelson-Hall).

Taylor, C. (1990) *Dangerous Society* (East Lansing, MI: Michigan State University Press).

Taylor, T., Peterson, D., Esbensen, F., and Freng, A. (2007) 'Gang Membership as a Risk Factor for Adolescent Violent Victimization', *Journal of Research in Crime and Delinquency*, 44, 351–380.

Thatcher, M. (1987) 'Interview for "Woman's Own" ("No Such Thing as Society")', http://www.margaretthatcher.org/document/106689 [accessed September 20, 2012].

The Job (2008) 'On the Heels of Violent Youths', *Author*, July 12–14.

Thompson, T. (2010) 'Inside the Child Gangs of London', *Evening Standard*, May 17, http://www.standard.co.uk/news/inside-the-child-gangs-of-london-6470176.html [accessed September 20, 2012].

Thornberry, T. (1998) 'Membership in Youth Gangs and Involvement in Serious and Violent Offending', in R. Loeber and D. Farrington (eds) *Serious and Violent Juvenile Offenders: Risk Factors and Successful Interventions* (Thousand Oaks, CA: Sage).

Thornberry, T., Krohn, M., Lizotte A., and Chard-Wierschem, D. (1993) 'The Role of Juvenile Gangs in Facilitating Delinquent Behavior', *Journal of Research in Crime and Delinquency*, 30, 55–87.

Thornberry, T., Krohn, M., Lizotte, A., Smith, C., and Tobin, K. (2003) *Gangs and Delinquency in Developmental Perspective* (Cambridge: Cambridge University Press).

Thrasher, F. (1927) *The Gang: A Study of 1,313 Gangs in Chicago* (Chicago, IL: University of Chicago Press).

Tita, G. and Papachristos, A. (2010) 'The Evolution of Gang Policy: Balancing Intervention and Suppression', in R. Chaskin (ed.) *Youth Gangs and Community*

*Intervention: Research, Practice, and Evidence* (New York, NY: Columbia University Press).

Tita, G., Cohen, J., and Endberg, J. (2005) 'An Ecological Study of the Location of Gang "Set Space"', *Social Problems*, 52, 272–299.

Tremlett, G. (2006) 'Row Erupts in Spain over Treatment of Latin Kings, *The Guardian*, October 4, http://www.guardian.co.uk/world/2006/oct/05/spain. gilestremlett [accessed September 20, 2012].

Tsang, L. (1998) 'Postcards from "Home"', in C. O'Hearn (ed.) *Half and Half: Writers On Growing up Biracial and Bicultural* (New York, NY: Pantheon).

TUC (2012) *Youth Long-Term Unemployment Rises by 874 Per Cent since 2000*, http://www.tuc.org.uk/economy/tuc-21125-f0.cfm [accessed September 20, 2012].

Van Duyne, P., Pheijffer, M., Kuijl, H., van Dijk, A., and Bakker, G. (2001) *Financial Investigation of Crime: A Tool of the Integral Law Enforcement Approach* (The Hague: Koninklijke Vermande).

Van Gemert, F. (2001) 'Crips in orange: Gangs and groups in The Netherlands', in. M. Klein, H. Kerner, C. Maxson and E. Weitekamp (eds.), The Eurogang paradox: Street gangs and youth groups in the U.S. and Europe (Dordrecht: Kluwer Academic Publishers.)

Van Gemert, F., Peterson, D., and Lien, I. (2008) *Street Gangs, Migration, and Ethnicity* (Devon, UK: Willan).

Varese, F. (2001) *The Russian Mafia: Private Protection in a New Market* (Oxford: Oxford University Press).

Varese, F. (2010) 'What Is Organized Crime?', in F. Varese (ed.) *Organized Crime: Critical Concepts in Criminology* (London: Routledge).

Varese, F. (2011) *Mafias on the Move: How Organized Crime Conquers New Territories* (Princeton, NJ: Princeton University Press).

Venkatesh, S. (1997) 'The Social Organization of Street Gang Activity in an Urban Ghetto', *The American Journal of Sociology*, 103, 82–111.

Venkatesh, S. (2008) *Gang Leader for a Day: A Rogue Sociologist Crosses the Line* (London: Penguin).

Venkatesh, S. and Levitt, S. (2000) 'Are We a Family or a Business? History and Disjuncture in the Urban American Street Gang', *Theory and Society*, 29, 427–462.

Viterna, J. (2006) 'Pulled, Pushed, and Persuaded: Explaining Women's Mobilization into The Salvadoran Guerilla Army', *American Journal of Sociology*, 112, 1–45.

Wacquant, L. (2001) 'Deadly Symbiosis: When Ghetto and Prison Meet and Mesh', *Punishment and Society*, 3, 95–133.

Watt, N. (2012) 'Gang Members Show Entrepreneurial Zeal, Says Chuka Umunna', *The Guardian*, June 26, http://www.guardian.co.uk/society/2012/jun/26/gang-entrepreneurial-zeal-chuka-umunna [accessed September 20, 2012].

Watt, N. and Oliver, M. (2009) '"Broken Britain" is like The Wire, Say Tories', *The Guardian*, August 25, http, [accessed September 20, 2012].

Webb, V. and Katz, C. (2003) 'Policing Gangs in an Era of Community Policing', in S. Decker (ed.) *Policing Gangs and Youth Violence* (Belmont, CA: Wadsworth).

Weber, M. (1978 [1915]) *Economy and Society* (Berkeley, CA: University of California Press).

Webster, D., Vernick, J., and Mendel, J. (2009) *Interim Evaluation of Baltimore's Safe Streets Programs* (Baltimore, MD: Johns Hopkins Bloomberg School of Public Health, Center for the Prevention of Youth Violence).

Weerman, F., Maxson, C., Esbensen, F., Aldridge, J., Medina, J., and van Gemert, F. (2009) *Eurogang Program Manual: Background, Development, and Use of the Eurogang Instruments in Multi-Site, Multi-Method Comparative Research*, www.umsl.edu/~ccj/eurogang/EurogangManual.pdf [accessed September 20, 2012].

Weinstein, J. (2005) 'Resources and the Information Problem in Rebel Recruitment', *Journal of Conflict Resolution*, 49, 598–624.

Weinstein, J. (2007) *Inside Rebellion: The Politics of Insurgent Violence* (New York, NY: Cambridge University Press).

Weisel, D. (2002) 'The Evolution of Street Gangs: An Examination of Form and Variation', in W. Reed and S. Decker (eds) *Responding to Gangs: Evaluation and Research* (Washington, DC: US Department of Justice).

Wheeler, V. and Brooks, N. (2010) 'LA Gangs Take Over UK Streets', *The Sun*, April 15, http://www.thesun.co.uk/sol/homepage/news/2932813/London-gangs-are-aligning-themselves-to-LA-based-Bloods-and-Crips.html [accessed September 20, 2012].

White, R. (2008) 'Disputed Definitions and Fluid Identities: The Limitations of Social Profiling in Relation to Ethnic Youth Gangs', *Youth Justice*, 8, 149–161.

Whitehead, L. (2011) 'The Law on "Gangbos"', *Law Society Gazette*, http://www.lawgazette.co.uk/in-practice/practice-points/the-law-gangbos [accessed September 20, 2012]

Whitworth, A. (2012) 'Inequality and Crime across England: A Multilevel Modelling Approach', *Social Policy and Society*, 11, 27–40.

Whyte, W. (1943) *Street Corner Society: The Social Structure of an Italian Slum* (Chicago, IL: University of Chicago Press).

Wikipedia (2012a) *Crime in London*, http://en.wikipedia.org/wiki/crime_in_london [accessed September 20, 2012].

Wikipedia (2012b) *Danny Dyer's Deadliest Men*, http://en.wikipedia.org/wiki/danny_dyer%27s_deadliest_men [accessed September 20, 2012].

Wilder, L. (1941) *Little Town on the Prairie* (New York, NY: HarperCollins).

Wilkinson, R. and Pickett, K. (2008) *The Spirit Level: Why More Equal Societies Almost Always Do Better* (London: Allen Lane).

Wilson, J. and Chermak, S. (2011) 'Community-Driven Violence Reduction Programs: Examining Pittsburgh's One Vision One Life', *Criminology and Public Policy*, 10, 993–1027.

Wilson, J. and Kelling, G. (1982) 'Broken Windows: Police and Neighborhood Safety', *Atlantic Monthly*, 249, 29–38.

Wyness, M. (2000) *Contesting Childhood* (London: Falmer Press).

Yablonsky, L. (1959) 'The Delinquent Gang as a Near Group', *Social Problems*, 7, 108–117.

Young, J. (1999) *The Exclusive Society* (London: Sage).

Young, T. (2009) 'Girls and Gangs: Shemale Gangsters in the UK', *Youth Justice*, 9, 224–238.

Youth Justice Board (2006) *Antisocial Behavioural Orders* (London: YJB).

YouTube (2007) *Police Officer Shoots Him Self in the Leg!* http://www.youtube.com/watch?v=rAVYFRM5Tl8 [accessed September 20, 2012].

Zahavi, A. (1975) 'Mate Selection: A Selection for a Handicap', *Journal of Theoretical Biology*, 53, 205–214.

Zahavi, A. (1977) 'Cost of Honesty (Further Remarks on Handicap Principle)', *Journal of Theoretical Biology*, 67, 603–605.

Zahavi, A. and Zahavi, A. (1997) *The Handicap Principle: A Missing Piece of Darwin's Puzzle* (Oxford: Oxford University Press).

Zhang, L., Welte, J., and Wieczorek, W. (1999) 'Youth Gangs, Drug Use, and Delinquency', *Journal of Criminal Justice*, 27, 101–9.

Zimbardo, P. (2008) *The Lucifer Effect: Understanding How Good People Turn Evil* (New York, NY: Random House).

Zimring, F. (2011) *The City that Became Safe: New York's Lessons for Urban Crime and Its Control* (New York, NY: Oxford University Press).

## Filmography

*American Gangster* (2002) Dir.: Ridley Scott.

*Beef I* (2003) Dir.: Peter Spirer.

*Cidade De Deus* (2002) Dir.: Fernando Meirelles.

*Child's Play 3* (1991) Dir.: Jack Bender.

*Collateral* (2004) Dir.: Michael Mann.

*Crips and Bloods: Made in America* (2009) Dir.: Stacy Peralta.

*The Dark Knight Rises* (2012) Dir.: Christopher Nolan.

*Gangs of New York* (2002) Dir.: Martin Scorsese.

*The Godfather* (1972) Dir.: Francis Ford Coppola.

*Goodfellas* (1990) Dir.: Martin Scorsese.

*The Interrupters (2011)* Dir.: Steve James.

*Lock, Stock and Two Smoking Barrels* (1998) Dir.: Guy Ritchie.

*Paid in Full* (2002) Dir.: Charles Stone III.

*Scarface* (1932) Dir.: Howard Hawks.

*Scarface* (1983) Dir.: Brian De Palma.

*State Property* (2002) Dir.: Abdul Abbott.

*Taxi Driver* (1976) Dir.: Martin Scorsese.

*The Breakfast Club* (1985) Dir.: John Hughes.

# Index